D0340163

EIGHT O'CLOCK FERRY TO THE WINDWARD SIDE

EIGHT O'CLOCK FERRY TO THE WINDWARD SIDE

SEEKING JUSTICE IN GUANTÁNAMO BAY

CLIVE STAFFORD SMITH

Nation Books
NEW YORK

I dedicate this book to the prisoners and
their families who have been subjected
to the tragic world of Guantánamo Bay and,
with my eternal love, to Emily.

To donate to Reprieve please go to www.reprieve.org.uk

Copyright © 2007 by Clive Stafford Smith
Published by
Nation Books, A Member of the Perseus Books Group
116 East 16th Street, 8th Floor
New York, NY 10003

Nation Books is a co-publishing venture of the Nation Institute
and the Perseus Books Group.

First published in 2007 by Weidenfeld and Nicolson (London)

All rights reserved. Printed in the United States of America.
No part of this book may be reproduced in any manner
whatsoever without written permission except in the case
of brief quotations embodied in critical articles and reviews.
For information, address the Perseus Books Group,
387 Park Avenue South, New York, NY 10016-8810.

Books published by Nation Books are available at special
discounts for bulk purchases in the United States by
corporations, institutions, and other organizations.
For more information, please contact the Special Markets
Department at the Perseus Books Group,
2300 Chestnut Street, Suite 200, Philadelphia,
PA 19103, or call (800) 255-1514, or e-mail
special.markets@perseusbooks.com.

Designed by Input Data Services Ltd, Frome

Library of Congress Cataloging-in-Publication Data is available

ISBN-13: 978-1-56858-374-7
ISBN-10: 1-56858-374-5

10 9 8 7 6 5 4 3 2 1

CONTENTS

'The only thing I know for certain is that these are bad people. ....'

President George W. Bush, of the Guantánamo Bay prisoners, at a press conference held jointly with Prime Minister Tony Blair on 17 July 2003.

ACKNOWLEDGEMENTS

First and foremost, this book belongs to the Guantánamo prisoners. Some have been freed, returning home to face local prejudices often created by the mistakes of the American authorities. Others continue to endure, after five years of abuse and privation in US custody. There are many more individuals held in secret prisons elsewhere whom I have never met – we will reach you yet. There are some, no doubt, who regret their past acts, but I am not willing to be their judge, certainly not without the guarantee of a fair trial.

Then there are the families of the prisoners, who are indubitably innocent of any crime: the parents, the wives, the brothers, the sisters and, of course, the children. I hope that the sons and daughters of my clients will grow up to be compelling and peaceful advocates against the kind of injustice inflicted on their fathers.

There are almost five hundred lawyers now who have sallied forth in defence of the people and the important principles at stake. Here I will be partisan, and recognise the tireless work of everyone at our Reprieve office in London, including Annabel Harris, Zachary Katznelson, Marc Calcutt, Clara Gutteridge, Cori Crider, Ordesse Hamad, Hayley Ichilcik and Sam Hew, in addition to the scores of Reprieve volunteers who have worked on behalf of the clients over the last few years. I also want to single out some of the many American lawyers: Professor Joe Margulies, Tom Wilner and his team at Shearman & Sterling, and Michael Ratner, Gita Gutierrez and all the staff at the Center for Constitutional Rights in New York. These were the people willing to stand up from the very beginning when the battle was so unpopular. From the start, I have wanted the book to focus on the prisoners, so the legal teams get little credit in the text, but their contribution to this work and their dedication to their clients should be sung from the rooftops.

Greater justice has been achieved for the Guantánamo prisoners in the courts of public opinion than in the courts of law. There have been many journalists whose work stands out – and from whom I have borrowed on occasion (and, I trust, with attribution). There are many other organisations and individuals, and even a small but increasing number of politicians who have held up their hands when it mattered.

There are also charitable foundations – particularly the Open Society Institute, the Joseph Rowntree Charitable Trust, the Roddick Foundation, the Impact Fund, Echoinggreen, the Jeht Foundation, the Oak Foundation, the Baring Foundation, and Unltd – whose directors have had the courage and vision to support this work.

I also wish to acknowledge those individuals, including members of the US military, who have worked at Guantánamo itself and who have recognised the tragic mistake it represents, as well as those who support the mission but who have tried to act with decency inside that paradigm. To paint them all with the same brush would be unfair.

Various people have conspired to assist and encourage me in turning my notes into this rough chronicle, including Sara Fisher at A.M. Heath; Alan Samson, Lucinda McNeile and the people at Weidenfeld & Nicolson; Martin Soames (who ensured that I complied with the reprehensible British libel laws); the US Major who vetted the entire book under the military censorship process; and others who took time to give me helpful criticism, including David Rose, Ian Katz and Sarah Hann.

I cannot conclude without a word for those closest to me. Until his death on 22 January 2007, my father Richard had been a constant inspiration to me. He was of the steadfast opinion that consistent spelling shows a lack of imagination; fortunately, my mother Jean was the one who checked the book over. And without Emily there would not be much point doing anything at all.

This book is a necessarily incomplete account of what I have seen and heard in the course of my representation of prisoners at Guantánamo Bay. I am prevented from presenting a more complete picture by the US censorship rules, to which I have rigorously adhered, and by my obligations to my clients.

I am under no illusion that I have the skill to do justice to the stories of these prisoners, but the greatest sin would be not to try.

– Clive Stafford Smith, April 2007

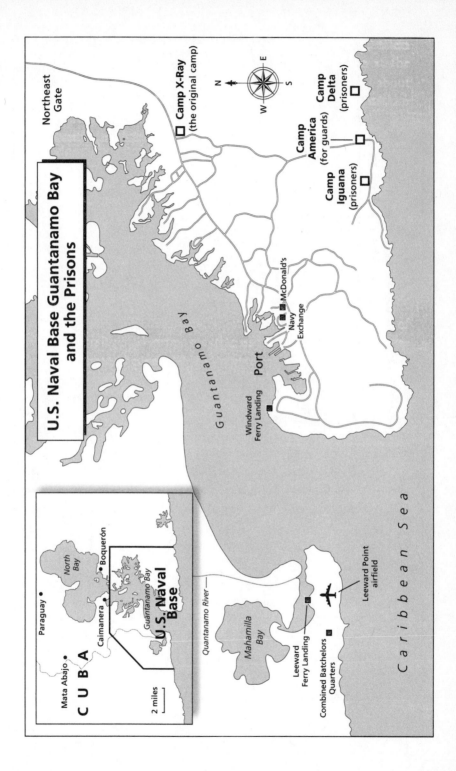

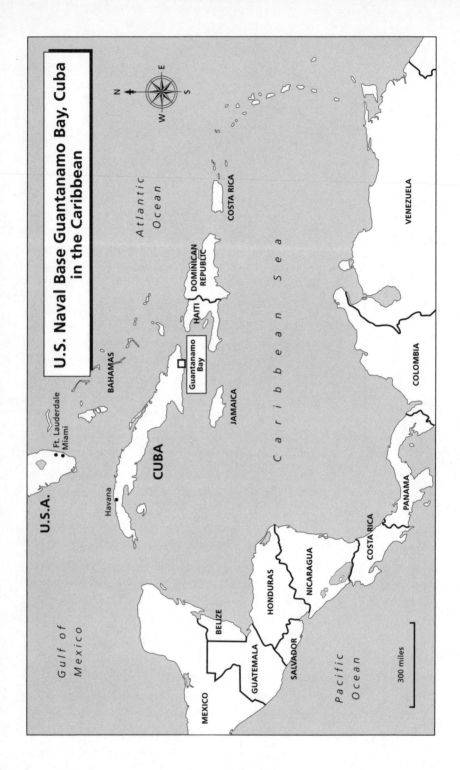

U.S. Naval Base Guantanamo Bay, Cuba in the Caribbean

PREFACE TO U.S. EDITION

The Bush Administration's "Secret Prison" strategy has been unraveling at a rapid pace. Faced with the shocking crime of September 11, it was perhaps unsurprising that our political leaders reacted in the heat of the moment, without sufficient reflection.   Nine months into his first term, President George W. Bush had little experience running a country, let alone a country in crisis.   He has had to act quickly, and he has repeatedly made the fatal mistake of abandoning core American principles.

Guantánamo Bay has been the flagship among the secret prisons, and it is a tribute to the resilience of these American values that the ship has been sinking so fast — at least since lawyers were allowed in, and so many uncomfortable truths began to come out. Yet, well after it closes, the story of Guantánamo will have important lessons to teach us about the illegal acts that our government is still committing.

Guantánamo is a diversionary tactic, the lightning rod not only for criticism but also for global attention. The world has largely ignored the other secret prisons where many more prisoners are being held in even greater isolation. These other detention centers are flourishing. The U.S. takes prisoners daily in the 'War on Terror' — in Afghanistan, in Iraq and the Middle East, in the Horn of Africa, and beyond — and something must be done with them.   There is, therefore, not the slightest chance that the Administration will abandon its broader secret prison program even when it trumpets the closure of Guantánamo.

Indeed, the Bush Administration does not retreat willingly from any of its misguided 'War on Terror' policies.   In the congressional arena, the Administration has tried to trump the Supreme Court each time the Court has reaffirmed the rule of law. In 2004, in *Rasul v. Bush*, the Supreme Court held that the writ *habeas corpus* reached into Guantánamo; the next year, the Bush Administration championed the Detainee Treatment Act

(DTA), which it hoped would evict the writ again.   In 2006, in *Hamdan v. Rumsfeld*, the Supreme Court held that the DTA could not retroactively steal the prisoners' rights. Within five months, the Bush Administration pressed through the Military Commissions Act (MCA), trying to over-rule *Hamdan*. As this book goes to press in the late fall of 2007, the Supreme Court will hear a third challenge to the Bush Administration's claim that prisoners can be denied all constitutional rights.

In Washington, the Administration has been forthright in its oppos-ition to due process. The rearguard action in the trenches has been more insidious, and has attracted much less criticism. From the start, the Department of Defense has mounted a vigorous PR campaign assert-ing that Guantánamo was the "most transparent" prison in the world — a somewhat improbable claim given that the prisoners were held wholly incommunicado for the first three years. When independent lawyers were given limited access to clients, the government imposed rules that required every word a prisoner said to his lawyer to be passed through censors. The rules were created by the government for the government, and changed at will. For example, initially any statements regarding torture or abuse were deemed classified on the grounds that they reflected "methods of interrogation". Gradually, under the threat of litigation, these rules were relaxed and the truth began to filter out. However, in 2007 the government began to clamp down aggressively once again, apparently because there had been too much "bad news".

The entire secret prisons operation eschews open government. Rather than demand that the government justify every limit it would impose on free speech, the government would have the lawyers justify every word that they may speak. Surely there can be no legitimate reason to censor proof that prisoners in U.S. custody are being abused, yet the government has erected a new presumption that such evidence is classified.

The ebb and flow in Guantánamo is an object lesson in the Admin-istration's broader plan. If we understand the methods used here, it is possible to predict and challenge many of the illegal tactics employed in the other secret prisons.   At *Reprieve*, we are busy tracking down these other prisons, and their still more unfortunate prisoners. Guan-tánamo is therefore only the first chapter. Sadly, several more chapters will need to be written.

Clive Stafford Smith

July 2007

1

HONOUR BOUND

Security on the twelve-seater civilian flight to Guantánamo Bay is relaxed. In Fort Lauderdale the passengers assemble at the commuter terminal and the crew steadfastly refuse to search anything. Finally one of the pilots waves a wand over each of the men, pointedly excluding both the women and all the baggage from the search. Curious, I ask why only the men receive the security check. The pilot confidently replies that most weapons are hidden around the ankles and men wear long trousers. I point out that here all five of his female passengers have spurned the skirt. He nods, smiles and walks away.

I am surprised to find such minimal security on the way to this island prison, reputed to house the most dangerous terrorists on earth. If anyone wants to commandeer a plane to attack Guantánamo, he only has to take a beginner's course in hijacking. But it would not be a task for the weak-bladdered terrorist, as the pilot reminds us that there is no toilet on the plane, casually estimating the flight at somewhere between three and four hours. The co-pilot points out the cooler full of complimentary fizzy drinks that blocks the exit aisle, a temptation to the unwary. Before we arrive, one of the men will sheepishly apologise as he covers his lap, filling an empty bottle.

We fly over blue sea and the occasional sandy archipelago. Most passengers have military haircuts and snooze once we get underway. I drown out the engine with my headphones and work on my laptop. I am heading down for another week at the naval base, as one of the volunteer lawyers representing the Muslim prisoners there. I am always excited to come to Guantánamo, as visiting the clients is my favourite part of the job. It is where theory meets reality, the human cost of President George W. Bush's executive order establishing this secret prison full of 'bad men' shortly after the invasion of Afghanistan began in October 2001.

On the way down, we stop for fuel at Exuma in the Bahamas. As we come in to land I notice a plane, of similar size to our own, sprawled in the undergrowth at the end of the runway. I wonder what happens to the island, perhaps ten feet above sea level at the pinnacle of a sand dune, when a hurricane sweeps through at this time of year. I assume that the plane must have been torn from its moorings and tossed among the stunted palm trees.

As I step out of the cabin for the refuelling, I ask the (very young) co-pilot if he knows the fate of the wrecked plane. He brightens. 'Yeah, it was just last week. The pilot didn't land till more than halfway down the runway and that was that. You see, they're too cheap to keep the landing lights on here at night. Can you imagine? Don't even keep the lights on!'

He seems thoroughly amused by this. In the breeze-block waiting room that serves as a terminal, there is a large map of the islands on the wall. There are three airstrips marked and another passenger asks where we are. The same young pilot looks doubtful. He waves vaguely between the three, saying that the Bahamas are really all one island.

There is a lot of blue sea between them.

Eventually we are curving round the eastern tip of Cuba, keeping out of Fidel Castro's airspace, and coming directly in towards the Guantánamo Bay Naval Base. Cacti struggling in hostile soil contrasted with the tropical foliage of the estuary remind me of parts of Spain, as the plane sets down on the very large and empty runway. It was built long enough to accommodate those huge planes that brought cargoes of orange-suited prisoners, starting in January 2002.

The base is divided into two unequal parts, windward and leeward. The main base and the prison are on the windward side, across the bay from where we land. As we touch down, I can see the ferry plying its way towards us, backed by Cuban hills to the north. At the airport we are on the leeward side, which has little else but housing for non-military personnel. Soldiers are standing by the plane as it comes to a halt, managing to project a vague sense of menace into their boredom. As I look around at nothing happening, I realise that the arrival of this little commuter plane is probably the most exciting moment of their day.

They search my bags and I am careful to make no jokes. Even pleasantries seem to sound like security threats here. Soon, I am allowed through to meet my military escort, an NCO who is charged with keeping an eye on the lawyers. He tries to affect a respectful stand-offishness. Most of them want to be friendly, but they are under orders to be careful around us. Loose lips sink ships on a naval base and the lawyers have been identified as 'the enemy'.

Today, one of the most affable escorts has come to meet me. I won't identify him as the military are paranoid about names. The Pentagon seems to think that if we publish a soldier's name, an al-Qaeda cell will swoop in and level the Midwestern town where he was born. He and I banter about the threat that the legal profession poses to national security: lawyers have to sleep on the leeward side, safely away from the main base. He drops me off at the motel where a sign boasts that it is 'The Pearl of the Antilles'.

Here, for twenty dollars a night, I get a two-room suite with four beds. The first time I visited my Guantánamo clients was in November 2004 almost three years after we first sued to get the prisoners the right to counsel. I was here for four nights along with my friend and colleague Joe Margulies. A lawyer gets the entire 'suite' to himself and Joe tried out each bed. He discovered that every one was equally uncomfortable. Normally a military bachelor must share with three other soldiers. Even in the slightly less homophobic age of 'Don't ask, don't tell', where gay people can serve in the military so long as they don't admit their orientation, the name – the Combined Bachelors' Quarters or CBQ – is incongruous.

I am an old hand, now, after several trips and have my favourite 'suite'. On the upper floor of the west wing there is a view over the placid Caribbean. The two rooms are joined by a kitchenette and a bathroom. Each bedroom has a table, a chest of drawers and two beds, all in sterile white, all cheaply prefab. Half the slats have fallen off the footboards of the beds.

The employees at the front desk are Filipinos, glad of their sub-minimum American wage. We have long since made friends, and they store my printer and supplies in a cabinet. Soon I have an office away from home set up in my room and try to sign on to the Internet. I have to set the computer on automatic redial, as the system is over-loaded and constantly engaged, and it is fifty or sixty times before I hear the happy static of the connection. It is my lifeline to the outside world.

I check in with friends and family. Bizarrely, I sometimes feel more intimidated here on an American military base than anywhere else on my travels. Recently, I have been to various places categorised as dangerous by the US State Department – including Yemen and Jordan. I even got taken in for questioning by the secret police in Jordan, when I was there to seek out the families of the Guantánamo prisoners. But here, in the midst of the US military machine, I am more concerned about being detained on some trumped-up charge. I go to great lengths not to violate any of the US military's censorship rules, no matter how silly they may seem, but obeying the law does not necessarily provide protection, as some of my Guantánamo clients can attest.

I go outside, planning to walk down the road to find some kind of dinner. The motel sign bears the base motto: 'Honor Bound to Defend Freedom'. Freedom is a relative term. Iguanas are free enough on both sides of the island and if a soldier accidentally runs one over it's a $10,000 fine, since the US environmental laws apply in Guantánamo. Meanwhile, several hundred prisoners are more than five years into captivity. If a jailer feels the need to hit one of them, it's called 'mild non-injurious contact' and there are no consequences. For these prisoners it's a law-free zone. In 2004 we argued in the Supreme Court that it would be a huge step for mankind if they gave our clients the same rights as the animals on the base. 'Equal rights with Iguanas!' became our clarion call.

The 'chow hall' – the military terms seem like self-parody – closed some time ago, at six o'clock, so the only place left to eat is the Clipper Club, perhaps the most boring bar in the Caribbean. The Management's 'Standards of Appearance' sign prohibits 'clothing with bizarre, drug promoting, obscene and offensive insignia'. Patrons are warned that 'shirts must cover excessive body hair on the chest, abdomen, and under arms'. I pass the test, but they check my ID to make sure I am over twenty-one and give me a wrist tag so I can drink. The barman warns me not to take it off. I have interrupted him, as he sprawled watching a film on a two-metre plasma screen. I am the only patron there.

The food is inedible, chicken sticks of cardboard, pizza slipped into the microwave. At least they cannot do much to harm a bottle of beer.

Back at the motel, television is meant to be the diversion. There are two large televisions in each suite. The cable connection is distorted by static. This would spark a riot among the thousands of soldiers stranded for twelve months on the windward side, but there are too few people on the leeward side for their complaints to register. Only the movie channels are much of a loss, although I do like to watch the American Forces Network as an exercise in social studies. This is what the soldiers are meant to see: optimistic American voices booming positive news, where no setback in Iraq is significant and Israel's invasion of Lebanon is an interesting experiment with new weapons systems.

I check what films are playing tonight, without much interest since the TV is too blurred to watch. On the last two visits to the base I watched *Groundhog Day*, where Bill Murray wakes up over and again to the same morning. As his clock radio clicks over to 6 a.m. every day, Sonny and Cher are inevitably moaning 'I got you, babe'.

Guantánamo Bay is *Groundhog Day*. I go to bed early, as I am up for Reveille at six o'clock myself. I walk back down to the 'chow hall' for breakfast, arriving on the stroke of seven, as the doors open.

I sign in, pay my $1.95 and go to where the cook, who knows me from many visits, is already starting my cheese omelette. He asks me how long I am down for, as he nonchalantly treads on a scorpion that has wandered into the kitchen. Until I saw that I had not known what to make of the story told by my client Hisham Sliti, about the crunchy boiled scorpion that appeared in his meal one day. Now it seems credible.

I am surrounded at my table by more television monitors, one at each corner of the room, shouting the Armed Forces Network at me. The channels are indistinct here also, but the TVs are on full volume. 'Fashion may come and fashion may go,' says a fuzzy woman in a blurry uniform. 'But not overseas. Dress so you won't be noticed.' She tells of the dangers to Americans of being obvious, disparaging the long-haired hippies of the Seventies and the tight white trousers of John Travolta in *Saturday Night Fever*. She turns to a picture of a man in khaki trousers and a stiff blue-collar shirt, the Army's ideal of how one should blend into a foreign country. To me, the khakis scream 'I'm American!' in every language of the United Nations. I wonder whether there is anyone on the planet who would not be able to guess which country her model comes from.

I have always found breakfast TV disturbing and this is well before the time I would rather be having my breakfast. Each morning there is 'This Day in History', when we learn about the US military as superhero over the ages. After all the allegations of bias made against al-Jazeera by President Bush, I wonder idly whether anyone has ever done a content comparison between the Armed Forces Network and the Arabic station.

To make the eight o'clock ferry across to the windward side, I need to leave the chow hall by 7.35. There is a bus, but the Guantánamo thermostat has not yet risen to unbearable levels and it is a pleasant walk, allowing me some quiet time in which to plan my client meetings today.

I walk down First Street. On the leeward side there are two roads (First and Second Streets) running roughly in parallel until they converge near the ferry landing. Swimming Pool Road runs off up the hill. The sign points to a pool, a bowling alley and tennis courts. It used to offer something else, but that promise has long since fallen off, leaving only discoloration on the wooden uprights. I explored up there once on my evening stroll. The pool is empty and cracked. The leeward side is full of ghosts from fifty years ago, as Castro came to power and the importance of the only US base on communist soil suddenly magnified. Buildings once constructed to accommodate the influx of soldiers that coincided first with the CIA-sponsored Bay of Pigs invasion, and then the Cuban Missile Crisis, have now been allowed to decay.

The foot-long banana rats are blundering around in the grass this morning. They advertise their activities so loudly that if there were any predators on this island they would be doomed. But there is nothing that wants to eat them and the environmental laws also protect them from being crushed by patrolling military Humvees. Behind the banana rats lie vestiges of earlier wars. The reinforced-concrete skeleton of a massive tower holds only a spotlight, long since disused. Peering out over the scene is a World War Two bunker, the heavy wooden beam cracked, only barely holding up the earth that covers the roof. I wonder whether the ten-foot snake that was outside my motel door this morning lives in there somewhere.

The 7.41 bus passes me in the wrong direction at precisely the same place on the road each day as it winds up from the airport to fetch passengers for the morning ferry, including the other lawyers who prefer not to sweat on their way to see their clients. I wave to the driver. The tarmac begins to steam as the sun rises over the Cuban hills, stillness and beauty clashing with the rusted barbed wire.

I can see the ferry steaming stolidly across the bay. As it approaches the landing, tinny music pierces the drone of the engine. Last time I was here, every morning for a week it was Jimmy Buffett belting out 'Margaritaville', always that same song. It is the same again today. I remember from college that on this Buffett album there's a song called 'Let's all get Drunk and Screw'. It amuses me to think that the US Navy might not have noticed and I fantasise that one day we will progress a track or two. But we remain stuck on the same song.

A retired naval jet stands on metal stilts next to where we wait for our time to board the ferry. The plane has recently been repainted, with a clover – only three leaves – on its tail. There is a sudden rush towards the boat as a crew member beckons to the passengers. Most of the lawyers complain about staying on the leeward side, and the daily commute, but I enjoy the twenty-minute cruise each morning.

As we pull out into the river, I look back towards the three orna-mental palm trees that tower over what was once a boating pier. The roots of the pier prod out of the water, the walkway long since rotted away. The palm trees are tall and mature, put there for show many years ago. On the other bank of the river, the side towards the Cuban border, the foliage is lush. The trees lean into the water like a tropical forest.

The ferry passes the Oil Spill Response Unit on the estuary bank. Three more palm trees lean over the white concrete building. As the pilot steers us out of the river and into the bay, towards the windward dock, high in the hills four wind turbines slowly rotate. They are majestic, supplying a quarter of the electricity for the base. Beside the windward landing is the water desalination plant; further up the road, the recycling centre. The environmental correctness of the base is out of place set against this terrible prison.

The military escorts meet their flock of lawyers at the dock, as they must shepherd us at all times on this side of the base. We stop off at Starbucks, then drive down to McDonald's. At the door, a soldier smartly salutes his superior, 'Honor Bound, sir!' The officer salutes his reply, 'To Defend Freedom, soldier!' The first time I saw this I chuckled, thinking they were joking. But it's mandatory. It's hard to believe they are still doing it, all these years into the Guantánamo experiment, but the naval base is deeply oblivious to irony.

Some escorts are more talkative than others. I ask one, a veteran of two real battlefields, whether he plays along with this charade.

'They're lucky if I show up in the morning,' he says with a snort.

There is a new area marked off with a green netting in the Morale, Welfare and Recreation section of the base. In an area four times the size of a tennis court there are various inflated shapes. The escort is not sure what this new entertainment for the troops could be.

We pass along to Recreation Road, which runs alongside the Guantánamo golf course, besieged by the semi-desert around it. Officers lay a rubber mat on the gravel for each shot towards the green, a minimalist saucer of grass. Our escort says anyone who plays should rent clubs. 'You don't want to have to pay to play a round and have to replace your whole set as well.' Local rumour has it that the course was ruined by the Haitian refugees, themselves housed here in makeshift camps in the early Nineties. Like so many of the Guantánamo rumours, this is false. God just did not design Guantánamo for golf courses. Another more optimistic military rumour had two pros donating hundreds of thousands to fix up the course. Actually, they just flew down some new equipment to encourage the men stuck on guard duty. One of the pros was Frank Lickliter II, whose link with the base goes back three generations. He still has the rifle his great-grandfather used during the Spanish-American War, when Guantánamo was originally taken by the US. Later, his father flew in P-3 Orions for the Navy during the Cuban Missile Crisis.

Once we leave the golf course behind, Recreation Road leads to the prison camp. An escort points out an iguana, sunning itself on a rock above the road. The hillside to the right as we drive along used to be daubed with all kinds of puerile soldier graffiti. It has all been cleaned off for the benefit of the media tours. As I look in awe, I wonder whether there has ever been another entire hillside scrubbed clean. It must have been an enormous and thankless task, and I feel for the soldiers who had to do it. Then I notice that they did it with camouflage paint. The graffiti have been painted over, with the colours matching the background.

I cannot write about the layout of the prison camp, as this would violate the security rules. Apparently there may be a plot afoot among al-Qaeda to traverse the Atlantic and storm the beaches. There is no rule, though, against saying that each camp has a given name. 'Romeo' is where the military forced the prisoners to wear only shorts, sexually humiliating to a devout Muslim. Forty Muslim men, forsworn from alcohol, live in 'Whiskey'. I can't decide whether the names are inadvertent, as is generally the case in Guantánamo, or deliberately demeaning.

For the past two years, meetings between clients and lawyers have generally been held in Camp Echo. Before June 2004, when the Supreme Court ordered that the prisoners be allowed lawyers, this used to be the harshest camp, where prisoners were held in total isolation. Each cell, sealed off from the others, is divided down the middle – the prisoner lived on one side and was only brought into the other half for interrogation sessions.

For a short time the legal visits were held in Camp Five, but they are back at Echo again now. I am going to stay there all day, until 4.30 – 16.30 hours here. The rules are more restrictive now than two years ago, when the lawyers were allowed to arrive earlier and stay longer. Back then, our arrival used to coincide with the national anthem. At precisely 7.55 a.m. each day the siren sounds on the tannoy, giving the five-minute warning. At eight the world comes to a halt and the soldiers stand rigid, saluting the nearest flag until the anthem is over. One of the soldiers explained to me that if you get inside, you don't have to take part in the ritual and you can go about your business. At the siren there is a rush to get into a building.

Now we are not allowed to arrive before 9 a.m.

Visiting in Camp Echo feels like school, in a way. There is no going to the 'latrine' without permission and an escorting soldier. So I make a last visit to the toilet on the way in, with the hope of holding out. Inside the men's toilet are the uniforms of the ERF squad piled up on the left of the door, ready in case they are needed in Camp Echo. 'To be ERFed' has entered the Guantánamo lexicon. The Emergency Reaction Force is sent in to control unruly prisoners. My clients call it the 'Extreme Repression Force', and describe how five soldiers come rushing into their calls with shackles and brandishing pepper spray. The uniforms are black boiler suits, with hard plastic breastplates and Darth Vader helmets.

The pile of uniforms remind me that the verb 'to ERF' is very real. Omar Deghayes knows all about that. He's originally from Libya, but he has lived most of his life in England, a refugee. He was badly abused before he got to Guantánamo, but the long-lasting damage has happened here. He got ERFed and they rubbed pepper spray repeatedly into his eyes. He already had a childhood injury to his right eye, where the patient work of a Swiss doctor saved his sight. Now that eye is a milky white and Omar sees only gradations of light. The flickering neon lights, never turned off, cause him constant pain.

I go into the camp and wait. In the early days, when the guards prepared the client for a visit, the prisoner used to be called a 'package'. The static on the radio would tell us when the 'package' was ready. Thankfully, we have moved on. Now the prisoners have been elevated to numbers and the guards are identified in the same way. The lawyers had protested that it was impossible to bring complaints against those who used excessive force, since none of them had tags. It amuses me, in a childish way, to play snap with the prisoners and guards, trying to match their numbers.

Five years since they arrived here, fewer than half of the prisoners have met a lawyer. Today there are three lawyers waiting to be allowed in. The guards live a monotonous life and most are friendly. One tells me he saw a report on CNN recently where I had said most of the military were decent people consigned to a terrible task. He smiles as he asks me whether he is one of the bastards doing a terrible job.

Another confides that he has been told to keep his distance from the lawyers, as we are deemed 'the enemy'. I am curious about the Cuban minefield that apparently still separates the naval base from the Cuban communists. The 75,000 mines on the American side were finally removed in 2000, under orders from President Clinton.

'Every now and then you hear an explosion at night,' says the soldier. 'Those are Cubans trying to escape to freedom.'

I laugh. I assume he is kidding me. There have been at least five Cuban deaths in the minefield (the skeletal remains were dubbed, simply, 'Fence Jumper'), but the last one was thirty years ago. He is serious. I suggest that any mine that goes off probably signals the demise of an errant iguana. He is clearly unhappy. I am a cynic and he does not talk to me again for several days.

A guard comes over and takes off his hat, putting it on the table. To remind him of his mission, he has taken a black marker to the inner rim: 'Al Qaeda are Pussies'.

Finally the time comes to see the first client. As we go in there is a cooler of Freedom Springs water bottles on ice, the name fluttering on an American flag. A soldier tells us to strip off the plastic wrapper before passing a bottle to the prisoners, since they might be offended by the US flag. I smile. This is a new story. Last time they told me that the label should be taken off because otherwise the prisoners would desecrate Old Glory. Desecrating the flag reduces many Americans to spluttering apoplexy.

I spend the day talking to clients, normally one in the morning, one in the afternoon. Gaining the clients' trust is not easy. When we finally won the right for counsel to visit the prisoners the military tried to outflank us. They began by sending in interrogators pretending to be lawyers. Yusuf, one of my clients, was just a kid when he was turned over to the US military in Pakistan. He is smart and has taught himself English as he has grown up over the past four years, but as he tells me the story of his interrogators he is childlike again. One female interrogator insisted she was there to represent him and told him about the cases she had taken to the US Supreme Court. She told him she would be his mother for as long as he was in Guantánamo. Yusuf seemed unsure whether to believe her.

The military has adopted various duplicitous tactics. They told the prisoners that all their lawyers were Jewish, relying on perceived Muslim prejudices to drive a wedge between us.

'So you're Jewish,' says my client Shaker Aamer, with some accusation in his voice as soon as I enter the visitation cell. I am taken aback. Whenever I visit the base I plan for what could go wrong, yet some surprise always slaps me about the head. My father didn't get around to telling me that he was Jewish until I was thirty-seven years old. How could Shaker know? Technically, in a matrilineal society it would have to be my mother for me to qualify, but that is not a point worth debating. Shaker and I discuss my ethnicity. Ultimately we agree that a shared Semitic background between the Jew and the

Muslim is probably a good thing, and it is the Cornish half of me that he should worry about.

The next military gambit was arguably even sillier. 'They have been saying ...' Usama Abu Kabir hesitates, not wanting to go on. Usama is another client from Jordan.

'Tell me!' I smile at him, curious.

'They say ... they said to another of your clients ... he said ... the interrogators have been saying ...' By this time Usama is scarlet. He is a courteous man, unworldly in some ways.

'Come on, Usama, spit it out. I want to know what they're saying! You know it isn't going to be true.'

'Well ... that you like having sex with men!' He finally gets it out. Of course, I want to say that it should make no difference to him. I can't afford to, as so many of my clients here have been brought up in conservative Islamic countries, and we don't have time for a debate. I have to wave my wedding ring about and issue a denial.

Meanwhile, there are some entirely valid reasons for the prisoners to mistrust their lawyers. What is to distinguish the lawyer in the eyes of the client after years of deception? To represent a prisoner here you must be an American citizen. 'Hi! I'm from America and I'm here to help you.'

When a prisoner has a legal visit it is called a 'reservation', the same euphemism used for interrogation sessions. An American, who says he is a lawyer, comes in to see the prisoner, wanting to get the client's version of events. 'So, tell me, is it true that you went to Afghanistan to fight jihad?' The lawyer is hard to distinguish from an interrogator.

Some lawyers actually tell their clients that the meetings are confidential, protected by the attorney–client privilege from the snooping ears of others. The prisoners laugh to think that anyone could be so soft in the head as to make promises like this. Everyone knows that there are cameras in the cell and microphones by the door. When you buzz to be let out, the guards can hear you whether you hold down the button or not. So they can listen in whenever they like.

There are other problems that the lawyers accidentally bring on themselves. One showed up to see a client for the first time, not knowing that the firm was paying $1,500 a day for a translator who had previously worked for the US Department of Defense. The same prisoner had previously been introduced to the same translator by an interrogator working with US military intelligence. The only difference now was this man saying he was a lawyer.

Once gained, it is easy to lose your client's trust. The little world of Guantánamo Bay is a conspiracy theory in a goldfish bowl. Even routine legal rules that apply in any American case stir up problems among prisoners who have little idea of Western culture. For example, a lawyer is never allowed to file a lawsuit seeking a prisoner's freedom without permission of either the client, or a 'next friend' – someone close enough to him to act in his best interests. Obviously, the first option is not available, as all the prisoners who still need lawyers are being held incommunicado in Cuba and lawyers have no way of asking whether they want help. I spent several weeks travelling around the Middle East tracking down prisoners' family members, offering to find legal assistance for their sons and brothers in Guantánamo. Normally, the families would respond gladly, signing the forms necessary for us to file the legal papers. At the same time they would give me letters and family pictures to take to Guantánamo, to try to prove my connection to a prisoner's family.

The wife of one Middle Eastern prisoner gave me written authorisation to help her husband, and told me about his background.

'Why involve my wife in all this?' the prisoner complained, angrily when I met him. 'Why do you get her in trouble because I am here?'

She had provided an affidavit which included Western aspects of his life, to refute the US military's view that he was a bearded Islamic extremist. He used to watch every Jean-Claude Van Damme film ever made and wore his hair long, emulating his cinema idol. When he saw the statement he became even more angry. 'You are making me out to be a bad Muslim!' he said.

The clients' suspicions go far deeper than this. Sometimes a 'reservation' for a lawyer visit is worse than interrogation. One person I visited was Jamal Kiyemba. He is originally from Uganda, but he lived in England from the age of fourteen. He is quiet and well behaved, so the military generally kept him in Camp Four, where the conditions were relatively favourable. He lived in a cell block with ten other people and was allowed out into a common area during the day.

When he was first brought over for a legal visit, the military moved him to Camp Echo ten days before I was due to arrive to see him.

'Camp Echo is the most lonely place on earth,' he wrote. 'I was all alone for ten days. They brought me over here, they would not let me take my Qur'an and they put me in an isolation cell with nothing. There is no way to talk to any other prisoner, you're not meant to talk to the guards. There is a camera and microphones in the cell to make sure this is obeyed. The camera seems to shrink the cell and make you paranoid. Showers and recreation were greatly limited – I got to go into the outside cage once for half an hour in six days and got one shower. If I complain about Camp Echo, I am told that it is the lawyer's fault. If I did not have to come for a legal visit, I would not be treated like this.'

One client was held in solitary confinement in Camp Echo for eleven days after I left as well. I have never tried spending two weeks all alone, not knowing whether it would stretch into a month. Would it be worth a few hours with some lawyer who has failed to get me freedom, or even the promise of a fair trial?

I have dual British and American nationality, but I grew up near Cambridge. Because I have an English accent, I am taken less frequently for a CIA agent than many of my colleagues. But even this does not spell trust. Some prisoners have coherent theories about how the lawyers are dupes for Donald Rumsfeld, despite their good intentions. After all, what good does a lawyer do? By the fifth anniversary of the Guantánamo prison, there had been more than 750 prisoners held there, 350 of whom had been dribbled back home by the Bush Administration, generally as quietly as possible. Not one had been ordered out of prison by a judge. Some prisoners think that the US has let lawyers into the prison solely to make the government look good. These prisoners view lawyers in the same light as they see the International Committee of the Red Cross – the ICRC has been visiting ever since the prison opened in January 2002, yet they are not allowed to report any of the abuses to the outside world. It makes the military look good that it allows supposedly free access to the ICRC inspectors, but what good does it achieve for the prisoners?

Often, I talk with my client about the coercion and torture he has suffered at the hands of the US military. Most of the soldiers at the base seem to accept the Guantánamo reality without blinking; a minority have qualms that this is all un-American.

It is always a long day. With some clients I have to speak my questionable French and even bring my dubious Italian into play. We laugh a good deal, but I think half the time they are laughing at my accent and goodness only knows what they understand about their legal rights. How many visits will it take for me to be able to win someone's trust in a foreign language?

At 4.30 I have to leave. I reflect as I walk out. It is not surprising that the prisoners I see today are depressed. They have good reason.

The soldiers are depressed too. One military escort grumbles how life is so boring at the base, he'd rather be in Iraq. I like him. He has it tough, stranded away from his wife and children for almost a year, unable to help with the escalating problems of the kids' adolescence. He's done over a decade in the military, but it is still a long way till he would reach that twenty-year retirement date. He thinks it's time he got out for good.

We are driving away from the camp when the escort applies his brakes hard. We sit without moving.

'Is he completely off yet? I can't see,' the escort asks. There is an irritated horn behind us. It must be some neophyte to the island. Surely anyone else would know that a traffic jam on one of the two main roads of the base can only be caused by one thing: an iguana, unhurriedly making for the side of the road, perhaps – as in this case – pausing to turn a lazy and distinctly supercilious eye on the waiting vehicles.

En route back to the ferry landing, we stop at the NEX, the Navy Exchange. Posters advertise the imminent visit of Miss Teen USA, a reminder that the overwhelming majority of the soldiers are male. One escort remarks that the base is full of horny young men: ninety per cent of the base are male, he says, and as for the rest, half the women are lesbians.

'That don't leave much for the rest of 'em,' he says. I cannot pluck up the courage to ask how many of his macho marine buddies are gay. I don't want to offend him and I know I have yet to convince him that I am not a communist. Up to now, he has been suspending his disbelief, allowing his friendliness and good manners to govern our relationship.

I am surprised that the US military does not treat its own soldiers better. The soldiers work four days in five. They are up at 4 a.m., at the camp by 6 a.m. and they work until 6 p.m. Then they have to go on a training run before dinner and sleep. They cannot bring their families to the base and when they do get leave to visit their children every six months, many of them have to pay their own way back to the mainland. There is a new company running the chow hall, Del-Jen. Someone is making a lot of money out of this, but the quality of the chow hall food is notably worse than last time I was here.

Every soldier I meet has a calendar, checking off the days.

At one of the shops there are some T-shirts hanging outside. The escort says they used to have some bad ones, but the PR people made them stop selling them when the media came on a visit. There are still plenty on offer that might offend someone of ordinary sensibilities. I cannot resist a Lilliputian shirt for my seven-year-old nephew that says 'Future Behavior Modification Instructor'. I am not sure whether I will be liable if he beats up my brother. There is a new one I had not previously seen: 'Taliban Towers: A Five Star Resort'. Then there is the old staple, the 'Guantánamo Golf Course' T-shirt, which will be a curiosity at my mother's club in Suffolk.

We get back in the van to head down to the ferry landing. I almost don't notice the iguana that is relaxing in the late-afternoon shade beside the tarmac as we drive by. He was well clear of danger really, but as I look back through the rear window of the van, I see him scurry away towards a hole.

I also see two police cruisers. They follow us closely. We pass the speed detector sign that shows us hovering at the maximum twenty-five miles per hour. Just when I think we might be safe, their flashing red and blue comes on, ordering our escort to the side of the road.

One military policeman comes directly to the passenger side while the second, following procedure, stands off to the side, his right hand on his gun. The escort opens the van door.

'You came awful close to that iguana back there,' the officer says officiously.

'Yes, sir, it was in the shade, it was hard to see,' our friendly escort replies.

'I watched him run off into a drain, so he wasn't dead, I guess, but it was awful close,' says the policeman. 'You know how serious that could have been.'

'Yes, sir.'

'Well, you be more careful in future, you hear?'

'Yes, sir.'

And the two policemen leave, each in his separate vehicle.

'What a shit!' says a second escort, also with us in the van. 'Like they've got nothing better to do.'

The rest of the drive is uneventful, just five minutes to the landing. The ferry has stopped for the day, so in the evening we take a faster boat back across the bay. Strangely, it's called the U-boat. It stands for 'utility'. Waiting for it to leave, I walk over to the plaque thirty yards away. This is where Christopher Columbus anchored on his second trip, on 30 April 1494. He found nothing of interest in Guantánamo – no water, let alone gold – and left the next morning.

The trip back across the bay takes no more than ten minutes. We skirt behind a rusty Cuban tanker listing out to sea from the communist Guantánamo City. Snapping at her heels like a sheepdog, a fifteen-foot US Navy boat patrols, machine guns at the ready.

As I walk back up the hill to the CBQ, the iguanas eye me balefully. An exquisite scarlet and white butterfly bounces in the turbulence as a pick-up truck passes by. I am smiling to myself, thinking about the guard who searched me at the camp today. He was patting me down and he patted down my arm. That might have been more reasonable if it were not for my short sleeves. I walk past a parked Island Mechanical truck, with its bumper sticker: 'If 10% is enough for God, it's enough for the IRS' (the Internal Revenue Service).

Four Humvees pass by on patrol, machine guns trained in different directions. The last one has a soldier with a rifle aiming backwards. As the armoured vehicles drive away, for perhaps a quarter of a mile, his rifle aims constantly at my chest. I think how my mother told me never to point even a toy gun at a person. I have time to ponder the nervous habits of bored people, and wonder whether he is clicking the safety catch on and off, on and off. It is unsettling.

Endless tiny orange crabs scout their way across the road. They make the walk uncomfortable, as I have to concentrate to avoid adding to the orange smears of their predecessors. There is a banana rat on its back, staring at the blue evening sky, its stomach tipping out into the grass. Seven buzzards stand at attention, ugly in a circle, each waiting for a turn.

Up at the CBQ I change into shorts for a walk down to the sea. There is a dirt road that turns away through the metal fencing. Banana rat droppings are scattered like the pits of kalamata olives. Yellow flowers, counterfeit cowslips, are blooming along the roadside in the tall grass.

Chapman Beach is the first I come to, well kept military style, with concrete changing rooms so solid that they would stop a tank invasion. Only the Navy could have brought a crane round on a barge and moved massive boulders into a semicircle, creating a pool that is safe from any encroaching sharks. There is a concrete diving area, too, and the water is warmer in December than the English Channel in July.

I walk along the cliff towards the airport, to Hidden Beach. Here the red sign warns of dangerous currents and prohibits swimming. To emphasise the point there is a memorial to RMC Billy Armstrong Henry: 'He gave his life attempting to Rescue Another, 17 March 1986'. There is a Del-Jen barrel – 'We Recycle: No Trash' – at the top of sixty-three well-tended wooden steps down to the cove below. Several geckos scamper out of the way as I clamber down through the pine trees.

The beach is remarkable: an infinity of fossilised shells and coral thrown up in a bank by the storms. Here and there, flotsam: a 'Comfort' shoe sole, some plastic spoons and forks, and a blue pen top.

Going further along the cliff I come to Midway Beach, where the sign allows some snorkelling – 'Buddy System Required'. Visitors are admonished that 'Alcoholic Beverages are permitted from Sunrise to Sunset only'. This time there are no stairs down and I am a little paranoid as I walk through the high grass to the cliff, remembering the large black snake that was waiting for me outside the CBQ motel one morning. I walk as noisily as I can, only as far as the cliff's edge. My approach has troubled the large iguana on an outcrop below. He freezes and seems to survey the steep rocks that clamber down to the high tide. The snail crabs vanish inside their shells, hidden like limpets.

I come to the furthest reach of my walk and turn for home. Dusk is coming. Daring to come out for his dinner, another banana rat looks at me from twenty yards away. Lonely for someone to talk to, I greet him. But he is scared. He humps off like a chubby camel, ungainly, into the deeper scrub.

Rusty barbed wire from an earlier era, perhaps World War Two, pokes over the top of the grass. The evening birds use it for rest. As I walk back, I think of the conversation I had with one of the escorts, a black man from the Deep South. He understands the prisoners' plight here better than most and even joins in with the lawyers when we talk about the prison. He tells me of his retirement dream: how the military should itself retire from Guantánamo, so that he can come back here and run a Caribbean resort. It has the name recognition and it has the facilities: a major airport, the motel and the beaches.

In a canvas of reds, the sky silhouettes the cacti and thorn bushes seem aflame. It is disarmingly beautiful after a long day on the bleak military base. I always take a walk, as that hour helps to evaporate the melancholy that descends on me as I walk out of the prison.

The tannoy crackles to life again. It's time for the bugle to blare the Retreat, the slightly defeatist end to every Guantánamo day.

When I get back to my room I turn on the television. Still blurred, it is the US Paintball Championships, the Hurricanes versus XSV (pronounced Excessive). I recognise the inflatable shapes I saw earlier in the Guantánamo recreation grounds. The obstacles are the same: the 'doll house', the 'car wash' and the 'snake'. They are being spattered with paint in Miami, as the teams battle it out. 'Two brothers on the field,' said the commentator excitedly, 'with a combined eighteen years in paintball. XSV are now down two bodies, it's three on five.'

I go to sleep thinking about this place. Al-Qaeda means 'The Base' in Arabic. Guantánamo means 'The Naval Base' here. One of the military defence lawyers has developed his own response when a soldier confronts him with 'Honor Bound, sir!' He returns the salute sardonically: 'To defend the US Constitution'.

Guantánamo should consider a change of motto.

2

TICKING BOMB

The telephone call came in ten hours ago. The bomb is ticking somewhere in central London, but there are thousands of streets, endless alleys and an infinite number of secrets. There is no chance of finding it. The evacuation cannot be completed in time and thousands will die.

Scotland Yard has a man in custody. His name, he says with some pride, is Yusuf Surab. He says, boastfully, that it's a dirty bomb, high explosives underneath some radioactive material that will spread deadly radiation across the city. The detective in charge is confident that the man knows where the bomb is and almost certainly how to defuse it. But Yusuf has been read his warnings and he's not talking. He says he wants his lawyer. He does not seem overly concerned how long it takes. He says he's used to this kind of treatment and he knows his rights. He's calm.

Nobody else is.

'Fuck his rights!' one of the police officers exclaims. 'Let's force the bastard to talk. It's crazy not to. We got lives to save here.'

'We have to get a judge to issue a warrant to use torture, or get the PM's permission,' the detective reminds his colleague.

'So let's do it.'

In an emergency, getting the Prime Minister proves easier than a judge. The PM has called an urgent Cabinet meeting. As the second hand sweeps round the dial on the silent electric clock, the official portrait of Margaret Thatcher frowns severely; there seems no doubt that she would give a thumbs-up for the thumbscrew. Is there really any choice? Can the current PM condemn the city to death and destruction rather than inflict some transitory pain on a single man?

'We're about to be lynched with our own liberties,' intones the Home Secretary. There is a nervous edge in his voice. Nobody ever really believed it would come to this. 'Our first priority has to be to protect innocent people.'

The PM looks around the room. He does not need to say anything, or ask any question. With the vote for another term looming in only a few short years, the Cabinet members voice instant and unanimous agreement.

The PM will refer to 'enhanced interrogation methods' – with a nod to the American talent for euphemism. But he puts through the call without hesitation: 'Make him talk,' he says.

So Yusuf won't have a nice day, but you can't make an omelette without cracking a few eggs.

This is the one time when torture is provably worthwhile, the PM thinks to himself. If – when – Yusuf cracks, the police will be able to verify his story immediately. If the bomb is there, he is telling the truth. If not, it's back to the rack until he does. If it turns out to be a hoax, then it's his own damned fault for telling everyone there was a bomb in the first place, terrifying an entire nation.

Who, with the responsibility for so many lives, would make a different decision?

It was never meant to be like this. It was September 11 2001. After two decades defending capital cases across the Deep South and staving off execution dates, I was tired. I had planned to spend more time in England, closer to my family, where life would shift down a gear. Meanwhile, I had a capital trial coming up in Lake Charles, Louisiana and I planned to talk to the state's pathologist this morning. The law office I was running at the time, a small charity, had so many capital cases going in that parish that we had rented a small house. One of the volunteers helping on the trial had switched on the early-morning television and it was intruding, irritating me as I sat with my coffee preparing to meet the expert witness. There was something on about an aircraft hitting the World Trade Center in New York. The first reaction was to blame a small private plane and speculation about the pilot falling asleep or unconscious was substituting for factual news. I paid it little attention and left to meet the pathologist.

Twenty minutes later, as I turned back down the block looking for the address, the streets seemed unnaturally quiet. I found the beige single-storey building, but the front door was locked. It was almost nine o'clock and the pathology lab should have been open. Nobody answered the phone when I called on my mobile. Something was wrong. I drove back to the house.

America had suffered its first serious terrorist attack by foreigners, collapsing the Twin Towers and killing 3,000 people.

In the confused panic that followed, the gaggle of foreign prisoners seized on suspicion of terrorism began its inexorable expansion. Something had to be done with them. Four months later the Bush Administration announced plans for Guantánamo Bay. America was still looking around for the enemy, first nervously over a shoulder, then aggressively into the future.

The plans for this new gulag immediately pissed me off. Whose idea was it, in the name of democracy and the rule of law, to set up a prison in Cuba, where Americans have loudly complained that there has been no meaningful law for half a century? Whose idea was it to dissolve the US Constitution, leaving the prisoners with fewer rights than the local iguanas? Did nobody realise what a catastrophe this was going to be? Did they not see how all the goodwill that washed over the world after September 11 would soon dissolve in this kind of rank hypocrisy?

It was January 2002. There were plenty of prisoners facing execution in the Deep South who needed help, but I have never been very good at declining a new project. Jumping in with both feet seemed like a good idea at the time. I e-mailed round some friends in the death penalty world to find out who else wanted to sue Bush and put a stop to this ill-conceived plan.

For the most part response tended to be something about being busy, or how these people were terrorists who had attacked our country. The American mainland had not been invaded since the war of 1812 and already bombs were falling on Afghanistan in reply. The country was at war and – understandably – people were patriots first. A friend had tickets to the New Orleans Saints, the local football team. They always sing the national anthem before a game, but the 50,000 fans sang with increased solidarity now.

I certainly did not criticise America's shocked reaction to the horrors of 11 September but the Bush Administration's response seemed, to me, to be contrary to everything decent that America stood for. Eventually my e-mail messages did encounter two other people on a similar search. Joe Margulies was one. He had spent ten years in Texas, the toughest place to fight the death penalty, and now had a private practice in Minnesota. The other was Michael Ratner, head of the Center for Constitutional Rights, a legal charity in New York. We sued Bush on 19 February 2002 in Washington DC.

Almost three years later, when the Supreme Court had finally recognised the right for lawyers to visit the base, I paused, almost in mid sentence, when I was working on a memo I had titled 'The Torture Table'. It was a checklist of the coercive and abusive interrogation methods that the US authorities were using in the battle for democracy that the lawyers could use to interview the clients. A sense of perspective gleamed momentarily through my concentration. When I went to law school in 1981, it was not meant to come to this: listing arcane torture methods, each used at one time or another on my clients, or identified in official government memos as acceptable interrogation methods in our Brave New World.

I had been researching the pedigree of each technique, tracing each to the Spanish Inquisition, the Star Chamber, or an authoritarian regime in the Middle East. For example, tying the prisoner's wrists and hanging him from a hook may sound more benign than the rack, but the Inquisition recognised its value as a torture technique. They called it the 'strappado'. If they tied your hands behind your back and hung you by your wrists that way, it was the 'reverse strappado', an even more painful way to get your shoulders dislocated.

But what was I doing, frozen in front of the computer screen? What, more importantly, was the United States doing? And how had this come to pass?

There are some barbaric practices that take a long time to shake off. The death penalty is one of them, still used in thirty-seven states across America. At the turn of the millennium, though, criticism of torture had seemed to be almost universal; when the occasional tale of torture leaked out from a repressive regime there was unanimous condemnation.

Then came 11 September 2001.

*

Debating the circumstances under which torture might be acceptable used to be the exclusive domain of college professors, desperate to provoke their yawning students with philosophical conundrums ranging from the death penalty to abortion. They would talk about the recidivist murderer in support of capital punishment; they would pose the ticking-time-bomb scenario as the extreme example that challenged the comfortable assumptions of their students that torture was never justifiable.

But after 11 September the debate lurched out of the classroom and into both the halls of Congress and the British Court of Appeal. Torture was back on the public agenda. In late 2004, Channel 4 asked me to present a polemical documentary on torture. I had a visceral opposition to torture no matter what the circumstances and had not stopped to consider the other side, so I thought that talking to torture advocates might prove educational.

We began with one of the academics. I was going to sit across a dining-room table from Michael Levin, a philosophy professor at City College in New York. Back in 1982 Levin published a prescient article that now elevated him to a Moses among torture theorists. He had used the ticking-time-bomb scenario and argued that we should rethink the total ban on torture. Under limited, extreme circumstances, he suggested that the use of torture was not merely acceptable but morally required.

I had done my research and my prejudices were firmly intact. Advocating torture was not Levin's only philosophical peccadillo. He had also declared war on affirmative action, saying that he was 'sick and tired' of African-American people claiming that they should get a leg-up. He repeatedly expressed his opinion in his classes that African-Americans lag in the fiscal leagues because they have lower intelligence and motivation than whites, rather than because of discrimination. The college authorities warned him that he would be disciplined or sacked if he continued voicing his theories. He refused, sued and won his case. The court ruled that the First Amendment protected his freedom of expression.

Well before he arrived for the interview I had concluded that while he had the right to express his opinion, I did not have to like him, or his ideas. I should have known better. Levin was very obliging, agreeing to come down by train from New York to Washington DC for the interview. When he walked in he was immediately amiable. A short man with a wolverine face, Levin was the classic academic in his cord jacket. He was in his late fifties, trim from running marathons. He sat across the table, talked loudly and smiled through most of our discussion.

We were in an apartment borrowed for the meeting. The camera was over my shoulder and we faced each other over a cup of coffee. We were six floors up, so Levin was framed by the tops of the trees, behind them the Washington zoo.

We chatted as the cameraman set up. By American standards, Levin was not even very right-wing. He disdained President George W. Bush and most of his policies. But he remained a firm torture advocate. As we turned on the camera, I asked him to identify the circumstances when he thought the use of torture would be justified.

'Well, first of all I wouldn't be in the market for specific rules,' he began rather vaguely. 'But very broadly speaking, when there's a very, very great wrong that will be done, a great many people will be killed, I think it has to be that. There's no question about the guilt of the perpetrator. It's done in a preventive . . . for preventive purposes to keep the harm from happening.'

He had set out his theory clearly in his article.

> Suppose a terrorist has hidden an atomic bomb on Manhattan Island that will detonate at noon on July 4th unless – here follow the usual demands for money and release of his friends from jail. Suppose, further, that he is caught at ten in the morning on the fateful day, but he won't disclose where the bomb is. What do we do? If we follow due process, wait for his lawyer, arraign him, millions of people will die. If the only way to save those lives is to subject the terrorist to the most excruciating possible pain, what grounds can there be for not doing so?

Ask an audience whether they favour torture and the vote will be overwhelmingly no, but pose the ticking-time-bomb scenario and the vote tends to turn round. Take it out of amorphous theory and suggest that the bomber's target is the audience's home town, that it is their families who will die, and the torture majority widens.

It is disturbing. 'What about the level of torture?' I asked. 'Is there any principle you think that dictates, this is the worst thing we'd do to people?'

'Well, I'm inclined to think it ... to some extent ...' He paused contemplatively. 'It's sensitive to the harm we're trying to prevent. Well, if we're very clear that it is the perpetrator and so questions of innocence don't arise, I guess we could do anything up to death on his part ... excruciating physical pain. Once you open the door to torture, you've opened the door to whatever level of pain is necessary to elicit the information that you need.'

Of course, it is logically irrefutable. There are millions of people who are going to die because of a bomb laid by this terrorist and he holds the key to prevent all the suffering – he is hardly in a place to set limits on the pain that he might have to endure.

'I mean,' I returned to Professor Levin, thinking I would see how far he would go along the path, 'you're torturing me, I'm acting tough and you try the rack without success, you'd then move on with electrodes to the testicles?'

'I guess so, I guess so,' he said without hesitation. He was still smiling.

'Mmm. I'm feeling uncomfortable already,' I said.

He laughed. 'Just don't do anything wrong, and, er ...' He paused, recognising that he was on television rather than in the classroom. 'In some cases I'd have no objection to torture, but I'd also see a case for not doing it, so it could go the other way. But certainly in some cases it would be mandatory.'

'Mandatory?' I asked, startled. 'Mandatory for a prisoner ... for us to ... to ... to abuse him?'

'Yes.' No perceptible qualms. Of course, this is the logic of the torture advocate. They are not abusing people for the hell of it, but for the greater good. 'Right. How would you ... what would you tell the parents of all the children who died? – that, well, there are these rules and we had to wait until his attorney showed up before we could ask him questions, and in the meanwhile his ... your children died?'

'What do you think about the people who say torture is absolutely abhorrent even in the circumstances where you think it is the only option?' I asked, putting my own position. It sounded rather plaintive.

'Well, I'm inclined to say that . . .' He paused briefly, obviously wondering whether to say it or not. 'They are perhaps moral cowards. That's strong but . . . er . . . either moral cowards or perhaps they have . . . they're not thinking . . .'

'They're just morally wrong not to accept torture?'

'I don't say morally wrong, but they're not really thinking.' The professor returned to his comfort zone, wagging the finger that had obviously been applied to his students for many years.

I took a sip of my coffee and tried moving the theory down still further. 'If there's a circumstance when someone is going to blow up a bomb and, instead of having the person responsible for the bomb in custody, you have someone who had nothing to do with it, but knows where the bomb is. But the person you've got has children who are being held by the terrorist and the father knows his kids will be killed if he talks. Would you torture that father to stop the explosion?'

'That's a very difficult one . . .' He pondered. 'I'm inclined to say when the numbers get big enough it would be OK to.'

'You're in the situation where the perpetrator knows where the ticking bomb is,' I continued. 'The way you're going to get him to talk is you're going to torture his five-year-old child, would you do that?'

'Yes, that seems within the bounds.' He was more emphatic this time. 'Yes.'

'Yet the five-year-old is utterly innocent?'

'That's right.'

All this presupposed that Levin could be certain that he was torturing the right person. The professor was a strong proponent of the death penalty. I have fought executions for over twenty years and it always colours my view of people when they express that opinion. I can't help but think that they've never been close to an actual execution. It was a good jumping-off place to discuss the fallibility of the people making this torture decision.

'What proportion of innocent people are we willing to allow to be executed to preserve the death penalty as an institution?' I asked.

'Well, you ask a question as if there's a precise answer,' replied Levin. 'As Hegel said, there's a reason we cannot calculate the prob-ability of finding your horse in the wrong stable. But my impression is that it would have to be fairly high, say five or six per cent, before I'd even start to wonder.'

At the time I was talking to him there were 3,373 people on Death Row USA – so five per cent meant that more than 160 would have to be innocent before that would trip Levin's worry meter. Each one would be a human being with only one life to lose. An academic's answer, I thought to myself.

'Now translate the issue of innocence into the context of inter-rogation; what proportion of people are we willing to torture erro-neously, because we just got it wrong, before that invalidates the whole process of torture?' I asked.

'Well, I would think it would have to be a very small percentage, much smaller than the death penalty,' he said reflexively.

'So what you're saying is we're willing to torture fewer people who're innocent than execute them?' I was intrigued. I wouldn't want to be tortured, but I'd rather that than being tortured to death. I had witnessed two clients die horribly in the electric chair.

'Many fewer, because torture's not a punishment, right? It's not a punishment, it's to prevent harm. And so you really, in that case, you have to be very, very sure that there's harm on the horizon.'

That seemed a strained distinction. He had said he would hesitate before he would torture someone plotting to take thousands of lives. He wanted to be more careful about inflicting pain under those cir-cumstances – where innocent people suffer but they don't die – than he would be when society was executing a human and where history suggested society made plenty of mistakes. Perhaps he had a point, though: far fewer people would agree with 'torture' as a proposition than with the death penalty. But where did that leave us on Levin's theory about the ticking time bomb, the cornerstone of his torture hypothesis?

'Can you identify, though, for me ...' I began. 'Can you identify one instance, say, in the last fifty years where torture was a real practical thing we could have done to avert a ... a massive disaster?'

'Well,' Levin pondered. 'I can't think of anywhere, with 20/20 hindsight, we might be able to say – well, they suspected these guys at the aeroplane gate, they were acting funny, if only we had known and we'd squeezed the information out of them right then and there, diverted the flights ... of course, you couldn't know that until afterwards. Unless you've got a candidate, I can't think of one at the moment.'

So we had a theory, but it seemed to have no practical application. Meanwhile I had what I had come for: a relatively coherent advocate for the torture position. I found my discussion with him very disturbing. Far from being my imaginary bogeyman of neocon extremism, he had been pleasant and not totally unreasonable. I could see his students lapping all this up.

Professor Levin's article had been influential, yet he had spent his entire life in the academy and he was far divorced from the real world of the torture chamber. He was not the only one talking about torture and my plan was to work up the ladder of torture advocates towards those with more practical experience. Researching for the programme, I had been surprised to discover that Professor Alan Dershowitz of Harvard University had proposed the use of warrants to validate torture, even though he insisted he opposed torture itself. Dershowitz is a famous liberal, who helped defend O. J. Simpson. Surely, of all people, he should not be marching, resolute, towards the Middle Ages. We flew up to Boston. It was the end of November, cold, with a wan sun. We passed an hour before the appointed time filming filler shots of the campus, where law had been taught going back to 1636. Fifty-six years later, just twenty miles to the north, the witch trials put the village of Salem on the map.

'I am no more a witch than you are a wizard,' said Sarah Goode to the Reverend Richard Noyes, who tried to take her confession as she stood at the gallows. Goode was a homeless woman who would mumble as she begged for alms. Some thought she was cursing them when they refused to be charitable. Before the hysteria subsided Goode was hanged, along with eighteen others, and at least 150 more were imprisoned in the witch trials. Most either confessed under torture or were implicated by statements tortured out of others. There is presumably no stronger evidence that torture induces a false confession than the admission to being a witch.

Two of the three judges to sentence these miserable people to death were Harvard graduates. One, Samuel Sewall, recognised his mistake four years too late and in 1700 he went on to publish *The Selling of*

Joseph, the first influential American book that argued for the abolition of slavery.

Meanwhile, back in the twenty-first century, I approached my interview with Dershowitz, certain that his good sense had been dissolved by too many years proposing hypotheticals to his students. This time we set up the camera in a small library. The bookshelves were all dusty texts and in the half-hour we had to wait I found half a dozen condemnations of torture, published over four centuries.

Dershowitz eventually arrived from a prior meeting. I had seen him on television throughout the O. J. Simpson case, but I had never met him in person. He was very short and expostulated around the room with all the energy of Napoleon directing his early battles. We did the interview standing up, but the producer made me perch on the arm of a chair to de-emphasise my height.

Dershowitz laid out his position. Twice in rapid succession he demanded that I make clear that he was a professor: as such he has a different obligation: to inspire debate, without necessarily guaranteeing a practical response.

'I hate torture. I wish nobody ever used it. I wish it were never done. I also hate terrorism.' He bounced around in his vehemence, making it difficult for the cameraman to focus.

'Tell me, then, what you think about the American position on torture as we stand now,' I asked.

'Utter hypocrisy. We say, we proclaim, we declare, we sign treaties saying that under no circumstances will we ever use torture or anything like it, and of course we do. And Americans *love* it!' He almost shouted the word. 'When we took Khalid Sheikh Mohammed and subjected him to water-boarding there wasn't a single complaint.' Khalid Sheikh Mohammed (normally known by his initials KSM) was allegedly the number three man in al-Qaeda, captured in March 2003. The notorious water-boarding technique involved being strapped to a plank, and then having your head dunked under water. Those who use it have said it is 'simulated' drowning, but it is more accurate to call it drowning, where you are dragged out of the water moments before you would actually die. As Senator John McCain has said, it is clearly torture, and an ugly form of it. 'What the American people don't like,' Dershowitz continued, are people taking photographs of it, because that makes us look terrible to the rest of the world. It's all a pretext. It's a little bit like France during Algeria where they never punished anybody for torturing but they did punish somebody for revealing the fact that they did torture. That's hypocrisy at its most extreme.'

He was talking about General Paul Aussaresses, the coordinator of the French intelligence services during the battle of Algiers in 1957. Forty years later Aussaresses was an octogenarian with a strange, skin-coloured eye patch that made him look as if his left eyelid had been sewn shut. He wrote a book detailing his role in the death of prisoners during the Algerian war of independence. 'The best way to make a terrorist talk when he refused to say what he knew was to torture him,' he wrote, speaking of the Algerian rebels whom he abused or even summarily executed. 'I was indifferent. They had to be killed, that's all there is to it.'

'I didn't enjoy it, it gave me no pleasure,' Aussaresses said after the book came out, responding to public criticism. 'But I have no regrets. I would do it again today if it were against bin Laden.' He was stripped of his rank and the right to wear his military uniform, and lost other military honours – not for committing torture, but for disclosing state secrets.

American courts have never punished any American for committing torture either. The only torture cases to appear in the US courts have been attempts to punish foreigners for abusing Americans. So Professor Dershowitz explained that he wanted to bring everything out into the open and, to do that, he thought that law enforcement officers should have to get a warrant from a very senior official – the President or the Chief Justice of the Supreme Court – before torture could be carried out.

'It's always possible that a warrant would be abused,' he immediately conceded. 'It makes no sense whatsoever having a mere district court judge do it – they hand out warrants the way they hand out presents at Christmas. That's why I'd require the President of the United States or the Chief Justice of the Supreme Court to issue it. The President's gotta be willing to go on television and say, "This is that *one* case where we *had* to make an exception."'

Dershowitz argued that his torture warrant idea would generally limit the use of torture. As I watched him, I was surprised that such an obviously intelligent man could be so naïve. Given the slightest official encouragement, surely those who are inclined towards torture are more likely to stray down the path, warrant or no warrant. I could not figure out whether he seriously believed his theory, or perhaps he wanted his students to try on the idea in the pristine fantasy land of their classroom.

While I would be the last to want to see anyone censored, there is a responsibility that comes with free speech that escalates with a person's influence in society that sensibly encourages self-censorship. Sometimes there are very real consequences to simply expressing an idea. Dershowitz was now trumpeted by the neocons for 'supporting' the abuses that they wanted to inflict. Even if he had been mis-understood, he had to recognise the consequences of his advocacy. I found myself liking him personally, but it seemed like an intellectual game, one that my clients were obliged to continue playing.

Indeed, Dershowitz had famously suggested in his writings that the torturer might begin by sliding needles under the prisoners' fingernails.

'I think pain is tremendously exaggerated in our society,' he said, accusing the American people of going soft. 'If I had the choice of one of my children being sentenced to prison for, say, six months in one of America's terrible prisons or being whipped thirty medically administered lashes, I would have no hesitation saying, you know, whip 'em. Nobody dies from the whipping. Nobody dies from the needle underneath the . . . er . . . nail.'

The mere fact that the prisoner would not die seemed scant jus-tification for abusing someone, but Dershowitz had a good point when it came to 'torture'. People are blinded by the word itself.

'There's a fascinating experiment being done at William James Hall at Harvard University, the Psychology Department, at my suggestion,' he said. 'For years people have been asking the following question: you have a train and it's on the track and the brakes fail, and if it . . . something isn't done, if it continues on the track, fifteen innocent people will die. But the engineer, by shifting it to another track, can kill only one person – what would you do?

'And everybody, across all cultures, says you shift it to the other track. Better for one to die than for fifteen to die, even if it means the person has made the decision to kill him. And that decision is made with the rational part of the brain, and a PET scan is administered to test that.' He was referring to the Positron Emission Tomography scan, where a radioactive tracer travels through your brain to see which part is reacting.

'Then you shift the question. You ask the same people, what if you didn't have to kill the one person, you could just injure him? And they say, what a dumb question. Of course you do it, by just injuring him. And then you say' – he paused, gesticulating with his right arm to enhance the drama – 'ah! But the catch is the injury has to be wilful and deliberate, you have to *torture* him.'

He left the word to dangle, his eyes sparkling, keen to close the circle on his story. 'And as soon as you mention the word "torture" all the thinking shifts from the rational side of the brain to the emotional side of the brain. The "torture" word changes the way we think about choice of evil dilemmas.' Now, the people in the experiment chose fifteen deaths over one case of torture.

We closed our discussion on this note. Dershowitz was in a hurry, off to another meeting. We tidied the lights and cameras into the gathering gloom of a winter evening, and hurried to the airport for the flight back to Washington. I pondered some of his arguments in the van as we drove away. The position Dershowitz took rankled. There is nobody who is as harsh a critic of a liberal as a fellow liberal; I could more easily forgive someone like Levin for publicly endorsing torture, as he would hardly be identified as a known leftie. Dershowitz was doing great damage in the torture discourse simply because of who he was. The fact that someone with his reputation could even mention torture warrants would be seen as validating the concept for the right wing.

Yet he was undoubtedly right about the emotive response to the term 'torture'. Each side has its T-word: one side uses the word 'terrorist' to steep the world in fear and dissolve any chance of rational judgement; the other side uses the word 'torture'. Each word is dangerous, a distraction.

The War on Terror has been a godsend to anti-democratic regimes. It is worth remembering that today's terrorist may not just be tomorrow's freedom fighter – he may well be today's freedom fighter. Vladimir Putin has leapt on to the Bush bandwagon, tarring the Chechen liberation guerillas as terrorists. Only five years ago the West recognised that the Russians were committing war crimes in Chechnya.

Now, the mute button has been pressed on all criticism. The Chinese say the Tibetans and the Turkestanis are terrorists. Colonel Gaddafi says the same of anyone who opposes his tyranny in Libya. The list goes on and on. As with all despots, Gaddafi's time will pass. Before September 11 2001 the West understood that if we are to find a more reasonable replacement, we need to support the tyrant's opponents and help ensure a peaceful transition to something better. Now, Tony Blair visits Tripoli and tries to deport opponents of the regime back to Libya.

Meanwhile, at the same time the word torture obscures the debate on a multitude of levels. Dershowitz is probably right to say that shouting 'torture' pushes the listener beyond rationality, but even if we remain coldly logical, the word justifies as much misconduct as it proscribes. In 2002 the Bush Administration circulated some now notorious memos that defined torture, apparently with a view to legitimising lesser forms of abuse. Torture was forbidden, but 'enhanced interrogation techniques' were fine. The rack was beyond the pale, but water-boarding was not.

Specialist Sabrina D. Harman was a young reserve military police officer from Alexandria, Virginia, whose face became famous as one of the soldiers portrayed stacking naked prisoners into a pyramid at the Abu Ghraib prison. She described how her assignment was to 'break down' prisoners for interrogation. 'They would bring in one to several prisoners at a time already hooded and cuffed,' Harman wrote from Baghdad. 'The job of the MP was to keep them awake, make it hell so they would talk.'

Long before Harman achieved notoriety, in April 2002, Donald Rumsfeld finalised a 'list of techniques for interrogation officers to break resistance'. The aim, of course, was to overcome their will in order to gain important intelligence. All this talk of 'breaking' people twice begs the question: if the suspect is to be 'broken' by a series of acts, each of which falls short of torture, does this not amount to the same thing? At the same time, is there any reason to suggest that a statement extracted from a gradually broken suspect is any more reliable than something extorted more rapidly by harsher forms of abuse?

Harking back to my work with Death Row, I thought of Travis Hayes, a sixteen-year-old black kid who signed a false confession but never pretended to have been physically abused by the police, let alone tortured. He was simply intimidated by the white Louisiana cops and their promise to get him executed, so he falsely implicated his co-defendant, Ryan Matthews, in a murder. It took several years and six DNA tests to get Ryan off Death Row.

Focusing on torture – or even seeking to define it – tends to blind everyone to the fact that mistakes are commonplace when we use even minor methods of coercion.

Professors Dershowitz and Levin were both academics without much practical experience in the realities of interrogation. The fact that the professors construct theories in the classroom carried limited weight as far as I was concerned. I wanted to get much closer to the real world of torture.

I was excited about my next interview. It would be someone closely associated with the Republican hierarchy. He would not give an official view on the use of torture, but he was willing to go on record and explain the kind of thinking that veered the Bush Administration so strongly on to this course.

Richard Perle has been one of the driving intellects of the neocon agenda. He was once a liberal, he said, but he had been mugged by reality. However they might sneer at his views, Europeans could not look down at the cultured Perle, as they liked to disdain the parochial President Bush. Greying, in his early sixties, Perle maintained his holiday home in Provence, and his Washington home was littered with books and magazines on European culture. On the evening I visited him he was keen to keep the interview as concise as possible to avoid being late for an appointment at his Italian dining club, where the members took turns to prepare a meal.

Perle was an Assistant Secretary of Defense in the Reagan Administration. Some thought him the most powerful man in the Pentagon; others simply dubbed him the 'Prince of Darkness', since when it came to arms control, the main focus of his job, he generally opposed new agreements with the Soviet Union. When he left his job for a lucrative spell in the private sector, he was paid a large amount to write a book about his experiences, called *Hard Line*. In it he described how battles were fought within the US government, with cabinet members using their deputies as proxies.

'Since turf wars and ideological battles between the principals on such a high level attracted unwanted publicity, assistant secretaries did the fighting,' he wrote, describing his own role. 'Urbane guerrillas in dark suits, they fought not with AK-47s but with memos, position papers, talking points, and news leaks.'

Three presidents later, Perle returned to the old game, this time conducting his surrogate war from outside the administration, speaking for fellow hawks who had to stay silent because of their political positions. He would doubtless deny that his role was to serve as Bush's test balloon, but his situation did allow him to float ideas, watch the resulting flak, all the while allowing Bush deniability.

Perle's home was sheathed in bark tiles, a tree house on the ground. It was set in a quietly oppressive neighbourhood. There was a dissonance between outward appearances and the dangerous reality trumpeted by the Bush Administration. The local children seemed to be riding their bicycles happily in the street, but their nervous parents knew better. The kids were in appalling danger – not, as the observer might worry, because the bikes were weaving perilously on to the road. Not because Washington, the political capital of the United States, was vying with a handful of other cities for the title of murder capital. No. Looming over the heads of these children were the dark clouds of al-Qaeda, an ever-present threat.

We settled into his living room for the interview and I began by asking him why today was so different from times past when, for example, the Soviet Union trained thousands of nuclear warheads on the United States.

'Well,' he began in a briefing tone, 'very much unlike the threat of the Cold War, massive Soviet armies backed up by a huge nuclear arsenal and an intense revolutionary ideology, the threat today comes from religious fanatics, who want to remake the world in their own image, who want us infidels (and that includes most Muslims, by the way) to live by their extreme version of Islam.

'Bin Laden appeals to people who are driven to religious fanaticism, often, I think, because of personality disorders of their own,' he continued. 'Er, it's worth observing that a significant number of the hijackers on 9/11 seem to have had a lot of advantages, living in the West, decent educations, middle-class backgrounds, but a lot of personal conflicts and problems over their relationships with women, for example, their families.'

While blowing up innocent people in droves is clearly a madness of some sort, I was not sure I bought the idea that every extremist had a college degree and a sexual dysfunction. The twenty hijackers' social class could easily be explained in other ways. An illiterate peasant tending sheep in rural Yemen could hardly have passed himself off in a suit and tie to get on an American jet.

I wanted to move him on to the Bush Administration's cavalier attitude towards human rights.

'The question that I need to try to work out in my own mind', I began rather ponderously, looking for the right words, 'is this: does it not damage our credibility internationally when we stand for the rule of law, but then we don't allow lawyers to defend people?'

'The . . .' He paused, seeming perplexed by the question. 'The rule of law to which you refer is domestic law and it does not apply to non-American citizens. It just doesn't.'

'So British people don't have those rights?' I asked, remembering the people who would be watching the documentary we were making.

'Well . . . they . . . certainly don't have the same rights that Americans have in the American judicial system.' Perle stated this as a fact. There was no room for argument, no need for justification, it was simply the *civis Romanus sum* of the hyperpower.

Such a view goes down well to a domestic audience, but it leaves a foreigner feeling slightly left out and lonely. There is an American attitude that Europeans sometimes miss. In Europe, talk of human rights inevitably carries with it an enforcement mechanism, as legislation and conventions carry the human rights label. Not so in the US, where an aggrieved citizen may scream about the police trampling on his constitutional rights, but he'll never be heard to shout about his human rights. There is not a single human rights law that is enforceable against the United States in any international court, so in the US the term 'human rights' tends to be used by philosophers, not lawyers.

Running parallel with the semantic issue is an important distinction in the minds of the people, often even the liberals: human rights would obviously belong to all human beings. Constitutional rights do not. They belong to those who have signed up to the constitutional framework, in this case the Americans. And before the Europeans get too sanctimonious about this, Perle's view was certainly predominant in Britain when the colour pink spread across the globe. The bellicose Victorian Prime Minister Lord Palmerston would send a gunboat to enforce the rights of those carrying British passports, not just any old person with documents from a nineteenth-century League of Nations.

Having no human rights to worry about certainly helps avoid any legal problems that might be associated with coercive interrogations. But there still had to be a justification for it in the first place. Just like everyone else, Perle started talking about the ticking-bomb scenario, with the man in custody who could stop the deaths of thousands of innocents.

'The example I use is obviously the easy example, because I think most people would agree if you could save thousands of lives, even if it meant the harshest treatment with a single individual,' he said. Like any politician advocating torture, he certainly would not use the T-word. 'Harshest treatment' made it sound a little like school, where the headmaster was forced to punish disobedient boys. 'That would be justified. But it gets much more difficult in ... er, in lesser cases, and I think it can't be answered in the abstract.'

That was a waffle statement, since the 'abstract' is the only way that laws can be made. We can't legislate every time a real-life dilemma varies the facts. I pressed him, but could not get anything more concrete than a generalised endorsement of the 'harshest' techniques.

'Do you think the world, for an American, is more or less dangerous today than it was before 9/11?' I asked, trying to see where these techniques had got us.

'I think in one respect it's less dangerous, and that is because we are now conscious of, and organising to deal with, a threat that we didn't understand properly before September 11. In another sense we're now in a full-blown war with a radical ideology married to, er, suicidal, destructive acts. And so in that sense, our safety is very much in jeopardy.'

'Post the war in Iraq, is America a safer place?'

'I think we're safer.' Again no hesitation. 'I think leaving Saddam in place and hoping for the best was not a safe solution by any means.'

The interview did not last long. We did briefly discuss whether the US had sufficient laws to prosecute torturers, but in a way my question was moot: if torture was legitimate, there would be no need for a prosecution. Perle hurried off to his dinner engagement, leaving me to wonder about the evolution of such an obviously intelligent man.

Was it really true that September 11 and al-Qaeda pitched us into a Brave New World – or was the United States just unused to the battle being carried to her own territory? Since the war for independence in 1776, American soil has been attacked only three times. To be sure, there was the war of 1812, where the British burned the capital, along with the White House, but virtually no lives were lost since the city was evacuated ahead of the British advance. Then, on 7 December 1941 the Japanese instigated the day that would live in infamy, in Pearl Harbor, but even this took place among the far-flung islands of Hawaii. The loss of life was relatively modest when set in the context of the entire Second World War with 2,403 military personnel and sixty-eight civilians killed. Finally, on 11 September 2001 the World Trade Center in New York and the Pentagon in Washington were the objects of dramatic and devastating destruction by passenger planes. An estimated 2,996 innocent people died.

Other than this the United States itself has never been attacked. Obviously one should not attempt to underplay the tragedies (or perfidies) of Pearl Habor or September 11. There is no disputing the horror of the collapsing towers. Yet does the attack on the World Trade Center raise the stakes higher than the Cold War, when the Soviet Union joined America in a nuclear race, the theory of mutually assured destruction (nicknamed MAD) promising a nuclear winter that would wipe out humanity entirely? Have we forgotten, so soon, the chill of films such as *The Day After* and *The Third World War*?

So should we have tortured any Russian we came across, to try to learn anything and everything we could about Soviet plans to launch a nuclear attack? Did we? Or did the US hope to learn more by promising Soviet defectors asylum, a new home and a 1955 Chevy?

Other countries have faced far greater challenges than those that the United States confronts today. Can it honestly be said that Britain is in greater danger today than in 1940, when incendiary bombs tumbled down on London, replicating September 11 each evening, and Panzers lined up across the Channel? Londoners in the Blitz (or the still more desperate victims of Auschwitz) could have made a strong case for torturing every captured German to head off the next assault. The Russians, with twenty million dead and counting, could have been justified in joining the torture debate. Yet the excesses of World War Two seeded the political landscape for the very conventions that Richard Perle and President Bush would jettison today.

Professors Levin and Dershowitz were academics. Richard Perle struck me as a sofa soldier, making some rather sweeping statements from his Washington living room. Even though he was respected as an American conservative intellectual, I had found him unconvincing. But he conceded that he was only a 'consumer' of intelligence; I wanted to listen to the opinions of a hunter-gatherer.

A retired Marine Corps officer, Lieutenant-Colonel William 'Big Bill' Cowan spent three and a half years on combat assignments in Vietnam. In the 1980s he was selected to serve as the only marine in the Pentagon's most classified counter-terrorist unit, the Intelligence Support Activity (ISA), the activities of which still remain under the tightest security. Cowan served as a senior military operations officer and field operative on covert missions to the Middle East, Europe and Latin America. Today, he is a co-founder of the WVC3 Group, a company providing homeland security services, support and technologies to government and commercial clients.

Now in his late fifties, Cowan had hardly slowed down. We met in his office in standard American suburbia, just outside Washington, but Cowan looked far more comfortable in his pick-up truck as he swung into the parking lot. The bumper sticker advertised his arrival: 'I ♥ my AK-47'. The engine throbbed as he leant out of the window with his greeting. He was ready to roar once more into the forests and swamps of Vietnam.

Cowan had become a darling of the media, where he had gruffly described attaching crocodile clips to the genitalia of Vietcong prisoners to learn about enemy troop positions. He would intimate in interviews that he was no virgin when it came to real-life torture.

'I'll be honest by saying that I served a lot of time in Vietnam and in some cases, where I worked on prisoner operations, we did go a little bit beyond what normal interrogation techniques would give you, and we got phenomenal information,' he said one night on Fox TV.

In our interview, Cowan admitted only to a rather milder kind of abuse – threats that led to trembling, but never to actual screams; electrodes attached, but the current never applied. He did describe watching his South Vietnamese colleagues taking two prisoners, shooting one of them in the head, then turning to the second to demand information. 'It was very effective,' he said.

Big Bill presented his argument in a stark perspective. In the field his only obligation was to protect the lives of his men, and threatening physical torture seemed a relatively benign alternative to carpet-bombing, to the My Lai massacre, or even to the entirely legal efforts he was required to make to kill as many Vietcong and North Viet-namese as possible. When a soldier was walking out on patrol towards a crossfire that could cut short his life, adhering rigidly to the Geneva Conventions was like promising to apply the Marquess of Queensberry Rules in the boxing ring when your opponent climbs through the ropes with a hunting knife. The Vietcong were hardly known for their own respect for the rules.

Cowan felt that the Geneva Conventions were sometimes sissy regulations, unrealistic in practice, but he would contemplate torture solely under rules that were very narrowly drawn.

'Torture can only achieve results if the threat comes immediately upon capture,' he said. 'Within forty-eight hours the enemy will know that the prisoner has been taken and will already have taken steps to minimise the predicted dissemination of intelligence.'

When it came to Bagram Air Force Base, Abu Ghraib, Guantánamo Bay and George Bush, Cowan was a vitriolic critic. As far as he was concerned, abusing prisoners months and years after capture to secure information was senseless, simply gratuitous.

'We need to find Muslims who will support us, who will do things for us – and if we cause civilian casualties we lose that,' said Cowan, more realistic about the consequences of violence than his commander-in-chief. 'We may win tactical victories like Fallujah but . . . they are not helping us win the larger war for the support of the Iraqis. Not one city in Iraq had drinkable water eighteen months after we arrived. We should stop using contractors and just get a decent US Army Construction Battalion in there, do a show city, indicate how it can be done.'

Cowan's real-life experience presented a moral conundrum: is something as inherently savage as war subject to being 'civilised'?

Should there be a rule against attacking hospitals if the injured may later take the field once more? Why not bomb civilian targets if this will demoralise the enemy and end the war sooner?

Or do the Geneva Conventions hold out hope that if we agree now to take the harshest edges off war, one day perhaps we will outlaw it altogether?

I respected Cowan, as he had to apply theory to the real world. Based on the inconsistent versions that I read in various earlier interviews, I suspected that his stories of torture intelligence might have matured over thirty years in the telling. But he had been in the damp foxholes of Vietnam, never knowing when an enemy soldier would end his shivering life with a bullet out of the undergrowth. Maybe he actually had taken part in torture. All my life I have been transfixed and depressed by the surreal world of the front-line soldier. How would any of us react if, after months enduring shelling in a Somme trench in 1916, some staff officer sitting comfortably five miles behind the lines ordered us to climb out of the trench and walk slowly towards machine guns? Would we go back and shoot the officer instead? Or how would we respond, finding that we were among the lucky few who reached the enemy machine gun alive, if the German with his finger on that scything trigger threw up his hands in surrender just as we reached him? Would we respect the Geneva Conventions, or would we shoot the bastard who had just mown down dozens of our friends?

Big Bill Cowan's experience came at one end of the spectrum, the desperation of the battlefield. Under no circumstances would he carry his torture advocacy elsewhere. He saw no point, since he felt that torture just did not provide effective intelligence in the calm after the storm of battle.

Was he right? Next, I had an arrangement to speak with someone who should know. Mike Baker spent sixteen years with the CIA – called the 'Agency', the 'other service', or one of the various euphemisms that attach to America's main international intelligence office.

I met him in a stainless-steel hotel bar in Washington. It was time for morning coffee, although a battalion of liquor bottles lined the mirrors behind the bar. It would be difficult to guess from his average-American accent, but Baker holds dual nationality with Britain, where he was born. He joined the CIA shortly after university and when he left the Agency he turned to the private wing of the intelligence business.

Baker still looks like a clean-cut American student, betrayed only by a little grey over the ears. The camera had him in a slightly sinister light, which I thought unfair. Mike didn't look like someone who could climb over his own good manners to beat up a prisoner.

I was not quite sure why he took the time to do the interview, though I was glad he agreed to it. I told him that our conversation would deal with 'enhanced' interrogation techniques used by American intelligence operations. He chose his words carefully, balancing his desire to speak openly against his obligations to his former employers, always against the backdrop of the recent public relations disasters that the intelligence community had suffered from Afghanistan to Guantánamo Bay. Once he wondered aloud whether anyone would ever believe again that the intelligence community had any morals.

A photocopy of a CIA interrogation manual – marvellously entitled *The Human Resource Exploitation Manual* – lay on the bar top between us.

'In terms of experience, how many, er, subjects, or whatever word one might use, have you actually interrogated?' I asked, trying to choose my words carefully too.

'Er, you know what . . .' He hesitated.

'Oh, you're gonna . . .'

'Yeah, I am not, I mean,' he stuttered. I could see that he wanted to be polite, but could not answer questions about the specifics of his experiences. 'I am going to have to pull back on . . . on that one and just say that's the kind of specifics that they . . . you know we . . . don't go into.'

'OK.' I understood and certainly did not want to press him on this. I moved on. 'Would it be fair to say, I mean, that you have . . .'

'I am familiar with the subject, yeah.' After sixteen years of it, I was sure that was correct.

I asked him to describe in general terms how an effective operative would proceed with an interrogation. What was acceptable coercion? What were the lines that would loom but never be crossed?

'For an interrogation to be successful, it has to be a very controlled, very methodical, very thoughtful process and, I mean, a good interviewer is incredibly labour-intensive and the most methodical, the most patient, um, analytical person, because nothing happens in a bubble.'

'What kinds of techniques does one have to achieve that?'

'Well.' He shrugged. 'Take the way we're sitting.'

'OK.'

'That's ... that's a very good technique for interviews, or for business ...'

'Sitting in a bar?' I asked with a smile.

'No, mirroring, mirroring.'

'Ah.' The mirrors all around us confused me and I was not sure what he meant.

'Mirroring the person you are talking to,' he explained patiently. 'Sitting the same way they do. The sympathetic approach. I mean there's ... there's a lot of things that are done in daily life that the interrogator uses.'

We went through various techniques. He described something like a divide-and-conquer technique.

'Two people in a car are picked up, you immediately separate them, so they can't compare their stories,' he began. 'Um, and start double-tracking, start questioning them independently of each other. They ... you know, you say ... your friend has just advised us you know what the real story is. You know, you are ... seeing how that plays on the other person.'

'Another technique in the book' – I nodded towards the *Exploitation Manual* – 'is called double informers, which is about planting two informants in the suspect's cell, so when one is taken out, the first starts telling the suspect that the guy's a stooge.'

'Uh huh. Right, well, again the concept is that you have ... you are controlling the environment. You are in charge,' he said. 'But I mean, it's you ... you don't want to make it sound too much like rocket science, because it's not. It's just, in a sense, being creative and understanding of human nature ... and human nature is sometimes to talk, er, in a very unguarded fashion.'

So far, it all sounded like a polite conversation, the gentle art of persuasion. But I wanted to know how far the interrogator would ultimately graduate towards more violent methods.

'I love those euphemistic names those guys come up with for these manuals,' I said. 'There's another thing in this ... this ... "*Human Resource Exploitation Manual*". The book talks about different levels of duress and threats, you know.' I read from the CIA manual how for centuries questioners have employed various methods of inducing physical weakness, prolonged constraint, exertion, extremes of cold, along with deprivation of food and sleep. 'All of those sorts of things. Where does that type of stuff lie on the continuum between proper interrogation and abuse, do you have a sense?'

'Well, sleep deprivation to a degree ...' He nodded. That was something they would use.

'Mmm.' This gave me pause, because we had already crossed a line. In American criminal law, if a police officer intentionally uses sleep deprivation in an effort to edge a suspect towards a confession, any statement would be excluded, almost automatically, as being coerced.

'Um, temperature adjustments, sensory control, sound ... white noise, whatever it may be, in a sense you know, do I think that those methods are crossing a line into an area that should ...' Baker trailed off, thinking out loud about how these techniques are used and whether they really should be. He rapidly became resolute. 'No, no, because in a controlled environment, it has to be a controlled environment, ensuring that you are not crossing some line. You do it to a certain degree. I mean, it's very ... it's, it's very regulated, in a sense.'

He paused for a moment to reflect again, reaching for his coffee. 'You know, and that is not necessarily a pleasant way of putting it, but it's what you are looking to do. You are looking to break their will, within a set of parameters that allows you to keep that person ... as a credible source of information. Again, from a technical standpoint, you can easily walk in and get anybody to say anything.'

'Do you have any sense of where the line is where this becomes counter-productive?' I was already sceptical. If you broke the person's will, surely he would have no will to resist agreeing to any story put to him.

'Right, well, well, first you are correct,' he replied vaguely. 'I mean, the question is always what's coercion and what's something more, what's ... what's ... where does that line fit. And there's two reasons why you don't ... um, engage in what I suppose people would call torture. One is the moral reason. It's wrong. You ... you ... you don't do it as a civilised society.'

I got the sense that the more Baker stuttered slightly – really more of a hesitation – the further over the line he thought the process had actually strayed.

'The second reason,' he continued, 'which is probably more compelling for a lot of people who don't believe the intelligence services are actually moral, is that it serves no purpose in the larger scope of things. You cannot trust information that's gathered from a torture situation. When you cross the line from coercion, persuasion ... to torture, wherever that line is, the credibility of the information gathered is ... is right out of the window. If you've got a sophisticated, you know, intelligent individual, who is actively working against your interview interrogation process, threats are ... are of minimal use. I mean they just ... because all you have to do is ... is make one threat, not act on it, and you have really ... you ... you've lost your ability to control that environment and you've really lost the ... the upper hand in that relationship. And once you ... once you start to act on that, once you cross over, then immediately you're in this ... this area where you're saying, well hold on a second, you know, how ... how can I trust the information that person now is putting forward?'

Of course, the $64,000 question – the 'does the statement made by this prisoner give us a reason to invade Iraq?' question – is when intelligence can be trusted and how on earth you divine that. I asked him.

'I mean intelligence is not, you know, much like we'd like it to be like Tom Clancy books, it's not. I mean you ... sometimes you get a good piece of information, sometimes you get complete crap.' The word sounded harsh coming in his polished diction. It made him sound particularly hostile to bad intelligence. 'And you're very often making operational decisions based on the best that you can gather.'

What did he think when operational decisions were being made based on evidence extracted by the interrogators in Guantánamo Bay, or Iraq?

'Abu Ghraib was an abomination. With Abu Ghraib you had people running a correctional facility that were completely unprepared for that sort of function. Low-level individuals,' Baker said. He did not mean to patronise them, merely that they did not know what they were doing.

Yet even though Baker was so obviously intelligent and experienced, how successful would he be himself at setting the coercion line? As he agreed, the decision is all the more difficult when the interrogator begins the process with a series of presumptions based on the prisoner's arrest – an Arab seized in Afghanistan in November 2001, for example.

The US had been offering a $5,000 bounty for each 'foreign Taliban' turned over to coalition forces, an enormous sum by local standards, equal to several years' income. If the Northern Alliance turned the prisoner over to the US with a tale attached – an uncorroborated story either about the prisoner brandishing a Kalashnikov on the battlefield, or about plotting on a computer in an al-Qaeda safe house – would not the subsequent interrogation session be aimed at getting the prisoner to 'admit' that this was true?

'Potentially, if the interrogators applied sufficient pressure ...' I began. Baker knew what I was saying. They would inevitably get the confession that they expected.

'Uh huh,' he said. 'Maybe you'd have something to show a statement was true?'

The question hung there for a moment, as we both surveyed our rather cold coffee. Both of us knew how unlikely it was that there would be any way to tell what was true and what false – what was wheat and what chaff. In the end, what would the intelligence officer have to go on, except the statement by the Northern Alliance, now 'confirmed' by the prisoner's coerced admission?

I remembered one more question I wanted to ask. It involved the ticking-bomb scenario. As I laid out the facts he nodded, obviously unimpressed. He had heard this all before, torturing people to stop the bomb from going off in downtown Manhattan.

'Can you think in your entire career of one situation that's ever occurred, is there one example of that?' I asked.

'No, not in my ... not in my time,' Baker said. 'But it's always the argument that's thrown out there.'

Baker promised to meet in a London pub the next time he was over. I hoped he would look me up. While I could not agree with everything he said, he was my kind of spy, someone who thought that more would be achieved through patience and decency than hurried along at the tip of an electrode.

*

Various people I had interviewed had now made their case for torture and sometimes against. The ticking-time-bomb hypothetical, perhaps the most compelling argument in favour of torture, had been rolled out by every torture apologist I had encountered. Mike Baker denied that such an event ever took place during his time with the CIA. Indeed, with each person I interviewed – Professor Levin, Professor Dershowitz, Richard Perle and Big Bill Cowan – I gave them 500 years to come up with an example. Nobody could identify one instance where a catastrophic bomb had been defused by torture.

It is this ticking-time-bomb myth that is used to justify the nightmare of torture.

3

HUMAN RESOURCE EXPLOITATION

Perhaps the experts were wrong. Maybe there had been a nuclear bomb almost ready to go off in New York City.

US Attorney-General John Ashcroft was in Moscow on 10 June 2002, when he urgently interrupted his meetings to brief the world by satellite on a major breakthrough in the War on Terror. He announced President Bush's designation of an American called Jose Padilla, otherwise known as Abdullah al-Muhajir, as an enemy combatant.

'In apprehending al-Muhajir as he sought entry into the United States, we have disrupted an unfolding terrorist plot to attack the United States by exploding a radioactive "dirty bomb",' he said, introducing a new and frightening term to the nightmares of Americans. 'Now, a radioactive "dirty bomb" involves exploding a conventional bomb that not only kills victims in the immediate vicinity but also spreads radioactive material that is highly toxic to humans and can cause mass death and injury.'

Ashcroft was emphatic about the nature of the threat. 'Let me be clear,' he said, eyeing the camera. 'We know from multiple independent and corroborating sources that Abdullah al-Muhajir was closely associated with al-Qaeda and that as an al-Qaeda operative he was involved in planning future terrorist attacks on innocent American civilians in the United States. The safety of all Americans and the national security interests of the United States require that Abdullah al-Muhajir be detained by the Defense Department as an enemy combatant.'

The arrest was all down to some excellent intelligence work.

'I commend the FBI, the CIA and other agencies involved in capturing Abdullah al-Muhajir before he could act on his deadly plan,' Ashcroft concluded. 'Because of the close cooperation among the FBI, the CIA, Defense Department and other federal agencies, we were able to thwart this terrorist.'

On 13 June 2002 the Bush Administration leaked the name of Padilla's alleged accomplice, a man called Benjamin Mohammed, said to have lived in England before joining the plot. He and Padilla had apparently planned to buy some uranium somewhere in Asia, smuggle it into the US, and explode it among the millions of innocent people living on Manhattan.

So, the time bomb had almost been ticking in New York. Surely this was an unprecedented threat, where a terrorist was about to inflict on the United States something as terrible as Hiroshima and Nagasaki suffered in 1945? Here, at last, was an act of such horror that surely harsh interrogation techniques were permissible – even mandatory in the words of Professor Levin?

A postcard came directly to the London office of Reprieve, the charity I work for, from Guantánamo Bay. It was a surprise. Somehow it had been allowed out by the US military censors. It was brief, only a paragraph, handwritten:

> I have written a few times to try to contact you through the Army. Now I am sending you a postcard thru the privilege team and wait your response. I would like you to act as my lawyer.

Signed Binyam Ahmed Mohamed. He had written the note on 20 April 2005 and it finally got to Reprieve in London on 16 May which was actually two weeks after I first met him.

Binyam had found another way of reaching me. My client Shaker Aamer, also a British resident in Guantánamo, had heard from Binyam that he wanted help and had told me three months before. Binyam had lived in England. I was trying to take as many clients as possible who spoke English to avoid the cost of the interpreters, which could make the cost of one two-week trip as much as $25,000, and Reprieve certainly couldn't afford that.

When Shaker told me that Binyam wanted help I didn't stop to think whether I had time to take on another client. I wrote up a habeas petition for this man whom I had never met and sent it off to Washington, setting in action the process that would allow me to visit him. On Monday, 2 May 2005 I walked into the cell in Camp Echo to meet him for the first time.

Binyam was twenty-seven. He was tall and gangling, dark-skinned, originally from Ethiopia. He smiled and immediately told me how glad he was to see me. He spoke quietly, with a particular dignity. Some prisoners would take many hours of convincing that I was not from the CIA, but Binyam immediately opened up. I explained what we needed to do, and he started talking. He barely paused for breath during the three consecutive days we met. I have become so used to typing that the effort of handwriting notes was exhausting. Absorbing what he told me about being tortured would be far more difficult.

Binyam's father, Ahmed Mohamed Bushra, was a supervisor with Ethiopian Airlines. His mother was originally from Yemen. In 1992 the Ethiopian government changed and the military took over. They began arresting people who had been associated with the old government – Ahmed's political leanings meant that he and the family had to flee.

Originally they went to the United States. Then fourteen years old, Binyam stayed with his oldest sister for a little over a year, but he had heard good things about British tolerance of Africans and talked to his family about going there. His older sister and brother stayed on and became American citizens. Today, they share an apartment just outside Washington DC. His younger sister married, and lives near Atlanta with her husband and small child.

Binyam and his parents moved to London on 9 March 1994. He enjoyed life there and sought political asylum from Ethiopia. He was given leave to remain while this was resolved, but the lawyers were slow to press his case. Seven years went by without his claim being resolved.

Binyam found Britain more welcoming to a man with black skin than America. For five years he lived in Wornington Road, at the corner of Golborne Road in North Kensington. He studied at Paddington Green College, without managing to pass many of his courses, in part because he developed a drug habit. He was drifting slowly nowhere, and he watched unhappily as his life slipped by.

In late 2000 he was attracted to Islam and began to attend the Muslim Heritage Centre, five minutes from his flat. The US authorities may think that Binyam was being indoctrinated as an al-Qaeda agent there, but I doubt it. I went to the Centre, and found an imam so mild-mannered that he feared the most minimal controversy. Binyam did gain some strength from religion and his new friends helped him to kick his drug habit. He began to work at the Centre as a janitor, first volunteering, then being taken on to the payroll.

In early summer 2001 Binyam left Britain to travel because he felt he needed to get away from his old haunts if he was to maintain his resolution to remain drug free. He decided to go to Afghanistan to see the place for himself. There had been plenty of Western horror stories about the Taliban, but Binyam had heard another side. He particularly hoped that their rigid ban on drugs would provide a haven without temptation. Indeed, in May 2001 US Secretary of State Colin Powell had praised the regime's work to eradicate heroin, announcing a ten million US dollar grant to assist further efforts. Binyam thought he would go to see the truth for himself.

He arrived in Afghanistan in July 2001, oblivious to the dramatic events that would soon shake that country and change the course of his own life. This was his first mistake.

Two months later everything changed. The news was garbled in Afghanistan, but one message came through clearly: the Americans were planning an attack and Binyam wanted out. He had little trouble getting to Pakistan, but he did not return directly to Britain. In retrospect this might seem foolish, but at the time the war was hundreds of miles away and solid news was scarce. Nobody thought it would last. Indeed, the American bombing campaign seemed to be propelling the Northern Alliance to a rapid victory. So he did not immediately leave – his next mistake.

Six months went by and the situation in Pakistan was deteriorating, particularly for foreigners. The news was full of stories about the strange new Alcatraz that the Americans were building in Cuba. Rumours were rife about Pakistanis accepting bounties to turn over foreigners, particularly Arabs, to the United States. For far too long Binyam ignored the gathering clouds – indeed, the storm had escalated into a hurricane before he finally decided to go home to Britain.

His decision was complicated by his lack of a passport. His original Ethiopian passport had been stolen and, while it was not hard to cross the Pakistani border, getting back to England would be more difficult.

Binyam could hardly ask the Ethiopian government for help and he had no right to a British passport. In the end a friend from London said Binyam should use his passport instead.

It was 10 April 2002 and Binyam was at Karachi airport, with a ticket to Zurich and on to London. This was to be his last moment of freedom for many years.

Initially, Binyam was detained by the Pakistani immigration unit. They said his passport was invalid. He did not want to get his friend into trouble, so he initially gave a false name and said he had stolen the passport. He was held for three days. Then he was transferred to a detention centre.

It was here that he began the slide towards the dark chambers of the War on Terror.

As he began to tell me about his suffering, Binyam spoke in a curious monotone. 'What I am saying may not be exciting enough for you,' he said to me almost apologetically. 'But when I think about it, I am counting my rewards from God and I cannot express what I felt. I'm sorry I have no emotion when talking about the past, 'cause I have closed. You have to figure out all the emotion part – I'm kind of dead in the head. Perhaps I can work this out later.'

I was little more than his scribe. It began in Landi Prison in Pakistan on 13 April 2002. On 20 April he was taken to a Pakistani intelligence interrogation centre in Karachi. This is where he met the FBI.

'I refused to talk in Karachi until they gave me a lawyer,' Binyam said. He had lived in the West. He knew his rights. He did admit that he had initially given them a false name, but he said he had nothing to do with America and did not see what America had to do with him. 'I said it was my right to have a lawyer. The FBI said, "The law has been changed. There are no lawyers. You can cooperate with us – the easy way, or the hard way."'

Reconstructing some of the epic American misjudgements in the War on Terror is a challenge. The US authorities keep much of the evidence secret and they certainly do not advertise their mistakes, even if they recognise them. With Binyam, I think it was perhaps his obduracy in refusing to cooperate that first put him on the railroad to trouble. If there is one thing certain to register on the radar of any American law enforcement agent, it is the prisoner who refuses to talk. If he asserts his right to remain silent he must have something to hide. It is the second presumption of guilt – the first, of course, is the fact that he finds himself being questioned at all.

The cells in Karachi were small, each perhaps eight feet by ten. It was at this Pakistani intelligence unit that Binyam had a taste of torture. He was suspended for a week by a leather strap, required to soil himself more often than he was allowed to the toilet, lapsing into a semi-sleep, standing up. This strappado position, inherited from the Spanish Inquisition, and later used on Guy Fawkes, puts great strain on the shoulder joints, dislocating them in a particularly painful and drawn-out way. Binyam could only just touch the ground with his toes. He was lowered down to use the toilet twice a day. He was given food, normally rice and beans, every second day.

'I just thought it would end,' Binyam said, reviewing ancient history, separated from him now by months and years of escalating abuse.

Meanwhile, people who presented themselves as FBI agents came in for morning interrogations. There were four of them, 'Chuck', 'Terry', 'Jenny' and a light-skinned black man whose pseudonym Binyam has forgotten. The FBI seemed to think that because he had lived in the US for a short while he had plans to commit some crime on American soil.

'But I'm going to the UK,' Binyam would say.

As the days progressed, the FBI also seemed to think that he was some kind of top al-Qaeda operative.

'How?' demanded Binyam. 'It's been less than six months since I converted to Islam! Before that I was into using drugs.'

'If you don't talk to me, you're going to Jordan,' Chuck told him early in the interrogations. 'We can't do what we want here, the Pakistanis can't do exactly what we want them to. The Arabs will deal with you.'

Terry asked the same questions. 'I'm going to send you to Jordan or Israel,' he said. Then Terry threatened to send him to the British. 'The SAS know how to deal with people like you.'

It was after Terry's first visit that other Pakistanis started coming. They could not speak English and Binyam could not understand much of what they said. They would just come in and beat him. This time they used a leather strap. It had a wooden handle and the leather was jointed in some way, so the rounded end whipped back on him.

One Pakistani pointed a pistol at Binyam's chest. It was a semi-automatic and he loaded it in front of Binyam.

'He pressed it against my chest,' said Binyam, still speaking in a dull monotone. 'He just stood there. I knew I was going to die. He stood like that for five minutes. I looked into his eyes and I saw my own fear reflected there. I had time to think about it. Maybe he will pull the trigger and I will *not* die but be paralysed. There was enough time to think the possibilities through.'

Chuck came back in after that. 'He said nothing. He stared at me and left.'

Binyam has tried to reconstruct how this came to be his fate. He remains confused. 'The British talked to me in Pakistan.' They said they were from the MI6 and one called himself 'John'. Binyam does not remember whether the other gave a name.

'The Brits had checked out my story and said they knew I was a nobody. But they gave me a cup of tea with a lot of sugar in it. I initially only took one. "No, you need a lot more. Where you're going you need a lot of sugar."' I must have looked confused as Binyam said this, so he went on to explain: 'I didn't know exactly what he meant by this, but I figured he meant some poor country in Arabia. One of them did tell me that it looked like I was going to get tortured by the Arabs.'

'How can I help you?' John had asked.

'I don't know,' said Binyam.

'I'll see what we can do with the Americans,' John had said, promising to tell Binyam what would happen to him.

'I have struggled with how I came to mean such a lot to them,' Binyam said. 'I have picked up that there was another Brit who had been abused and who was telling them all kinds of things. This may have been someone I had met who started putting my name in things. I don't know who it was saying all this. I wish I did.'

John never came back with the American reply. Whatever their source, the Americans had decided Binyam was a big fish.

A month later Binyam was still refusing to talk until he got a lawyer. The US authorities grew increasingly angry, but they left. Then the Pakistanis came back in with the money they had seized from him on his arrest. They had him sign a paper for his release from Pakistan. Binyam began to wonder whether his ordeal was nearly over and he was headed back to Kensington.

It was 19 July 2002, a Friday. A hundred days into his ordeal, Binyam was taken from Karachi to Islamabad on a PIA flight with two officers. It was a civilian plane, perhaps the first step towards deportation. He was led on to the plane at the rear and sat in the back row. There were officers around him, but he was not even in cuffs. His spirits rose. Arriving in Islamabad, he was handcuffed and taken in a bus to a pick-up truck. They drove a short distance to the Special Branch office, where he was left in a room with a Pakistani prisoner until the Sunday night at about 10 p.m.

On 21 July he was taken to a military airport in Islamabad. There were two others with him. He was blindfolded, but it was very quiet. He was held there for about two hours. He hardly dared to hope, but perhaps now the plane was taking him to safety.

Just as his hopes reached their apex he heard American voices and guessed that a Middle Eastern destination was back on his itinerary. They stripped him naked and took photos. Next, they put fingers up his anus, purporting to search him. The Muslim prisoner looks back in utter humiliation at being sodomised by the soldier's finger, far more so than most Westerners. I once quizzed a group of Muslim men whether they would 'rather' be tortured with electric shocks or have the finger treatment. The majority chose the electrodes. Americans might pretend that it is part of a bona fide search, but such searches are generally conducted for drugs in a US prison. It is hard to accept that a prisoner would secrete a shank there. For Binyam, it was just a foretaste of things to come.

The US soldiers were dressed in black, with masks, wearing what looked like Timberland boots. They re-dressed Binyam in a tracksuit, shackled him with headphones over his ears, pulled on a blindfold and hooded him for good measure.

He was tied to the seat for the flight. He spent the journey wondering what his fate would be, and also trying to estimate the time and the speed of the plane, perhaps eight or ten hours. At 500 mph they could be taking him as far as 5,000 miles, a circle which might run from Indonesia to West Africa or Europe. All the indications suggested the Middle East, perhaps Jordan. But he was only guessing. All he knew was that eventually the plane landed somewhere.

Where was he? It was summer and it was hot. They certainly had not taken him to England.

'At the airport I was put in what I believe to be a Reynolds van. I was told to lie down. My cuffs were changed to plastic ones and they drove for half an hour or forty-five minutes.' Binyam was already learning that he could not judge much by this. Perhaps they drove round in circles just to confuse him. If so, it was time wasted, as initially he did not even know what continent he was on. But he counted the days as best he could, to give himself some sense of time, if not place.

Soon he worked out it had to be Morocco, but at that stage nobody told him. On the rare occasion that a guard came to his door, nobody would answer his questions. Yet the look of the people, and their accents, made him think that was where he was.

'Where I was first held, from 23 July 2002 to about 15 August, there was a series of houses which were dug down, almost underground,' Binyam began, when I asked him for a careful description of where he was being held. 'There were six rooms per house and at least five houses in a group, with more further away. Three of the rooms were for the prisoners, one for interrogation, one for the guards and one empty.

'When I arrived there were already two other prisoners in the other rooms. I was in the middle room of three. The wall was white-washed. There was a large window, but it was shuttered. I was then moved, from about 15 to 22 August, to the end room, which was next to the toilet. This was the dark, "torture" room with wood panelling. Outside there was a metal fence all round. The trees were about ten metres high.'

Binyam was steadily introduced to the team in charge of getting information out of him. I asked him for details of each of them,

'My lead tormentor was Marwan,' he said without any irony in his voice. Marwan was just that, a tormentor. 'He was the one who was in charge of much of the actual abuse. He was six foot two, at one point he said he weighed ninety kilos, he had brown skin, brown eyes and was clean shaven. He was Moroccan.'

For the most part Marwan would stand back and smoke Marlboro Lights deliberately. During the more intense beatings Marwan would light one from another as he watched, eyes lidded, from behind the whaling arms and fists of the bruisers. 'He slapped me a few times during the interrogations. He had a Motorola Wing telephone,' Binyan added.

A second man went by the name Mohammed. He was also Moroccan, about six feet tall, and Binyam described him as 'built'. He had blue eyes, brown hair, very white skin and was maybe twenty-eight to thirty years old.

Third there was Sarah, who said she was Canadian. She was about thirty to thirty-five years old, white, blue eyes, blonde hair, about five foot six, and Binyam described her as 'average weight'. Among the millions of Canadians this was not going to get us very far, particularly since in the James Bond world of torture and spies, it was questionable whether she was Canadian and unlikely that her name was Sarah. I pressed Binyam and he said he thought she had spoken some French to him to 'prove' she was Canadian. This made me even more sceptical. Why would someone do that? I spoke some French but that didn't mean I was Canadian. It sounded like part of the game.

The fourth member of Binyam's torture team did not give a name. Binyam dubbed him as Smoke-Too-Much, from the Monty Python skit. It was a strange link with home during his torture sessions. The one who smoked too much was another Moroccan, about five foot ten, darker brown skin, black hair, brown eyes.

'Scarface' was the fifth, another anonymous abuser whom Binyam named after the 1983 film.

'He was scary-looking,' said Binyam. 'About five-ten. He was masked all the time. He had brown skin round his eyes, a deep voice. He did much of the questioning and the beating.'

Later Binyam would describe the man's fists as he saw them arcing deliberately in his direction.

The last and most senior person Binyam called the Boss. He did not have much to do with the direct torture. He was about six feet tall, with very pale white skin and brown eyes. His hair was black but flecking to grey; he had a trimmed beard and looked solid. Binyam heard much later that this man had been to Guantánamo to interrogate the Moroccan prisoners held there.

These six formed the basic shape of the torture team, though there were plenty of hangers-on who played cameo roles in the next eighteen months.

It was all threats to begin with, descriptions of what might be coming. Binyam believed them; then he didn't, unable to fathom how far away from his Kensington universe he must be.

Initially three guards took Binyam into a room and the plastic cuffs were cut off, replaced with metal cuffs, 'Made in Spain'. The sun was already up and he asked to be allowed to pray. They let him wash and told him the direction of Mecca. The room was about ten feet by ten feet, with a bed and a table. The large window was shuttered so he could not see out of it.

'I was not of this world,' Binyam said, when I asked how he felt at the beginning, if he could still remember it. 'I did not believe this was real, that this was happening to me. It never, never crossed my mind that I'd end up being hauled halfway across the world by the Americans to face torture in a place I had never been.'

The first shift of guards spoke some English – 'How are you?' – and were white with Arab features. Binyam's Arabic was very weak then, but they seemed to speak classical Arabic. The second shift were very Moroccan, speaking mostly Arabic and French. They tried to communicate the facts of life to him, as best they could make themselves understood. 'They told me, "If you cooperate with them, they won't torture you,"' Binyam recalled. 'Inside, I knew I was going to be tortured. I was pissed off that the US interrogated me, then took me across the world.'

His inner qualms could not suppress the faint hope that they had spirited him more than 4,000 miles for some reason other than torture. Indeed, for the first few days it seemed that they were just observing him. They would ask him a few innocuous questions and leave him to talk with the guards.

'What kind of torture do they do in this place?' he asked one.

'They'll come in wearing masks and beat you up,' the man replied dispassionately, factually. 'They'll beat you with sticks. They'll rape you first, then they'll take a glass bottle, they break the top off and make you sit on it.' It sounded beyond imagination. Perhaps it really was only to scare him.

But Binyam looked at the man as he talked. 'When I looked in the eyes of the person who said they'd make me sit on a broken glass bottle, all I saw was – nothing but certainty deep inside that they *were* going to do it. I hoped it was just a threat, but some people back home had told me about this happening in Morocco, they were known for it. I just didn't think they were going to do it to someone who was not Moroccan, who had nothing at all to do with Morocco.'

Still he hoped.

It was Friday, 26 July 2002. One of the Moroccans came into the room. 'This is just a welcome.'

'Who are you anyway?' Binyam demanded, making a show of looking pissed off. The bravado did not get him far. 'All I did was ask what kinds of tortures were available. I went back to my room.'

Two days later Smoke-Too-Much came in with another man. Binyam was in the interrogation room and there was some kind of international swimming on television. He asked whether he was there for interrogation.

'This is just talk. If you want interrogation, we'll interrogate you.' They asked about the mosque in North Kensington where he worked from October 2000 to about May 2001. They showed him pictures and asked about people who had been there.

Binyam obstinately refused to talk. 'I'm not Moroccan, it has nothing to do with you,' he said politely. 'The Americans may think I have a problem with them. And it sounds like the Brits have questions. If they do, they should ask themselves, not you.'

Smoke-Too-Much smiled at him. 'Why do you think the Brits sent you here?'

They asked about Moroccan groups in Afghanistan. Binyam told them he knew nothing. The interrogator was smoking impatiently and launched the first direct threat. 'He told me that I had better speak to them at once,' Binyam recalled, 'or he would get up and smack me about.'

'I know I'm here to be tortured, so you may as well get on with it,' Binyam said with more bravado. 'I have nothing to do with you, or your Moroccan groups, as I'm not Moroccan.'

They sent him back to his cell and left him alone all that night. Binyam had a lot to think about. Today's questions were clearly derived from information coming from London. Why were the British helping the Moroccan torturers? What did they have against him? Surely they already knew the truth – that he was nobody, as they had said in Pakistan.

At one point a guard – a young kid, maybe only twenty-two years old – came in, seemingly to warn Binyam. 'If you don't speak to them now, you're just going to see people coming in with masks and they're going to beat the hell out of you.'

They left him all the next day – Monday – to think about it. Nothing happened.

On Tuesday he was taken for questioning again. It was all about his links with Britain.

'The interrogator told me that they had been working with the British. "We have photos of people given to us by MI5. Do you know these men?"' Binyam said. It was now clear that the British were sending questions to the Moroccans. 'I was at first surprised that the Brits were siding with the Americans. I sought asylum in Britain rather than America because it's known as the one country that has laws that it follows.'

Over the day the British betrayal became clearer. Binyam had been travelling on someone else's passport and they asked him how he had got it. He had told the Americans in Pakistan that he stole it, as he wanted to protect his friend from getting into trouble. The Moroccans corrected him. His friend had been questioned by the British and had admitted how he had given the passport to Binyam.

They knew his former address, on Lancaster Road, W11. They asked him very specific questions about his kickboxing trainer, who worked at the North Kensington City Challenge in Ladbroke Grove. They told Binyam that he had studied at Paddington Green College, with personal information they must have got from his former girl-friend. They even told him what his grades had been.

By the end of the day, Binyam knew that the British had turned on him. 'To say that I was disappointed at that moment would be an understatement.' He was alone in a secret cell, in a country he had never before visited, and nobody in the world who cared for him knew where he was.

That evening the guards started talking about torture again. They talked more about the beating and the rape. 'I tried not to show them the fear that I had.'

They left him to dwell on it some more. With help from Britain gone, who would prevent the worst from happening? Binyam's hopes were slipping away and he asked for a Qur'an as a different kind of support. He had to wait some more – two days – before they eventually brought one.

'It had been dipped in something like diesel,' Binyam said, sniffing as if he remembered the smell. 'I had to leave it to evaporate before I could read it.' This was a difficult moment, because he had known that the Moroccans would be Muslims and he had hoped there might be some sense of solidarity. But this was a clear indication of their hypocrisy. 'These people were not real Muslims.'

Binyam had not learned much Arabic at this point, but he had been taught to recite some of the verses. 'Just having the Qur'an gave me tranquillity.'

Sarah, the 'Canadian', made her first appearance on 2 August 2002, pretending to 'mediate' between Binyam and the Americans. Binyam had refused to speak to the Americans, or their Moroccan proxies, so they thought they would try something else. Sarah said she was meant to play the role of 'third party' between Binyam and his adversary, whom she identified specifically as the US authorities (not the Moroccans, who were actually making the threats). She said they had to delay his interrogation for four days to get her there from Canada. Did they really expect him to believe that the Canadians were running some kind of charitable intervention: 'Torture Busters – Will Fly Anywhere to Help the Suspect Avoid the Rack'? Binyam thought she was probably just an American or a Canadian in the US military, and this was just part of the interrogation process.

Binyam said he would not talk today, but would think about it.

The next day she returned. 'I told "Sarah" that I never asked for a "third party",' said Binyam. 'She got angry.'

'You don't know what's good for you,' she said, shortly. She had Binyam taken back to his cell.

A Moroccan came to his door and told him that they had waited all this time while she had been brought from Canada.

'How can I talk to them?' Binyam said, plaintively now, to this guard. 'I know nothing about what they want.'

'Ask them for pictures,' he replied. 'You're the one who should ask them questions, how you can help them.'

By now the waiting game was taking its toll. Binyam strongly believed in spirits, or *jinni*. He had lived in England long enough to know that any story about genies would possibly get him sectioned, but *jinni* are very real for many who believe in Islam. A *jinn* who is disobedient is called a *shiatan*, or satan.

'That night I felt that I was visited by spirits of some sort,' he explained, and it was physically real. 'I felt paralysed, I was being held down, they were strangling me. I tried to recite the Qur'an, but something trapped my tongue. I wondered if the Moroccans were somehow doing this to me. I was terrified and gasping for air.'

The next morning Sarah came in with Mohammed, the Moroccan.

'How was your night?' she asked. Binyam immediately knew that they had somehow sent the *jinni*.

Obviously, too, the guard had reported back that he wanted to cooperate. Sarah brought pictures. 'This is the British file,' she said. Sarah picked up the pictures of two British people and told their whole story, about how they were suspected of being al-Qaeda.

She also brought pictures of about twenty-five men whom Binyam understood to be the big names of al-Qaeda. 'I don't know these people,' said Binyam. 'I am interested in my own case. What is it that you want to know?'

But this was not good enough. According to his interrogators, he did know Khalid Sheikh Mohammed, Abu Zubaydah and other big names, and if he denied it he was lying.

'I'm giving you a last chance to think about cooperating with the US,' said Sarah. Again, they left him alone to think about it, with no interrogation.

Two days later it was Sarah and Mohammed again. They came in, sympathetic, bringing Binyam breakfast. But time and a tentative sense of optimism – perhaps there really never would be any broken bottles – had reinspired Binyam to obstinacy. He said he was not talking. They persisted, in a better humour for a while, and talked about politics and wars of the past.

At one point Binyam said that he had thought about going to Chechnya to help the Muslims there. He explained how he had seen the television footage of Muslim civilians being slaughtered and how even President Clinton had been highly critical of the Russian excesses.

'I don't care if you go to Chechnya and die there,' Sarah said. 'I want you to answer the Americans' questions. Then we'll drop you in Chechnya.' She talked on and on, all about how Binyam should be a witness against people. The other man, Mohammed, said that when they were through they would send him back to Britain. Binyam was rather more conciliatory, but he still did not understand what he was meant to do.

Binyam's obstinacy is sometimes mixed with the naïve. I have met several victims of torture in the past few years and have developed an unscientific theory based on those I have met: cynical or perceptive people tend not to get tortured as much as others. They quickly figure out what the torturer wants to hear and just say it. The ones who suffer most are either those who are simply not smart enough to figure out what is expected, or those who cannot bring themselves to accept that this is how the game is played.

I suspect I would have fallen into the naïve category myself, particularly in 2002, because I would never have believed that an American would be in the business of torture. Binyam was the same. He knew he was a 'nobody' and as the sea rose and fell around him he clung to hope that the threats had to be a bluff.

The night when Sarah left for the last time, he thought their bluff had been called. 'I thought I was going to be transferred out of there,' he said. 'They came in and cuffed my hands behind my back.'

But he was not going anywhere. When he was shackled, three men came in wearing black masks, some kind of ski mask that only showed their eyes. They had military trousers and different coloured shirts.

'When they came in my head stopped,' said Binyam. 'I ceased really knowing I was alive. One stood at each of my shoulders and the third punched me in the stomach. The first punch I didn't expect it. I didn't know where it would be. I'd have tensed my muscles but I didn't have time. It turned everything in me upside down. I felt I was going to vomit.

'Within ten minutes I was almost gone. It seemed to go on for hours. I had prayed the sunset prayer, but I don't know what time it went on to. I was meant to stand, but I was in so much pain I'd fall to my knees. They'd pull me back up and hit me again. They'd kick me in my thighs as I got up. I really did vomit within the first few punches. I hardly spoke through it all. I didn't have the energy or will to say anything. I just wanted for it to end.'

Westerners think that they are inured to violence. They think they see it all in the movies, but most have never come close to a rib-fracturing, concussion-inducing, physical beating. Perhaps different people respond differently. Binyam felt his mind dissociate from his body and watched what was happening from the ceiling, above where he was shackled.

'I could see the hands that were hitting me. They looked like the hands of someone who had worked as a mechanic or chopped with an axe. They were heavy hands. There was dark black hair on the back of the hands and the fingers. I don't remember any rings. The wrists were thick, with shirtsleeves buttoned down all the way.'

Sometimes Binyam was able to look at his main assailant.

'I looked in his eyes. I saw no sympathy,' he said. 'They never said a word. They just beat me up that night and left me.'

Binyam collapsed as they went out. He later remembered hearing the key turn in the lock, but meanwhile he stayed on the ground, lapsing in and out of consciousness. His legs were dead. He could not move, did not want to move.

When he awoke he was still on the floor. He gradually noticed that he had vomited and pissed on himself.

'The "first-class treatment" was over,' he said sardonically. He was not allowed to go to the bathroom. For the next day he was given no food. Eventually the door opened. He thought they were back. They were not. He was taken for interrogation.

'Are you going to cooperate or not?' asked the man. Binyam said nothing. What was there to say, he thought. They took him back out, but it was to a different cell now, next door to the other one.

'They left me there. I lost it at this point. I was numb,' said Binyam. 'I was full of pain. I still have a permanent stomach problem and my ribs hurt if I sit for long. Something is broken inside. But back then I was just numb.'

Soon, there would be more broken inside. It was the cycle of torture. They would come in to question him. He talked. 'They'd ask me a question. I'd say one thing. They'd say it was a lie. I'd say another. They'd say it was a lie. I could not work out what they wanted to hear. They'd say there's this guy who says you're the big man in al-Qaeda. I'd say it's a lie. They'd beat me. I'd say, OK it's true. They'd say, OK, tell us more. I'd say, I don't know more. They'd beat me again.'

The same people came back. The same man punched Binyam till he couldn't stand. Binyam was making noises, groaning, he couldn't breathe, he managed to stutter out a plea for them to stop. They didn't care.

After a while, suddenly one of them acted with a moment's sympathy. 'Let's leave him,' he said, as far as Binyam could understand the Arabic.

'We've got to finish the job,' said another with conviction.

Eventually they did leave him lying on the floor. He lay there for fifteen minutes, maybe half an hour – how could he really know? A guard came in, uncuffed him and gave him food.

'It's all over. You don't have to worry any more.' Binyam wanted to believe the guard. He couldn't.

This time they left him for a week. He got regular meals. He was in pain and could not get up for prayer. But they left him alone.

One week later one of the guards came in. '*Faraj*,' he said. By now, Binyam knew that meant freedom. 'You're going to leave.'

The first thing that occurred to him was that he was going to Cuba, the already legendary island prison run by the American military. He was relieved. He thought it would be public there, so this abuse could not happen.

'Half an hour later I was taken blindfolded in a vehicle. I was taken up some steps, along a hallway, into another room. Was it the waiting room at the airport?' Binyam wondered. 'When I could see again, it was about three metres square, white, with a window, opaque, high up. There were hooks in there. Now, my first thought was that they were for hanging people.'

For two or three days he was treated OK. Again, he began to hope that it might be over. 'That's what they kept on telling me.'

But it turned out to be the phoney war, the lull before the next assault.

'One night they came back in and tied me with a rope, back to the wall, hanging. They put shackles on my ankles. My feet were just on the ground again. They left me for about half an hour. I thought maybe I'd be left there, or maybe they'd start beating me with sticks again. I just didn't know.'

It was Marwan who came in. 'Give me the whole story all over again.'

Binyam did what he could.

'If this is the best you can come up with, you haven't seen any of the tortures yet.' Marwan was dispassionate about it. He called the three goons in. He gave an order, something in Arabic. It obviously was the go-ahead. Marwan stood behind them, watching while they applied the next beating. He was just standing there, watching, smoking cigarettes, eyeing Binyam coldly.

Now Binyam's life was measured in Marwan's cigarettes. 'I guess this went on for a couple of his cigarettes, I don't know exactly how long.'

'Is this what God has promised you?' Marwan asked.

'God has promised me heaven,' Binyam answered.

Marwan cursed the Qur'an. Binyam knew he had unsettled the man, so he smiled. It was unwise, a mistake. Marwan stepped forward and backhanded him across his right cheek. In a strange way Binyam felt victory over Marwan again for a moment. He'd got under his skin.

Marwan walked out and left Binyam hanging. 'I thought they'd just leave me there, but an hour or so later they came back in and started beating me up again. When they were doing it, it was only like a sting by then. I was semi-conscious. I wasn't really there. I had memorised some verses of the Qur'an, just the first chapter, and I was trying to think them.'

They hit Binyam in the chest, the stomach. They'd knock his feet out from under him. Binyam still complains of a shoulder pain as his arms were almost pulled out of their sockets by the rope.

'I was left again, maybe a couple of hours. I was almost asleep standing up when they came back. They came back in, with their masks on again.' Binyam paused without any interjection from me and began to think aloud. 'They were not wearing masks to prevent themselves being identified. It was to create fear. I'm sure of that. In their eyes, they were just doing a job. They were just getting paid for doing this.

'This time it seemed to go on all night. They came in four times that night. Towards the end they seemed to get really pissed off. I called them hypocrites I think. I think I must have recited a verse about hypocrites or something. I don't really remember. But the one who was punching, he hit me on the jaw and knocked me out.

'I think I reached heaven then, but I came back. That was the problem,' he continued flatly, after a pause. 'I came back. I think I came back after only a few seconds and he was just there waiting for me. I didn't really know what was happening, but he must have knocked me out again. The next thing I remember was seeing guards come in. They took me down and left me on the floor all day. I was happy. I could just sleep now.'

Vaguely, during that next day, Binyam remembered a guard telling him that to get tortured was not how to prove he was a good Muslim. The guard showed some kindness, and brought him tea and sweets, but he couldn't take much of it.

The Spanish Inquisition ultimately learned that second-degree torture – making someone watch or listen to the instruments being used on others – was often far more effective than physical abuse itself. As Binyam was learning, the more he was beaten the less he could think about anything, even telling a story that might save himself from future abuse. The waiting was the worst. When he was given time to anticipate the next instalment he had time to consider how he might avoid it.

The guards let him know that it had only just begun.

'They'd tell me there's worse to come. I could hear people screaming across the hall and next door all that night. There were two things crossing my mind. Either that these people are getting raped, or they are getting electrocuted. I just didn't know what to feel or think. At that point I was just wishing I was dead.'

But nothing happened. Still he could find room to hope that he was through the worst of it. But he could hear also what was happening to others, unknown victims close by. They left him for a week, maybe two. He could only guess at time by now. One day was like a week and sometimes a week would be like a day. He would sleep, but then he would wake at night because of the screams. The guards were running up and down the corridor, wearing heavy boots. They'd open the door every half an hour or so as well, to keep him from sleeping.

At one point, as he began to recover from his physical injuries, Binyam asked a guard why they were doing this.

'America's really pissed off at what happened and they've said to the world, "Either you're with us or you're against us." We Moroccans say we're with you. So we'll do whatever they want. They want revenge for everyone who died on 9/11.'

The Moroccans were just doing a job for the Americans. Binyam kept asking what he was meant to say.

'Some of the time they said that some big people in al-Qaeda were talking about me,' he said. 'Some of the time they told me that the US had a story they wanted from me and it was their job to get it. They talked about Jose Padilla and they said I was going to testify against him and big people. They named Khalid Sheik Mohammed, Abu Zubaydah and Ibn Sheikh al-Libi. I was meant to be working with these people, giving them ideas like the dirty bomb. It is hard to pin down the exact story, because what they wanted changed all the time. First in Morocco it changed, then when I was in the Dark Prison, then in Bagram and again in Guantánamo Bay.'

As Binyam told me this a thought occurred to me: why those three names? Why not Osama bin Laden, if they were really going for the big guns? Then I realised that by the spring of 2003 there was a consistency among the names he mentioned, Padilla, Khalid Sheikh Mohammed, Abu Zubaydah, and al-Libi: all were in US custody. There was no way Binyam could have known this. It seemed very unlikely that a low-level nobody like him would be in a small conspiracy with such major figures. It would, on the other hand, have been important for the US to secure witnesses against each of these people if, one day, they wanted to bring them to some kind of trial.

In cases like these there is a danger that the lawyer will get too close to the facts, allowing the minutiae to obscure the larger picture. Take a long step back and sometimes the government theory makes no sense at all. That struck me as true here. Someone who had only just converted to Islam, and who showed up in Afghanistan days before the war when al-Qaeda was most paranoid about Western infiltrators, was hardly likely to be the trusted ideas man for al-Qaeda's top operatives.

'One thing is sure,' Binyam continued. 'I've never met anyone like Khalid Sheik Mohammed, Abu Zubaydah or Ibn Sheikh al-Libi. How would I? I spoke virtually no Arabic when I was in Pakistan. And I didn't know Jose Padilla either. I never heard his name till they told me.'

But that was certainly not the story Marwan wanted to hear in Morocco.

'How are you?' Marwan asked.

Binyam was thinking if he said he was all right they'd beat him. Perhaps they'd left him to heal so they could start all over again. 'I'm in pain,' he said after some consideration.

Marwan started talking about what he referred to as Binyam's case. 'You're doing good. But we need to prepare you for other stuff.'

'I've got no problem saying whatever you want me to say,' Binyam offered.

'That's good. When I say something, you say yes.'

But then Binyam's obstinacy would surface again. All this subservience got to him and he couldn't stand it. Marwan acted like such a big shot, in charge of it all, like he was something so smart.

'Why do you think the Americans brought you to us?' Marwan asked at one point.

'I have no idea,' Binyam said, but then he could not stop himself, he simply could not resist saying what he believed. It just came out. 'I have no idea why they did. You're not intelligence, you're Moroccan. The British have intelligence, maybe. You don't.'

Marwan swore and left the room.

American officials have talked about 'enhanced interrogation techniques', or 'torture lite'. Is a beating torture? Do days of sleep deprivation constitute torture? Is forcing a prisoner to stand for hours torture? Binyam would assure you that they are, but academic discussions on the definition of torture were about to become moot in Morocco.

That night Marwan came back. He brought his three thugs and had them tie Binyam, hanging him once more up against the wall. 'Strip him.'

They cut off Binyam's clothes with some kind of doctor's scalpel. He was totally naked. 'I was afraid to ask Marwan what would happen, because it would show fear. I tried to put on a brave face. But maybe I was going to be raped. Maybe they'd electrocute me. Maybe castrate me.' He just did not know, but the brutes were being deliberate, giving him time to think through the options.

'You don't think I'm a man, not with intelligence,' Marwan said, sneering at Binyam. 'Show him who's a man.' He nodded at the other men.

'One of them took the scalpel to my right chest. It was only a small cut. Maybe an inch. At first I just screamed because the pain was just . . . I was just shocked, I wasn't expecting . . .' There was a pause while everyone looked at Binyam.

'Then they cut my left chest. This time I didn't want to scream because I knew it was coming.'

Marwan got agitated. 'Just go ahead,' he said.

'One of them took my penis in his hand and began to make cuts,' Binyam said, speaking evenly. I asked him whether he was OK to go on. He nodded. His voice was still flat as he continued. 'He did it once and they stood still for maybe a minute, watching my reaction. I was in agony, crying, trying desperately to suppress myself, but I was screaming. I remember Marwan seemed to smoke half a cigarette, throw it down and start another.'

Binyam has no real idea how long this went on for, or even how many times they cut him after that first time. He estimates maybe two hours and twenty or thirty cuts, but it is no more than a guess. There was blood all over him.

'I told you I was going to teach you who's the man,' Marwan eventually said, walking out.

One of the thugs said it would be better just to cut it off, as Binyam would only be breeding terrorists. They followed their leader out.

A long, long time later, Binyam asked for a doctor.

'"The doctor's off," I was told.'

It was a long time again, but eventually a doctor came. He was around forty-five years old, very white, five foot nine, stocky, and carried a briefcase. 'You're all right, aren't you?' was all he said. 'But I'm going to say a prayer for you.'

Later a second doctor came. A little younger, with a goatee and moustache, and wearing white overalls. Binyam told him about his penis.

'I need to see it. How did this happen?' Binyam told him. He looked at the wounds, as if this were just another patient. 'Put this cream on it two times a day. Morning and night.' It was some kind of antiseptic.

'He advised me to do anything I could to avoid torture,' Binyam remembered.

The 'torture heavy' had begun. It would not end for a long time. Binyam stayed in Morocco until January 2004, a total of eighteen months. Once they began, they continued to give him the razor treatment, irregularly, when he might just be starting to hope that it was over.

'What's the point of this?' Binyam asked a guard, begging for answers again. 'I've got nothing I can say to them. I've told them everything I possibly could. What's the point?'

'As far as I know, it's just to degrade you,' the guard explained. 'So when you leave here, you'll have these scars and you'll never forget. So you'll always fear doing anything but what the US wants.'

Despite the doctor's orders Binyam found he could not avoid torture. 'Three days later Marwan came in again and the thugs tied me up,' said Binyam. 'I did not curse or say anything. Last time, look what happened.'

Politeness did Binyam no good. And there were even worse things to come. Binyam described some to me, but asked me not to repeat them. He began to fantasise about trying to escape. He was afraid, but not of dying. He wanted to be shot, longed for it, but if they caught him and brought him back . . .

Meanwhile there was something Pavlovian about his training, even if the torture came at intentionally random times. About once a week he was taken for interrogation and they would go over what he had to say. They would tell him that if he told the story properly he would go to court only as a witness and all this torture would stop. His obstinacy was gone now and Binyam repeated the story as he was instructed.

Finally they did get round to bin Laden. They told Binyam to say that he had been with the al-Qaeda leader five or six times. 'Of course, that was false.'

They told him to say that he had told bin Laden about places that should be attacked. 'Of course, that was false too.'

They told him to say that he had sat with many of bin Laden's top people. 'That was a lie. Overall there were meant to be about twenty-five of them. They told me all their names.

'They told me that I must plead guilty. I'd have to say I was an al-Qaeda operations man, an ideas man.' For a while he insisted that this was silly, as he had only been in Afghanistan a short while and did not speak Arabic.

'We don't care,' was all they'd say.

Binyam learned his lessons. This diminished some of the physical abuses, although the scalpel treatment continued intermittently. Then they began what Binyam came to know as the brainwashing.

'I was taken in a car to another place,' Binyam went on. 'The room was bigger, maybe two and a half metres by four. It had its own toilet and a window which was opaque. There was a metal door with a flap. The walls were painted white and there was a pinkish-white mattress on the floor that was made in either the UK or France, I forget which. I had two blankets, one dark brown and red, the other dark and light brown. There was no pillow. They gave me a toothbrush and Colgate toothpaste. There was a bar of soap for washing clothes with a peacock on it. It was French, with the name Laus or Laos, or something like that. It was dark yellow or brown.'

Binyam had just endured a cutting session, but was allowed to recover for about two weeks, and the guards made no threats of future abuses.

One day they came into his cell, cuffed him and put earphones on him. 'They played hip-hop and rock music, very, very loud,' Binyam said. 'I remember they played Meatloaf and Aerosmith over and over. I hated that. They also played Tupac, "All Eyes On Me", all night and all day.'

Binyam could not take off the headphones as he was cuffed and they were firmly taped on his head. He had to try to sleep with the music on and even pray with it. The first time the music lasted several hours before they removed the headphones. A couple of days later they did the same thing, with the same music at deafening volume for hours. Soon it would become days on end. For weeks, then months, there was not one night when he could sleep properly. He would go forty-eight hours without any sleep at all. Even when they were not forcing loud music on him they would bang the metal doors, or just come right in and shake him awake.

Next, they took Binyam to a room that smelled overwhelmingly of urine. There were holes in the toilet and it had obviously been leaking out into the room for a long time. The walls were mouldy and damp. Binyam realised that they were putting drugs in the food. He had been dragged down into addiction in London and knew what dependency would do to him.

'It's best for you to go back to your old ways. You need to be a Muslim only in name,' one of the guards advised him.

'I found myself laughing my head off, drunk, or something wrong with me after eating. I did not know what to do. To begin with I told myself I had no choice but to eat. This went on for two weeks and it got so bad I decided I had to go on a hunger strike. I went four days without food or water.'

When it came to force-feeding prisoners three years later in Guantánamo there would be outraged doctors around the world citing the Tokyo Declaration – it is unethical to force-feed a competent hunger striker – and the US military would have to resort to euphemisms to disguise what they were doing.

Such niceties did not delay the Moroccan torture team, secure in their secret prison. They force-fed him drugs instead of food.

'Then they came in again and strapped me to a mattress. They put an IV in my arm. First one, then a second. There was some kind of yellow liquid. This I think must have been heroin, though I've never tried it so I don't know for sure. I was out of this world. I didn't exist. They alternated. They'd do a plain IV, then the heroin IV, then the plain one, then the heroin one. My body started reacting. I started shivering. It was like constantly going cold turkey on drugs. This went on maybe ten or fourteen days, but I lost track of time. By then my body needed the drug and if I didn't have it I'd go nuts, shaking, paranoid. I wasn't hungry. I didn't eat at all.'

In the end Binyam agreed to eat and they stopped the IV. The food that came still seemed to have something in it. Bad though that was, it was better than having the other drug injected straight into his bloodstream.

The perverse imaginations of the Moroccan torturers knew few limitations. When they knew it was the time for prayer, they would turn up the volume on the sex films they were watching. 'They brought in women. They would be naked, or part naked. I was high or drunk. I remember one woman, she was beautiful, with brown hair. They were just enticing me. Mocking my faith.'

Binyam found this mental torture worse even than the physical torture. He gradually came to recognise that they were now working on his brain. 'I think I came to several emotional breakdowns in this time, but who was there to turn to?'

Meanwhile the interrogations, more like trainings, continued. Scarface, the interrogator, eventually explained to Binyam what was going on. 'We're going to change your brain,' he said.

The physical abuse continued as part of the brain work. Binyam suffered the scalpel again and again.

'The last time they cut me, they tied me up and slashed me twelve times or so,' he said, speaking of the last round of fine razor cuts that he had to endure. Of course, at the time he had no idea that it would stop. 'I had lost hope that I could even talk to them. It had become like a routine. They'd come in, tie me up and spend maybe an hour doing it – they used to be very slow, deliberately slow. One would cut me, they'd take a rest. They'd have a cigarette, talk in some Moroccan dialect that I couldn't understand. Then another would take his turn. They never spoke to me, not a word. Then they'd tip some kind of liquid on me – the burning, the stinging, was like grasping a hot coal ... but not with my hands, even. The cutting, that was one kind of pain. The burning, that was another.'

In all the eighteen months Binyam was in Morocco he never went outside. He never saw the sun. He never saw any human being except the guards and his tormentors, unless you count the pictures they showed him.

'When the Americans told me in Karachi, "Our friends the Arabs know how to deal with you," I didn't really know what they were talking about,' Binyam reflected, as he came to the end of his Moroccan story. 'Now I understand why the Americans call the Moroccans "Our Arab Friends".'

I was hardly qualified to help Binyam work through this horror. When I watched my British client Nicky Ingram die in Georgia's electric chair in 1995, the word 'torture' was clearly descriptive of what happened. The elaborate shaving ritual that Nicky endured, followed by infinite minutes of dying in the chair, cut a scar across my brain. It had never occurred to me that month upon month of conscious, focused, intentional torture would rise up out of the Middle Ages and leer into twenty-first-century America.

I was finally able to get Binyam's dreadful story unclassified by the censors – some people were sceptical, reasonably enough. The world had seen the pictures from Abu Ghraib, but the flat denials of torture continued to dribble out of the White House and the Pentagon.

I make no claim to omniscience, but I spoke with Binyam for many hours and used various techniques to determine whether he was telling me the truth. Binyam told me that he flew from Islamabad to

Rabat, in Morocco, through the night of '21–2 January' 2002 and was taken from Rabat to Kabul on 21 July 2004. His story precisely matched the records for CIA flights into Rabat and out again. More than this, he described the one female soldier among six men who photographed the scalpel's handiwork before they left Morocco. Again, this matched the records of the US military personnel on the plane.

On one level Binyam was a broken man when I met him in January 2004. Some months before, I began to study the subject of torture and the victims of torture. In addition to the checklist of torture methods I had developed a list of the psychological damage that one would expect to find in a torture victim. Most of the memo was plagiarised from the *Psychological Sequelae of Torture* (Plenum Press, 1993), where two experts suggest the 'Psychological Symptoms Commonly Reported Following Torture'. The complaints were similar to PTSD, post-traumatic stress disorder. They would never leave the torture subject.

Binyam displayed all the signs of a torture victim. Then there was common sense: what other possible explanation was there for the US authorities to take Binyam to Morocco? Binyam was not Moroccan and he had nothing to do with Morocco. To be sure, Morocco's northern border is the Mediterranean, but it seemed unlikely that he had been brought to Rabat for an all-expenses-paid, eighteen-month Club Med holiday. He was brought to Morocco because the US wanted him interrogated in a particularly harsh way, but were unwilling to dirty their own hands doing it.

Still, on one level Binyam was stronger when he flew out of Morocco on his second CIA rendition flight. 'What kept me going were the stories of Stephen and Jesus and Mohammed. That and thinking that nobody goes through torture except that he is in the right. And I always thought that the truth shall prevail.'

So what was the truth? Had Binyam ridden shotgun on a dirty bomb plot intended to wipe out New York? Did the American and the Moroccan authorities feel they had some urgent justification for doing these appalling things to him?

When he had dramatically interrupted his Moscow visit to announce that the dirty bomb plot had been foiled, then US Attorney-General John Ashcroft gave a statement that had the desired effect –

the media turned into a piranha pool. Nobody objected to the Bush Administration designating Jose Padilla, an American citizen, as an enemy combatant and detaining him without formal charges. The name Benjamin Mohammed was leaked as the second suspect, but nobody even asked who he was, let alone where he might be or whether he was being tortured.

Padilla, who had briefly been assigned lawyers, was transferred to a military brig where he could have access to nobody but his interrogators. His lawyers spent two years fighting to get back in to see him.

Binyam never got close to a lawyer for three years. When I did eventually meet him he insisted that he had never met Padilla. How did Binyam become a central suspect in the highest profile conspiracy since September 11?

There were some indicators of the quality of the intelligence against him. I had been struck in newspaper reports by the fact that the Bush Administration could not even get Binyam's name right – they kept calling him Benjamin and making mistakes with his last name. Four years later, after months spent drawing up allegations against him, the US military lawyers were still struggling to spell his name. This inspired little faith that they had been investigating with care.

And of course there was the issue of common sense. How was this dirty bomb plot going to come to fruition? In the early releases to the media the US authorities insisted that Padilla had gone on a trip around Central Asia 'in April' 2002 in search of radioactive material for his bomb. It all seemed rather improbable. Was he meant to buy some uranium or plutonium, slip it into his suitcase and hop on a plane for America? Padilla would have needed a crane to winch the leadlined case into the overhead lockers on the Boeing 747. The sensors as you pass through airport security will sometimes pick up radiation from a recent X-ray; they are hardly likely to miss the amount you would need for a bomb, estimated to be around thirty-five kilograms of plutonium oxide.

Next, the US authorities insisted that Padilla and Binyam had dinner with various high-up members of al-Qaeda the night before Padilla was to fly off to America. According to their theory the dinner party had to have been on the evening of 3 April in Karachi. In turn, this meant that for Padilla's Central Asian search for nuclear fission material to have been 'in April', it had to have taken place on 1 or 2 April, helpfully encompassing April Fools' Day.

Binyam insisted that he spoke very limited Arabic, so he could hardly have been a participant in these dinner discussions. According to the US theory, Binyam was meant to have dined with Khalid Sheikh Mohammed, Abu Zubaydah, Sheikh al-Libi, Ramzi bin al-Shibh and Jose Padilla. The CIA hive was swarming in Pakistan. The notion that four of al-Qaeda's top six leaders congregated in one room in Karachi, a thousand miles by road from the al-Qaeda hideouts in Peshawar, simply to bid au revoir to Binyam and Padilla seemed unlikely. Indeed, the scenario was made more absurd by the fact that two of the conspirators were already in US custody at the time — Abu Zubaydah was seized six days before, on 28 March 2002, and al-Libi had been held since November 2001.

Naturally, as time went by those intent on charging Binyam would try to clean up their story, eliminating the glaring mistakes. The 'Dirty Bomb Plot' would become nothing more than the conspirators' idea; there would be no dinner party and so on. It was important to look for the earliest statements made by government witnesses that contained these details.

It was not until mid 2006 that Padilla's lawyer, Andy Patel, sent me the affidavit that had been used against Padilla on 8 May 2002. The statement was sworn by Special Agent Joe Ennis of the FBI, based on the intelligence they had at that time, and had been used to justify Padilla's arrest.

Binyam was not referred to by name, but it was clear that he was meant to be 'Subject-1'. Every single representation in the statement was either false, or inconsistent with other public statements that the Bush Administration had made. I was interested that, according to Ennis way back then, Binyam was not meant to be a member of al-Qaeda. This made the alleged presence at the al-Qaeda CEO dinner party in Karachi seem all the more unlikely. But it was the last of Ennis's sworn statements that made Binyam laugh the most: in a separate interview, Subject-1's wife told law enforcement authorities that Subject-1 would often become emotional and cry when he discussed his willingness to die for his God.'

'But I'm not married and I never have been!' Binyam said, confused.

We concluded that the FBI must believe in arranged marriages. Maybe they had arranged one for Binyam.

I was surprised at Binyam's resilience and humour, although he would show moments of paranoia. He would look me in the eyes and calmly tell me how he had no idea whether I was working against him with the CIA, but he felt he had no alternative but to work with me. And, he said, he just didn't care.

'I have nothing to hide, but I also don't care if they execute me. You can tell them that.' He paused. 'No, you should tell them that. I don't care if they hold me here in this torture island for the next fifty years. Tell them that also.'

The torture Binyam described was the most dreadful I had heard, but the potential consequences of that abuse made his case even more important. When a criminal suspect is coerced into falsely confessing it is an enormous tragedy – he has only one life and that 'confession' may mean that he spends every remaining day of it in prison. But when someone like Binyam is coerced into confessing about a radio-active bomb plot, the resulting panic filters into the lives of millions of people around the planet. It does not only result in the conviction of a potentially innocent man, but can change government policy, too.

There is a better known case of this, involving al-Qaeda suspect Ibn Sheikh al-Libi. In early 2002, he was taken to Egypt, where 'enhanced interrogation techniques' induced him to confirm a link between Saddam Hussein and al-Qaeda, allegedly teaming up on weapons of mass destruction. Of course, it proved to be the torture talking rather than the truth, but the falsity of the confession was not proven until long after President Bush had used it as one of the wobbly legs to support his plans for war with Iraq.

In Binyam's case, there are few people in America today who have not heard of the 'Dirty Bomb Plot'. It is almost certainly a fantasy, built in part on Binyam's tortured confession. How many people live in fear, thinking that Hiroshima may come to Hoboken, New Jersey? To what extent is the Department of Homeland Security able to ride on this phantom fear, charging around the United States dissolving civil liberties?

If there really had been a dirty bomb plot between Jose Padilla and Binyam Mohamed, the torture advocates would be one step along

EIGHT O'CLOCK FERRY TO THE WINDWARD SIDE

the path to justifying use of the rack. If, on the other hand, torture was used and the result, perhaps unwittingly, was to compound an interrogator's fantasy, then this was another strike against the ticking-bomb argument.

How could we establish the truth? In Western democracies the most powerful engine for resolving such conflicts is the trial. But would the kind of trials available in the War on Terror be adequate for that task?

4

CON-MISSION

By the time they got around to charging any prisoner in Guantánamo, almost four years had gone by. Binyam Mohamed was one of just ten men, two per cent of the prisoners on the base at the time, to face a military commission. Whether that would resolve the truth of the case against him remained to be seen.

Guantánamo Bay did not represent the first time that the victors in war have set up tribunals that will inflict a rough kind of justice on the vanquished. During World War Two, millions died. Unsurprisingly, there was strong desire for revenge.

Among the major Allies, civilians in the United States had arguably suffered the least, yet as early as 1942 ninety per cent of Americans opposed giving the Nazis trials, and one in ten wanted to torture any German unfortunate enough to be caught. Two years later a third of Americans polled wanted to destroy Japan completely and one in eight wanted to kill all the millions of Japanese. Very few citizens at the time had qualms about wiping out 100,000 civilians per atomic bomb.

The Nuremberg Tribunal eventually began on 20 November 1945, but it was not always certain that there would be trials at all. During one of the early meetings between Winston Churchill, Joseph Stalin and Franklin Roosevelt in 1943, the Soviet leader proposed executing a set number of German officers, between 50,000 and 100,000. Roosevelt thought he was joking and countered that perhaps 49,000 would suffice.

Stalin was serious. His initial plan was the total elimination of Nazis who might continue to cause trouble. By this point in his career as Soviet leader he had considerable experience in such purges.

'When it is a question of annihilating the enemy,' Stalin's chief prosecutor, Andrei Vyshinsky, once suggested during the 1938 show trials in Moscow, 'we can do it just as well without a trial.'

But Stalin soon came round to the idea of holding trials of some sort. He understood the importance of a public show, although he viewed trials as part of the work of Ministry of Propaganda rather than any independent judicial process. Between 1936 and 1938, a succession of remorseful defendants admitted the error of their ways, generally to avoid some horror being inflicted on their families. The trials were carefully scripted to provide a superficial appearance of fairness. As one commentator summed it up, 'Stalin took steps to, "simplify" the judicial system. He eliminated the right of defence. He sped up trials and often held them in secret. He suppressed the right of appeal. He expanded the death penalty to cover hundreds of offences . . .'

There is victor's justice; similarly, history is written by the winner. Today, we tend to see the Nuremberg Tribunal as an admirable exercise in restraint, with understated British jurists joining with the Americans to avert some of Stalin's excesses. But in some ways, Churchill was more extreme than Stalin. During extended negotiations the British leader strongly opposed holding trials at all, preferring instead a simple policy of summary executions.

By 12 April 1945, as the war drew to a close, Churchill was still opposed to the idea of a war crimes tribunal. He continued to advocate summary justice, rounding up the top seventy Nazis and having them shot. He feared that any trial would become a soapbox for the Nazis. 'Agree the trial will be a farce,' he jotted in notes. 'Indictment, facilities for counsel. All sorts of complications ensue as soon as you admit a fair trial. I would take no responsibility for a trial – even though US wants to do it. Execute the principal criminals as outlaws – if no Ally wants them.'

Some voices in America also proposed a harsh policy of labour camps and 'de-Nazification'. General Dwight D. Eisenhower wanted to execute the entire German general staff, all the Gestapo and every member of the Nazi party above the rank of mayor – at least 5,000 people. US Treasury Secretary Hans Morgenthau Jr suggested eliminating all members of the Nazi party. When he was told they would number thirteen million he replied that this was an exaggeration –

saying there were 'only five million', as if this were a reasonable number for the hangman.

Despite this the Americans were generally the moderating influence. US Secretary of War Henry Stimson proposed a series of proper trials for the worst offenders. Despite Churchill's continued concerns, by the Yalta Conference in February 1945 the general scheme was mapped out.

'In the Soviet Union, we never execute anyone without a trial,' Stalin said piously, now countering Churchill's qualms.

'Of course, of course,' Churchill is said to have ultimately agreed. 'We should give them a trial first.' He still thought that expeditious executions should follow.

Such proceedings could have turned into the kind of show trials that had become eponymous with the Soviet leader, but President Harry Truman, who succeeded Roosevelt in April 1945, was insistent on true due process. He persuaded Supreme Court Justice Robert H. Jackson to take a leave of absence to fill the role of chief prosecutor, to ensure that justice would be seen to be done.

'Undiscriminating executions or punishments without definite findings of guilt, fairly arrived at, would ... not sit easily on the American conscience or be remembered by our children with pride,' Jackson argued. His heart was set on the kind of due process for which America was famous. 'The only other course is to determine the innocence or guilt of the accused, after a hearing as dispassionate as the times and horrors we deal with will permit, and upon a record that will leave our reasons and our motives clear.'

The 'Major War Criminals' trial began, as I have said, on 20 November 1945. This trial focused on those thought to be the 'worst of the worst' Nazis in custody. The trial would last the best part of a year, with the verdicts returned on 1 October 1946.

Jackson began his opening statement to the military judges who would hear the case on 21 November 1945.

He paused frquently. He spoke calmly, without drama. At one point, critics of his low-key style thought he would lose the trial for the Allies. Yet his purpose was to avoid showboating and simply lay out the facts. He knew the dangers of victor's justice and recognised that the rule of law would more likely be the victor if the trials were dispassionate. Europe had witnessed six years of Blitzkreig, the greatest loss of life during any war in history among military and civilians alike. Yet the prisoners at Nuremberg did not have to wait several years for justice. Just five months after VE Day twenty-one allied countries, from Australia to Norway, had agreed on a process and started the trial. Jackson was determined that the trial should be fair, and that its fairness should be obvious to all.

'When I say that we do not ask for convictions unless we prove crime, I do not mean mere technical or incidental transgression of international conventions,' said Jackson. He spoke pedantically, pronouncing his words with great care. We charge guilt on planned and intended conduct that involves moral as well as legal wrong. And we do not mean conduct that is a natural and human – even if illegal – cutting of corners, such as many of us might well have committed had we been in the defendants' positions. It is not because they yielded to the normal frailties of human beings that we accuse them. It is their abnormal and inhuman conduct which brings them to this bar.'

Indeed, the crimes charged were horrific, as extreme as any human misconduct could ever be, including mass genocide against the Jewish race and war of aggression on an unparalleled scale.

Jackson had not chosen petty criminals for this, the flagship of war crimes trials. He had plenty to choose from, as millions of Germans had fought and still more had been complicit in the war effort. But no soldier was going to get prosecuted because he was not wearing a proper uniform when caught; no civilian, because she was Adolf Hitler's secretary.

Twenty-one prisoners were selected for the Major War Criminals trial, and they were the leaders of Nazi Germany. One defendant was Reichsmarschall Hermann Goering, who had been an early Nazi and a top aide to Adolf Hitler. Goering was a large man, physically and metaphorically. He had been an ace pilot in World War One, but during the recent war he had peacocked about in his Luftwaffe uniforms, written off by some as a vainglorious ass who spent most of the war pillaging artwork for his private collection.

'It is hard to say whether the spectacle of Germany's Number 2 leader urging his people to give up every comfort and strain every sinew on essential war work while he rushed around confiscating art by the trainload should be cast as tragedy or comedy,' Jackson argued. Yet few could deny that Goering was well qualified to be a defendant in the Major War Criminals trial. As early as 1933 he had advocated killing all opponents of Nazism, and by 1934 he proposed (or, to use Jackson's word, 'sired') the concentration camps, first for political opponents, and subsequently for any number of unwanted human beings. He pressed millions of captive foreigners into forced labour camps. He asserted the obsolescence of the rules of warfare, resulting in the indiscriminate bombing of civilians. The list of his crimes could continue for many pages – and did, during his trial.

The other defendants included such men as Rudolf Hess, formerly the Deputy Führer. It was most important for the credibility of the trial, Jackson said, that those accused should have been genuinely responsible for the horrors of the Nazi regime.

'The case as presented by the United States will be concerned with the brains and authority behind all the crimes,' he continued. 'These defendants were men of a station and rank which does not soil its own hands with blood. They were men who knew how to use lesser folk as tools. We want to reach the planners and designers, the inciters and leaders without whose evil architecture the world would not have been for so long scourged with the violence and lawlessness, and racked with the agonies and convulsions, of this terrible war.'

In seeking convictions, Jackson was adamant that the prosecution would not rest on unreliable testimony – evidence extracted through torture, evidence from the recently oppressed looking to visit a little oppression in return, or witnesses who had been well rewarded for their services.

'We will not ask you to convict these men on the testimony of their foes. There is no count in the Indictment that cannot be proved by books and records,' Jackson emphasised. 'They arranged frequently to be photographed in action. We will show you their own films. You will see their own conduct and hear their own voices as these defendants re-enact for you, from the screen, some of the events in the course of the conspiracy.'

One defendant, Hans Frank, had been Governor-General of Poland. It did not take an informant to prove the case against him. 'The Jews are a race which has to be eliminated,' he wrote in his diary in 1944. 'Whenever we catch one, it is his end.' Speaking of his work, he confided frustration to his diary: 'Of course I cannot eliminate all lice and Jews in only a year's time.'

Frank was not satisfied with only killing Jews. He also oversaw a slave labour programme. 'I have sent 1,300,000 Polish workers into the Reich,' he boasted in a public speech on 25 January 1944.

Despite the indisputable fact that someone had to have been responsible for the horrors of the Nazi regime, Jackson called for restraint since he knew that justice was itself on trial. Some of the Nazis' victims might have joined Churchill's call for summary executions but, Jackson said, they were not the plaintiffs here.

'The real complaining party at your bar is Civilisation. In all our countries it is still a struggling and imperfect thing,' Jackson argued. 'The usefulness of this effort to do justice is not to be measured by considering the law or your judgement in isolation. This trial is part of the great effort to make the peace more secure.'

Given the shocking evidence that was presented over the ensuing months, the Nuremberg Tribunals were modest in their vengeance. Eleven of the twenty-one major defendants were condemned to die and ten were actually hanged on 16 October 1946. The exception was Goering, who committed suicide by cyanide the night before.

Three defendants were acquitted outright. Three were sentenced to life, but even for war crimes life did not really mean life. Only Rudolf Hess served anything like a full term, committing suicide in Spandau Prison in 1987 at the age of ninety-three. The other two were released on compassionate grounds after ten and twelve years respectively. Today there are howls of tabloid outrage if a criminal is released on parole.

The four other prisoners were given terms ranging from ten to twenty years and none died in prison.

Following the Major War Criminals trial, there were eleven other trials in Nuremberg between 1946 and 1949. Two more prisoners committed suicide. Of the 188 prisoners who saw their trials through, thirty-seven were fully acquitted, representing almost one-fifth of the total, a far higher acquittal rate than most US criminal courts today. Thirty-five were sentenced to be hanged, a relatively small number, given the horrors alleged against them. Fourteen of these death sentences were later commuted.

That was then, this is now.

In September 2001, despite the tragedy of 3,000 deaths, there was no chance whatsoever of the United States being destroyed by al-Qaeda. Today we should be better prepared to deliver true justice to the vanquished, or a criminal suspect. We have benefited from fifty years of human rights law – the term would have been barely recognised in 1945, yet now conventions are named after it. The modern Geneva Conventions date from 1949 and promised a step along the long path of civilising warfare.

Following the honourable tradition of Nuremberg, what kind of military tribunals could we expect in the early years of the twenty-first century?

On 4 November 2005 I was surprised when Binyam's name appeared (misspelled again) among those slated to face a military commission in Guantánamo Bay. As far as I knew, the only evidence against him came from statements tortured out of him, which would make his tribunal very embarrassing to the United States authorities. It seemed an unwise decision on their part.

Almost simultaneously US citizen Jose Padilla, held in a South Carolina brig as the 'Dirty Bomber' for more than two years, was transferred to a proper federal court in Florida, where he would face criminal conspiracy charges. The indictment was released on 17 November 2005, so the final decision to charge him must have been made at the same time as the decision on Binyam.

Notably absent from Padilla's charges was any mention of the dirty bomb plot, and he was instead charged with a far less significant conspiracy involving raising money for criminal activity. The government immediately held a press conference to explain away the extraordinary fact that a man who was meant to have been planning a radioactive attack on the United States would not be facing that charge.

'The decision not to charge him criminally in connection with the more far-ranging bomb plots was prompted by the conclusion that Mr [Khalid Sheikh] Mohammed and Mr [Abu] Zubaydah could almost certainly not be used as witnesses, because that could expose classified information and could open up charges from defence lawyers that their earlier statements were a result of torture,' officials said. Without that testimony, the officials suggested that it would be nearly impossible for the United States to prove the charges.

Clearly, the government did not want a public hearing in a real court about how Khalid Sheikh Mohammed (KSM) had been subjected to water-boarding but it seemed improbable to me that this was the real reason for dropping the worst of the charges against Padilla. After all, KSM had not been captured until 1 March 2003, many months after Padilla's arrest, so he could hardly have been the one who provided the critical information. Abu Zubaydah, allegedly bin Laden's chief of military operations, had been shot during his capture, and was apparently subjected to terrible abuses. The question was whether Abu Zubaydah was truly the source of the case against Padilia, or whether Abu Zubaydah had simply agreed to parrot a story fed to him by his interrogators.

Yet the sequence of events raised another obvious question. If the government insisted that it was impossible to charge Padilla, supposedly the lead 'Dirty Bomber', without exposing the torture committed against KSM and Abu Zubaydah, how did the military expect to prove the same charge against Binyam as the second conspirator? One obvious conclusion was that the military expected to be able to prevent the defence from presenting evidence of such abuses in a tribunal in Guantánamo.

When I learned about the charges, I wanted to get down to see Binyam as soon as possible. The best I was able to do was to leave England on the day after Christmas, meet Yvonne Bradley, the military lawyer assigned to defend Binyam, in Florida and then fly down to Guantánamo on a military plane. I left the low-slung grey cloud of East Anglia in the morning, arriving in Jacksonville, Florida that night. I had not met Yvonne before and was somewhat apprehensive. I had a hard enough time keeping my clients' trust, without having a soldier along, but everyone charged in a military commission was required, under the rules, to have a military defence counsel.

We met in the hotel bar that evening. Yvonne was a major in the US Air Force, in her late thirties, quiet to the point of diffidence. It soon became clear that she voted Republican and was a sincere Christian. She was African-American and I guessed that her own experiences of racism would help her relate to Binyam, who had met his own difficulties trying to live in the dark skin of an Ethiopian. Overall, though, getting Binyam to accept that Yvonne was on his side was going to be a tough sell. I decided that I'd better spend the first day with Binyam alone, trying to explain why it could be helpful to have an officer in uniform on our side.

When we boarded the small military plane, though, I was grateful for Yvonne's presence – there was only one other person on the flight, a gung-ho senior officer who loudly demanded my opinions about the War on Terror. Yvonne was clearly terrified that if I was cornered into giving my full opinion she might be caught in the crossfire for the whole flight, so she ran interference. I pleaded that the engine noise made hearing too difficult and disappeared into my headphones to avert the crisis.

The next day I discovered that legal visits had been moved from Camp Echo to Camp Five, the state-of-the-art maximum-security prison that had been built a short distance away. Outside the front entrance was a brass plaque from the proud builders, advertising the fact that KBR (Kellogg, Brown & Root, the Halliburton subsidiary, best known as the company formerly run by Vice President Dick Cheney) had taken their slice of the profits.

Inside, the guards were the same, although the atmosphere had changed incrementally. Some still struggled to be polite and pleasant as they carried out their duty, but they had received a sterner lecture on avoiding lawyers. One smiling soldier told me that he had only fourteen more days to go before he left the island. I congratulated him and began a discussion about the New Year. One of his colleagues gave him a fierce look. He turned away from me, embarrassed. He should not have been talking. I was sorry to have put him on the spot and stood lonely by myself, waiting for half an hour to be shown in to see Binyam.

I was taken through to a cell for the meeting. As in Camp Echo, Binyam had to sit on the other side of a table, with his ankle shackled to the floor. I had been excited, glad even, that Binyam had been charged. It was an opportunity for him, the first time he would be able to make a public statement in the tribunal about his years of abuse, a statement that would be reported by the media. I had somehow expected him to feel the same, but of course that had been foolish. While he got up to shake my hand, he looked beaten down. He had been through torture, isolation and now this – being chosen among the two per cent of prisoners given 'special treatment', and where might it lead?

'Is it true that they don't want the death penalty?' was his first question. I was taken aback.

'What have they told you?' I asked.

'They just came to my cell back at the start of November and told me I was being charged, that was all,' he said. 'I heard later that they did not want the death penalty on me, but I didn't know that for sure. I was waiting for your visit.'

Normally, Binyam was always calm. He had suppressed his emotions so deeply that the flatness of his demeanour could be disconcerting, broken only when he would switch on a wry smile at the mention of some military inanity. He was agitated now for the first time since I had met him.

I recognised how insensitive I had been. I had it all neatly worked out in my own mind how it would actually be better if the military did seek the death penalty, as the opponents of capital punishment would then flock to our banner; but Binyam was the human being in the middle of all this. It reminded me of the trial of Scotty Loyd in Louisiana, several years before. I had been questioning the potential jurors about whether they had made up their minds in the case. More than one hundred said they would vote to execute Scotty without a trial. I was happily ploughing forward, because I knew that each person who said this would be ejected for bias and this would get us a change of venue to a town where we could get a fair jury. In the middle of the sixth day I turned to Scotty, who was pale and looking sick. Scotty had listened to a hundred people, none of whom knew him, publicly saying that they would like him summarily executed. I was happy that we were winning the battle to achieve a change of venue, but of course he was devastated by what he was hearing.

With Binyam, I had forgotten that basic lesson again. He was more depressed than he had ever been in Guantánamo Bay. The resilience of the human spirit is such that even after four years' torture and abuse, Binyam held on to the hope that somehow there would be a return to normality, along with the established rules of law and life. Being singled out for this charge was another punch to the stomach.

The military rules said anyone charged with any military offence was death eligible. They had not told Binyam that they had elected to forgo his execution – they had simply made a statement in the media.

'Well, let's start at the beginning,' I said, breathing in. 'There isn't going to be any death penalty involved here. They haven't said anything formally to me, but they said that in the media, the military did. So you don't have to worry about that.'

That still left the possibility of life without parole. For an alleged conspiracy to kill millions with a radioactive bomb in New York, forgoing the death penalty was bizarre and anything short of a life sentence would be politically impossible.

I felt that my first duty was to explain to Binyam that given the political realities, the commission process was a sham from the start. The military had originally insisted that he could be held indefinitely without a trial at all. Even if Binyam had a military trial and by some miraculous turn of events was found innocent, under the rules he could still be held indefinitely. I read to Binyam from the transcript of a press conference on 21 March 2002, where William Haynes, a lawyer for the Bush Administration, made the situation very clear.

'Do these procedures guarantee that if a defendant is acquitted, the defendant will be set free?' asked one journalist.

'The procedures don't address the outcome of a trial, except to say that a sentence will be enforced quickly,' said Haynes, trying to fob off the question. Of course, if the accused were not convicted, one would expect there to be no sentence to be enforced.

'Does that mean that if you are acquitted, there is a chance that you will not be set free?' the same journalist asked, determined to have his question answered.

'Well, it's . . .' Haynes could see no way to avoid the question twice. 'We're talking about hypothetical two or three times removed. If we had a trial right this minute, it is conceivable that somebody could be tried and acquitted of that charge, but may not necessarily automatically be released. The people that we are detaining, for example, in Guantánamo Bay, Cuba are enemy combatants that we captured on the battlefield seeking to harm US soldiers or allies, and they're dangerous people. At the moment we're not about to release any of them unless we find that they don't meet those criteria.'

In other words, yes, if a prisoner were convicted the US military could hold him for ever and if a prisoner were acquitted he could be held for ever. Not that there was really any chance of Binyam being acquitted. That was obvious from what some of the military prosecutors had said about their own task.

'The prosecutors on your case are people who were hand-picked for the job by the military,' I told him. 'Any prosecutor is likely to presume you guilty, but these are a special breed here. They are in the military and whether they would admit it or not they got chosen because the military thought they were the type who would get the job done.'

Despite being vetted, three of the chosen team of prosecutors had resigned rather than take part in a process they could not stomach. This was not something the military advertised. The officers' resignation statements did not come to light for some time after they were written. The first two were Captain John Carr and Major Robert Preston, both of the US Air Force.

'You have repeatedly said to the office that the military panel will be hand-picked and will not acquit these detainees, and we only needed to worry about building a record for the review panel,' wrote Captain Carr to his superior, Colonel Fred Borch. Carr went on to complain that the public was being misled into thinking that the prisoners were much more culpable than they really were. He was, he wrote, being asked to take part in 'a halfhearted and disorganised effort by a skeleton group of relatively inexperienced attorneys to prosecute fairly low-level accused in a process that appears to be rigged'.

Carr also revealed that exculpatory evidence – information that could help a prisoner prove his innocence – was being hidden from the defence in the documents withheld by the CIA for 'security reasons'. In other words any fact that might help the defence would be buried. For example, Captain Carr wrote, the prosecution team had told the defence that there was no evidence of torture of Ali Hamza al-Bahlul of Yemen. To achieve this, the prosecution team had 'lost' an FBI report of an interview in which al-Bahlul claimed he had been tortured and abused.

His colleague, Major Preston, likewise wrote that he could not in good conscience author a legal motion saying the proceedings would be 'full and fair' when he knew they would not. He wrote that the trials were 'a severe threat to the reputation of the military justice system and even a fraud on the American people'.

Soon after these memos became public, a third resignation message surfaced from Air Force Captain Carrie Wolf. She also wrote that she could not continue with her assignment 'because of concerns it was unfair'.

'Binyam, you don't have to believe me when I say the system is rigged,' I said, after going over all this. 'The prosecutors say it themselves.'

Colonel Frederick L. Borch was the senior prosecutor and the person alleged to have made the statements about the foregone conclusion of any trial. He sent his own e-mail round the prosecution team responding to the charges made by Major Preston and Captain Carr. Borch said he had great respect and admiration for both officers, but their accusations were 'monstrous lies'. He did not address any specifics.

'I am convinced to the depth of my soul that all of us on the prosecution team are truly dedicated to the mission of the office of military commissions,' he wrote, 'and that no one on the team has anything but the highest ethical principles.'

It took some courage for Carr, Preston and Wolf to spill the beans about a superior officer. The film *A Few Good Men* was set in Guantánamo Bay and I had recognised some of the locations. I imagined the three dissenting prosecutors, officers in brilliant white uniforms, confronting Jack Nicholson's character, Colonel Nathan Jessep.

These junior officers must have come under some terrible pressure. In *A Few Good Men*, Tom Cruise's character was the junior lawyer who had recently graduated from Harvard Law School. He dared to suggest that Colonel Jessep's few good men had gone a few steps too far, killing one of their number when discipline got carried away. Given the unswerving devotion to loyalty in the military, Cruise's insubordination went against the grain.

'I have two books at my bedside, Lieutenant, the Marine Code of Conduct and the King James Bible,' said one officer on the witness stand, a marine lieutenant played by Kiefer Sutherland. 'The only proper authorities I'm aware of are my Commanding Officer Colonel Nathan R. Jessep, and the Lord our God.'

Because it was a movie, Tom Cruise was courageous and ultimately victorious, bringing the officers to justice.

In the real Guantánamo Bay, when the *New York Times* asked him to explain all this e-mail traffic about rigged trials, Air Force General Thomas L. Hemingway said it had all been thoroughly investigated and he believed that the complaints were based on 'miscommunication, misunderstanding and personality conflicts'. The inspector general's report had not, he said, been made public.

Despite this stonewalling, it didn't look like Colonel Borch had won the day. While he had retired from the military, the three dissenting officers moved on to new jobs. At least one had been promoted. It would take someone with more credulity than I could summon up to think Binyam had a chance of a fair military trial.

So much for the prosecutors, but what about the people who would be sitting in judgement on Binyam?

'I don't even know their names,' I said. 'Except for one of them, that's Colonel Ralph Kohlmann. He's from the Marine Corps and he is the one in charge of your case. They call him the "Presiding Officer", something like a judge. Then there's six other officers – they're all colonels.'

I could see that Binyam was even more depressed.

'We don't really care too much about the seven colonels, Binyam,' I said. 'The court that's judging you is the court of public opinion, not a bunch of colonels in a court that has been rigged. After four years of keeping you gagged, finally they're going to let you speak for yourself.'

At last, Binyam became interested in how the tribunals would proceed. He quizzed me about the layout of the tribunal room, so that he could understand how it worked. The Presiding Officer would be in front of us, the prosecution to our right and the media behind us.

'The media are actually in the room?' he asked. He sounded surprised.

'Yes, of course,' I replied.

'Can I speak directly to them?'

'I have no idea,' I said. 'But whether you're facing forward, or back towards them, they're the people who are really listening to you, obviously.'

We talked for several hours that first day. I turned the conversation to Yvonne Bradley and explained how we had to have a military lawyer on our team. I pitched it as best I could, without any great expectation that Binyam would accept an Air Force major who was, according to the President, his sworn enemy. But he told me to bring her along the next day.

Emerging from the cell, I rued my various insensitivities. But perhaps we had made some progress.

It is the rare prisoner on trial who does not feel bound by the rules of etiquette in court. The prosecutor may be pounding the podium telling the jury how the defendant is an animal and deserves to die in the execution chamber, yet the client will listen politely, as if the prosecutor's behaviour were quite normal. I have often marvelled at this and I'm not sure why more people don't react. Mostly, the client wants to fulfil the expectations of the courtroom, but if he needs additional motivation to behave well, the threat of a contempt of court charge may rein him in. He faces an automatic six months in prison for every outburst.

Binyam was hardly going to shudder at a contempt charge when he had already spent four years suffering terrible abuse and when he had been promised that he would continue to be held in prison whether he was convicted or acquitted. And what sensible person could expect him to hold the process in anything other than contempt? Few observers respected the military commissions and even British Lord Justice Steyn had labelled them kangaroo courts.

So Binyam began to look forward to his first appearance in the commission. He was particularly pleased to learn that he had the legal right to represent himself – no matter what the colonel in charge of the commission thought, the United States Supreme Court had made this clear thirty years before. I explained to him that the lawyers were merely his assistants and that ultimately if he wanted to do the talking in court, that was his decision. He drew up his plans in his own mind and listened attentively as Yvonne and I explained how the process would operate, as best we could tell.

'I'm not gonna tell you what my strategy is, though, 'cos I don't want them being totally prepared for it,' Binyam said, nodding at the door of the cell, indicating he was convinced that the military were listening in.

There was a part of Binyam that clearly thought Yvonne or I might be going straight from the interview cell to talk to the authorities about his plans. As a lawyer, I want to control everything about the case. I justify this in my own mind because the client is generally at his first trial and cannot possibly be expected to know what to do.

Yet I came round to Binyam's point of view. There was no chance that he was going to be released by any military court, no matter what the weakness of the case or strength of his defence. His words, not mine, were going to be published by the media and would ultimately set him free. The more he represented himself, the better off he would be.

I worried that I could not forewarn Binyam what was coming, since these commissions were totally new to me as well. But it turned out to be easy to advise him. I was astounded when I received an e-mail from Colonel Kohlmann attaching the 'script' of the upcoming hearing. It was even called a script and it really was a script: nine pages long, single-spaced, with virtually every word that either side was meant to say in the tribunal. When I waved it at Yvonne, astounded that they should be so open about choreographing the process, she told me these kinds of things happen in the military, where apparently people are meant to do as they are told.

The words that each participant was meant to recite were typed out, with parenthetical alternatives where it might go one way or another.

'Please be seated' were the first words the presiding colonel was meant to say when he walked into the room and took his seat. 'This Military Commission is called to order.'

The colonel would then turn to the prosecutor. 'This Military Commission is appointed by Appointing Order No. 05-0005 dated 12 Dec 2005 as amended by Appointing Order No. 06-0010, dated 27 March 2006 copies of which have been furnished to the Presiding Officer, counsel, and the accused, and which (have been) (will be) marked . . .' the prosecutor was supposed to intone.

The very existence of the script was bizarre – I have sometimes thought that trials in Mississippi run as if the judge and prosecutor had concocted the whole process on the golf course, but here it really was preordained.

Binyam gave me a list of items that he wanted me to get for him, props for the day of the hearing. I tried to guess what he had in mind for each one. 'First, I'll need a piece of card and a large black marker,' Binyam said. It only had to be the size of a writing pad and that was easily procured at the Navy store. Its purpose seemed fairly obvious: some kind of placard. What it would say I had no idea.

'Next, I'll need a number ten shirt from the Dutch football team,' he continued.

'You want to be Ruud Gullit or Van Nistelroy?' I asked Binyam, joshing about the two famous Dutch centre forwards. Binyam simply smiled. I had a good idea what this was all about. Ten prisoners had been charged in military commissions and Binyam planned to adopt the number ten, with the orange Dutch shirt matching the iconic Guantánamo prison jumpsuits. The 2006 World Cup was two months away, so I was optimistic I would find it somewhere.

'What if I can't find a Dutch shirt, is there anything else that would do?' Later I was glad I asked, as I sent a Reprieve intern scouring the London shops without success.

'Well, if you can get a proper type of Islamic dress and colour that orange, that would be second best. You can bring that and the shirt to court, 'cos they won't let me have it here,' he said, gesturing at the cell.

He also wanted copies of cases that gave him the right to represent himself and on various other legal issues.

After going through his requests, I tried to give Binyam a sense of what he could expect with the hearing. I told him about the chief prosecutor we were dealing with. Colonel Moe Davis was someone who was doing the US military cause a great deal of harm. He had written a paper for the military on how it should deal with the press. Presumably this reflected the media expertise that had recommended him for his current assignment. In typical military language, it was called 'Effective Engagement in the Public Opinion Arena' and had been published in *Air & Space Power Chronicles* several months before.

In his article he wrote that his 'Rule Five' for dealing with the media was to 'take the offensive', advice that he illustrated through several paragraphs. 'Hearing bad news about someone from a third party often elicits schadenfreude, that wonderful German word that means taking pleasure in someone else's pain,' Davis advised in his article, expanding on his rule. 'The military cannot be the first one out of the chute every time for a variety of reasons. Many cases involve information on individuals that is protected by the Privacy Act. In those cases, taking the offensive may not mean being first with the news, but being ready to respond when the news hits. Have the

Privacy Act waiver ready and waiting. Have the relevant documents redacted, copied and ready to distribute.'

The way Davis interpreted taking the offensive was to be as offensive as he could. No trial had yet begun, nor would it any time soon. But there had been various pre-trial hearings in the nine cases besides Binyam's on legal issues that had to be settled early in the process. Davis had made various extraordinary statements in the press conferences that were held after each commission hearing. His most recent foray had been to compare the prisoners to Count Dracula. 'Remember if you dragged Dracula out into the sunlight he melted? Well, that's kind of the way it is trying to drag a detainee into the courtroom,' Davis had told reporters, apparently forgetting that all 500 prisoners had been crying out for a fair trial for several years now. 'But their day is coming . . . The defence has tried to hide. They're going to show up in the courtroom.'

Yvonne, Binyam's military lawyer, had a conflict of interest that put her in a hopeless position. I expected that working out a solution would take up much of the first hearing in Binyam's case.

Yvonne was in the Office of Military Commissions Defense, or OMCD as it was called. This was a military defence office with several other lawyers, each representing one of the nine other prisoners charged in the commissions. The military lawyers were very different. Some fitted the stereotype of the company man, tending to see problems from the government's perspective. But I wondered how some of them had made it in the military so long, as they were so willing to challenge any and all authority. They were very impressive. Inevitably, each lawyer had a different approach to the clients. Some recognised that it would take months of patient work to establish any kind of trust; some marched into the client's cell with a crew cut and a uniform, and started asking the client whether he was guilty or not.

All ten prisoners set for trial in the military commissions were accused of being in the same overarching al-Qaeda conspiracy against the United States and four, including Binyam, were meant to have worked together in a smaller conspiracy. They were supposed to have been working together to attack American soldiers in Afghanistan, in addition to the allegation that Binyam was plotting to explode his dirty bomb in New York. The structure of the OMCD presented a classic conflict of interest where many of the clients in the office were pointing the finger at others. That meant that one of the prisoners would inevitably be offered a deal to testify against the others, in exchange for a lesser sentence or total freedom.

To resolve this kind of 'conflict of interest' problem, in any civilian court a public defender office, the equivalent of the OMCD, would only be allowed one client. The judge would order that the lawyer for the other prisoners be appointed separately and be wholly independent of the public defender. The lawyers could not be in the same office because they would inevitably share confidential thoughts. I asked Yvonne to keep a log of all the chatter that was going on in the OMCD office, writing down the gist of what people were saying. It was a tough thing for her to do, as she would be viewed as an informant herself inside her own office. But it was the only way to go about it.

'Your guy is just a bad guy,' one of the lawyers had said to Yvonne, referring to Binyam, whom he had never met. 'My guy's no terrorist. He was just teaching schoolkids. Your guy's the bad one and he's been making statements against everybody.'

'I'd make statements too if I'd been tortured by a razor blade,' Yvonne replied. 'I'd give false statements and give up the people closest to me in the world if they did that.'

'Yeah,' the lawyer replied. 'If someone put a razor blade to my dick I'd confess that my father was bin Laden, and that he kept his beard and mask hidden in my closet. But that doesn't take away from the fact, your client's a bad motherfucker.'

And so it went on. Day after day the lawyers were talking about their cases. It was not their fault that they were put in this hopeless position – the OMCD had been set up in a hurry by the Bush Administration to carry out an agenda, ignoring decades of established law. Yvonne, who was bound by the civilian ethics of her home bar association in Pennsylvania, was forbidden from going along with this set-up.

I wrote to Colonel Kohlmann about it and it was his job to sort out the problem. But the odds were that he would try to sweep the issue under the carpet. Otherwise he would have to order the restructuring of the OMCD and that would derail the tribunal from its preordained course – to run over Binyam and the other nine prisoners as fast as possible.

Paradoxically, if Colonel Kohlmann ruled against us and ordered Yvonne to violate her civilian ethical rules – this would allow us to sue him, personally, in the United States on her behalf. A judge cannot order a lawyer to violate the law. The government would not let Binyam have a proper trial in the US, but Yvonne, being a US citizen, could sue in Pennsylvania and suddenly the US military would have lost control of the case to a federal civilian judge.

Indeed, we had to find a way to propel Binyam's case from Cuba over the Caribbean Sea to mainland USA, where we might find justice in a real court.

It was time for Binyam's first commission hearing, a very preliminary event that would address a few legal issues. Yvonne and I had been joined by Joe Margulies, who had volunteered to help out with Binyam's case. For many years Joe represented prisoners facing the death penalty in Texas, the buckle of the Death Belt, where the hostility to defence lawyers made my work in Louisiana and Mississippi seem tame. Now he had migrated back to his home in Minnesota and continued to take on unpopular cases as he taught law in Chicago. Joe was tall and skinny, like me, but unlike me he now wore rather high-quality suits. There was one aspect of him that had not changed. All the years I've known him he's had the scraggliest beard outside a rural Alabama filling station. It made him look like a grizzled, slightly greying Abraham Lincoln. Joe was the intellectual on the team and had been the lead counsel on the original case we had brought to the Supreme Court, Rasul v. Bush.

We had to go through an intense security procedure before getting into the commission building. I am not allowed to describe the security measures in detail.

We had arrived early – 7.30 for a nine o'clock start – to avoid the media rush and to have time to spend with Binyam before the hearing. The temperature was already well past the point where the English pass out from heat stroke. As lawyers, we each had to wear a suit and tie in the tribunal, and necks were sweating.

The guards were from the Marine Corps. They managed to remain cheerful as they spent a long, hot day conducting searches of anyone going into the commission building. As I completed the process and turned to walk up there I heard a loud shout behind me.

I had come in the same group as Dwight Sullivan, the senior officer in the military defence office, himself a Marine Corps colonel. 'Give me twenty!' Dwight had bellowed.

In unison, he and the soldiers had dived to the ground, and were now pumping up and down, doing their push-ups.

'Enough?' Dwight yelled, as he completed ahead of most of the younger men and women around him.

'No, sir!' they chorused. And everyone went at it again for another twenty.

I felt cooler already, as I counted off the fifty-four steps up to the commission building. I wondered whether Dwight had a different uniform to change into before court.

I went in to meet Binyam in the holding cell. Binyam was calm. I was impressed, as court makes me nervous even after twenty years. With a client's life or freedom at stake, if you don't get nervous you should no longer be in the job.

I had complied with Binyam's requests to the extent I could. The Dutch had not been selling their shirts in London, so a Reprieve intern had found a traditional Muslim shirt and dyed it prisoner-orange. The tribunal rules insisted that the prisoner 'appear in business casual attire or, if an accused desires, culturally equivalent attire'. Those among the other nine prisoners who had already had tribunal hearings had been dressed by their lawyers in Western clothes, but Binyam was on to the military's charade. Their PR people wanted the tribunal to seem like a normal courtroom, with everyone dressed the way Americans would dress in court. Therefore Binyam would do the opposite. For a long time, the military had forced him to dress in demeaning orange prison garb and he was not going to take part in the civilian fancy dress now that it suited the military's purpose.

Binyam happily dressed himself up in his 'culturally appropriate attire' while Yvonne, Joe and I went to the tribunal room. It looked like a modern American courtroom, although we all constantly resisted calling it a court as we did not want to dignify it with the name. I had been given the guided tour some weeks before as part of the well-intentioned effort by the military to act the good host. It had been an odd experience, re-emphasising my impression that this was all acting, each person being told his allotted part in the play.

The judge, or Presiding Officer, was in the normal position, in the centre of the room at the rear, the tall black swivel chair flanked by the usual American flags. At his stage right were seats for the commission members – in Binyam's case they would eventually hold the six other colonels, who would not appear until his actual trial began. At the Presiding Officer's left was a sealed cube where verbatim translators would speak huskily into their microphones, piped out to the earpieces of the participants. Beside this, directly facing the commission members, the prosecution table was cramped between the translation cube and a large concrete pillar.

The defence was well placed, at a long table spanning the front of the room, immediately inside the bar. For the 'public' seating area there was a militarily organised seating chart, with all the best seats reserved for the media, the NGO representatives (from Human Rights Watch, Amnesty International and the American Civil Liberties Union) slotted in further back. The seats on either side of the room were reserved for defence and prosecution staff, in a strange jumble apparently aimed at precise parity.

This meant that the media would all be sitting directly behind Binyam. Journalists from the best US newspapers had made the trip down, including the *New York Times*, the *Wall Street Journal*, the *Miami Herald* and the *LA Times*. I knew several of them since they were veterans of the War on Terror debate. I immediately leant on the bar of the court and began chatting.

'Excuse me,' said a soldier, who moved swiftly up to my right, addressing the journalist who was talking to me. 'You can't be talking to the people taking part.'

That was his mistake. He had cut off Carol Rosenberg from the *Miami Herald* in mid sentence. I would not want to be the soldier to get between her and her First Amendment right to freedom of the press. She gave him a ticking off, told him she had been coming down for months and knew much more than he did about the process. This was the way it was done. He beat a hasty retreat.

No media recording equipment was allowed in the room, though there were various cameras suspended from the ceiling that piped the proceedings to a media centre elsewhere on the base. This was for any overflow journalists or those who would rather be submitting simultaneous reports. A courtroom artist was seated at one end of the front row, sketching the participants. I asked her why the prisoners' faces always appeared as unfocused blobs in her pictures and she told me the military said to show their true identity would be a violation of their Geneva Conventions rights. This was the first time I had heard the Conventions invoked to protect a prisoner in Guantánamo. Binyam would want the world to see everything, so I wrote up a waiver for him to sign. Of course, the military would still enforce their rule, as it was just a pretext to prevent the world from seeing the prisoners as human.

The hearing was set to start at 9 a.m. – 09.00 hours – and Binyam made his entrance a minute or two before the allotted time. He was half carried on either side by heavy-set soldiers and forced to place one foot forward in front of the other, legs wide apart, his whole body leaning forward, stumbling like some kind of monster clambering out of the swamp. It was embarrassing for Binyam, as being shuffled into the tribunal in this way was demeaning. But as he was dressed in bright orange, the spectacle gave the media a clear image of how prisoners were frogmarched in shackles around the camp. I glanced behind me and saw the journalists' pens scrabbling with sudden urgency.

Binyam took his seat and I walked over to him to talk until the hearing began.

'Clive,' Carol Rosenberg said to me from her seat in the front row. 'Can Mr Mohamed answer some questions?'

'I don't care, if he wants to and nobody objects,' I said. This was precisely what Binyam would want to do. He turned round to her.

'First, do you mind telling me how you like your name spelled and your date of birth?' she asked, her interview beginning.

'Ahm.' A uniformed officer was approaching from the side of the room. 'No talking to the prisoner.'

Carol turned to argue with the man. I walked over to where Carol was continuing her debate. 'M-O-H-A-M-E-D and 24 July 1978,' I said.

'You can't do that,' the officer said.

'Why on earth not?' I asked as gently as I could. 'What rule says I can't tell a journalist how to spell my client's name so she can get it accurately?'

'You can't, that's the rules of this tribunal.' And he walked away.

Yvonne sat down next to Binyam at the defence table. She had to be there as she was under military orders. As Binyam had opted to speak for himself, Joe and I were to sit in the audience and we chose a place over near two prosecution paralegals. One of the military staff came across to ask what we were doing sitting there. We shrugged in unison. I pointed out to the official that according to his seating chart these were chairs for the use of defence personnel. I did not tell him that we were acting on Binyam's instructions, since that was none of his business.

By now the judge was fifteen minutes late. An officer behind the judge's seat eventually called the room to order and Colonel Kohlmann came into the commission room.

I had briefly met Kohlmann the day before. I had sought the chance merely to introduce myself. It had been difficult to get a read on him, as he was clearly uncomfortable with a defence lawyer coming into a meeting where he was talking strategy with some of the colonels in charge of other cases. He had been succinctly polite. He was a small man, with academic-looking glasses, hardly the tough Jack Nicholson type of marine. I could not see him dropping to the ground with Dwight Sullivan and the marines to do a few dozen push-ups. Now he came into the room, a black robe enveloping his uniform.

'This Military Commission is called to order in the case of the United States versus Binyam Ahmed Muhammad,' Kohlmann intoned. I had the script and he was reading directly from it. Kohlmann turned to the prosecutor, stage left.

While the colonel's name was fair game, under the incomprehensible military censorship rules I am not allowed to use the prosecutor's name, which has to be taken out of any public document.

I doubt the officer, whom I can only describe in the vaguest terms, cares much for his anonymity. He was a pleasant young lieutenant in the US Navy, smartly turned out in his well-pressed dress whites, who had shown himself to be impeccably polite as well – unlike his boss, the bizarre Colonel Moe Davis, who liked to compare Binyam to Count Dracula.

'This Military Commission is appointed by Appointing Order Number 05-0005, dated 12 December 2005, as amended by Appointing Order Number 06-0003, dated 1 February '06 ...' read the lieutenant, trying to make sense of the endless bureaucracy. 'And Appointing Order Number 06-0010, dated 27 March 2006, copies of which have been furnished to the Presiding Officer, counsel and the Accused.'

The lieutenant finished his lines, but the play was about to go off script. It was Binyam's turn to talk. He began by pointing out that his name was not Mr Muhammad, as set out in the charge sheet.

'This is four years of interrogations, highly intensified, or as they call it – he knows what it's called.' Binyam pointed across to the lieutenant at the prosecution table. 'Torture and they still don't get the right name. That means you've got the wrong person; a mistake, man. The man you're looking for is not here. I am not Binyam Ahmed Muhammad; that's not me. So I would like to ask the prosecutor has he got the right person? Has he got the right person at the table? Because if you are in Britain and you get arrested on the streets you have a name check.'

Binyam paused. Everyone strained to hear what he had to say. He had a great presence in the courtroom. The judge did not even begin to interrupt him.

'So now we have a problem,' he went on. 'I'm accused but I have evidence that's not me.'

Kohlmann was taken aback by Binyam's opening gambit, as the script did not include the prisoner insisting that someone should check into whether they had the right man. Binyam interpreted Kohlmann's silence as an instruction to remain silent.

'If you don't like me to speak, I can just give you the papers,' Binyam said. We had plenty of evidence to show that his name was not Muhammad. 'I'm not going to speak, there's no problem. I know the problem here is you don't want us to speak.'

'Right now, I don't want you to speak and I do not want your papers right now.' Kohlmann clearly wished to get on with his script. Simultaneously he recognised that this was the biggest stage on which he had ever played and he wanted to maintain decorum. 'I appreciate your offer. Thank you.'

'OK,' said Binyam. 'That's reasonable.' He was being polite in an almost exaggerated way. I could sense surprise among the tribunal spectators, who had expected some wild, bearded prisoner ranting about the Son-of-Satan George W. Bush.

Kohlmann turned back to the pages in front of him and asked Binyam a lengthy question about his rights. It was typical legalese that nobody but a law student would understand, let alone find interesting.

'Am I allowed to answer this question now?' asked Binyam, politely waiting for him to finish.

'Yes, I am asking you if you understand what I just told you,' said KohImann.

'So I hope you don't interrupt me,' said Binyam, as if he were beginning a lecture to an ill-mannered audience.

'You addressed me as Mr Muhammad,' Binyam continued. 'I keep referring to this because this is a big issue. You have the wrong person on the seat. I mean, I don't understand what kind of system, after four years of torture and renditions, still gets the wrong person to be on the stand. I am not Mr Muhammad, and if you are going by your books, I mean, how can you charge me with something and I am not the person. You got the wrong . . . the wrong man here.'

Kohlmann stared at Binyam with a rather owlish look. He was trying to work out how to get the prisoner in front of him off this subject and back on to the script.

'Do you understand what I'm talking about?' Binyam continued, this time accepting Kohlmann's silence as an invitation to continue. 'I think you're a reasonable person, that's why you're sitting over there. And to have in court a person who the cops put under interrogation for four years and then find out he's the wrong man, I mean, what kind of worthiness do these people have, man?'

Joe nudged me. Calling the judge 'man' was not going to go down well with the colonel.

'Ask yourself, what kind of worthiness do they have bragging about Dracula,' said Binyam, getting in his first dig against the speech Moe Davis had given to the media, 'and about this island that is getting them a lot of information, a gold mine? I'm innocent; I'm not – I'm not – I'm not supposed to be here. Mr Muhammad, as you call him, is not here . . . is not present, so how can we go on?'

He paused, but not for long. He wasn't giving Kohlmann the chance to take part.

'I don't know if that . . . I don't know if Congress gave you the right to change names, I don't know,' Binyam said, sounding entirely serious. I was thinking back to the time the FBI interviewed his 'wife' – the government certainly seemed to have had the power to marry him off without him knowing it. 'Sure. I mean, they give you the right to change laws and play around with them, but I don't know about names. And this is an issue. I can't call you Ralph Kallmann rather than Kohlmann, can I, and arrest you and put you in jail? Because that's not you? Four years of – what do you call it? – enhanced torture techniques, and we have the wrong person in court. I mean, that bothers me; I don't know how it doesn't bother you.

'We have a problem here. You can overlook it, I don't . . . I mean, you're the judge, but we have a problem.' Binyam finally lapsed into silence.

'I don't want to interrupt you, so . . .' Kohlmann began. Binyam had clearly taken control of the courtroom.

'No, no. I'm . . . I'm finished,' said Binyam graciously.

'Are you done now?'

'I'm finished. Go on, please.' He politely gave the colonel permission to speak.

Kohlmann did not respond to this speech, but turned back to the script in front of him, trying to steer the proceedings back to some form of normality.

'A couple of things you need to know, which I would hope your attorneys have told you, is that as you come here and sit here today you are presumed to be innocent under commission law.' Kohlmann had to be kidding. The process was rigged. The military prosecutors had said as much in their resignation messages.

'It's not my job to ensure that you are convicted or acquitted. Do you understand the word "acquitted"?' Kohlmann looked up, but quickly decided to explain anyway, rather than let Binyam have another burst. 'That means, found not guilty, OK? That's not my job and not my concern. My job is to ensure a full and fair trial. Now, if you are not the person that they allege you are, I would expect the evidence is going to demonstrate that or there won't be enough evidence to demonstrate that you are, even if you are, that person. And that would be something that's accomplished during the course of the proceedings, but it's not something that we need to, or will be, presenting evidence on at this time. And this process, unhappily perhaps, is going to take some time. Additionally, I will not allow us to do things out of order. We have a lot of things that we have to do before we get around to the evidence about whether you really are the person named in the charge or whether you did the things they said you did, OK?'

I nudged Joe. Binyam was doing very well, putting his point across. And now the Presiding Officer was saying that Binyam's innocence was not his concern, implying that the script was more important than whether they had the right man on trial.

'And I'm glad to hear you say you think I am a reasonable person,' said Kohlmann, now slipping back into his most reasonable voice. 'I think I'm a reasonable person too, but the fact remains that we need to do and we are going to do things in a certain order, whether you like it or not. Right now, we are going to move to the next piece of procedure, moving towards that time when we can hopefully receive evidence which will get us to where we need to be.'

Finally, we were back to the script. We were still only on page four and it had taken forty-five minutes to get this far. Kohlmann asked Binyam whether he was satisfied with Yvonne as his military lawyer.

'I mean, let's have this scenario,' said Binyam, tipped by the script that this was his next chance. 'You're an American and I'm not American. Why do I have to tell an American to defend me, man? But why that?'

'That's the rule,' said Kohlmann. The rule for civilian Defense Counsel, they must be a United States citizen.'

'Is this the rule on all the courts in the world or is it just . . .'

'That's the rule in this court.'

'. . . here? Well, I'm not . . . I'm not . . .'

'And, Mr Muhammad –' Kohlmann paused. 'Mr Muhammad, and that's what I would refer to you, and I understand your continuing objection to my use of that, OK, but I need to call you something and that's what I'm going to call you.'

'Well, you can call me Count Dracula like they call me,' Binyam said, gesturing towards the prosecution table. 'I'm content.'

There was laughter in the tribunal room, mostly from the media who had not forgotten the outburst by the lead prosecutor, Colonel Moe Davis, at the last press conference.

'Well, I won't be doing that.' Even Kohlmann smiled half-heartedly. He inclined his head, indicating that he did not want Binyam to go off on another rant about whether they had the wrong person in the tribunal again.

'We can go into the question,' Binyam went on, giving Kohlmann permission to get on with the case.

'OK,' said Kohlmann in some relief. 'Frankly, I forgot what your question was. Why don't you ask me again? I think it was a good one, but I just can't remember it.'

The question is, I am not an American . . .'

'Got it. I remember it.'

'. . . and I have problem with trusting Americans because I've been in custody of Americans for four years, directly and indirectly. I've been abused. So I have a problem in trusting an American. And that's your rules. In this military . . . this . . . I am not going to call it the name, but this room here.' Binyam laid heavy stress on the word 'room', unwilling to call it a courtroom. 'We have problem. How can I have . . . how am I supposed to trust her to defend me and yet she's under orders to be my enemy. I mean, it doesn't make sense. So why don't I have the right to my own lawyer, from my own nation, where I can have trust?'

'Right now, she is your Detailed Defense Counsel,' Kohlmann said, indicating Yvonne, who was sitting to Binyam's right.

'As far as right now, she said she cannot . . .' Binyam said, trying to explain that Yvonne's conflict of interest, as we had explained it to him, prevented her from working on his case.

I had expected to spend much of the day on Yvonne's problem representing Binyam, but this was the first mention of it.

'She said she is not able to talk on my behalf and she's explained that to me,' said Binyam.

'Yes. She may be mistaken in that regard, OK?' Kohlmann adopted a supercilious tone. 'At 10.10 on today she is your Detailed Defense Counsel, right?'

That was our first indication of where Kohlmann was planning to go. It looked as if he would try to steamroller over Yvonne's ethical obligations.

Meanwhile Kohlmann wanted to get back to the script, so he returned to Binyam's right to a lawyer. Once more Kohlmann had barely got the first sentence read before Binyam jumped in again. 'I'm . . . maybe I'm mistaken about . . . could you explain what the rights are?' Binyam asked politely. 'I mean, maybe I . . . I don't want to look stupid in court.'

'No, not at all.' Kohlmann was back to being polite. He was in control, he felt, educating the prisoner about the law.

'What is this rights you're talking about? Because I have been four years without rights and now all of the sudden I got rights. I am surprised.'

If Kohlmann had been listening carefully, he might have realised that Binyam was travelling on a different track.

'If at any time during these proceedings you are confused, OK, you should ask for recess and then you can discuss things with your counsel. In this case I am going to explain them to you again because they are actually pretty concisely stated here in the trial guide,' Kohlmann explained patiently. 'First, the one was – the right about a military – detailed military counsel, and I explained to you the right with regard to the Detailed Defense Counsel. And do you recall that explanation?'

'Yeah.'

'OK. Do you want me to read it to you again?'

'I don't want to . . . to go too deep into this because my interest is . . . you said I have a right. But where did that come from? I have – I've had – I haven't had rights for four years. If I had rights, I don't think I would have been touring the world. Could you explain what is . . . what is . . . what is rights? I mean, she can't explain it because I've asked her.' He nodded towards Yvonne.

Kohlmann again misunderstood what Binyam was asking and launched into a lengthy explanation of the right to counsel. Binyam sat patiently through this and Kohlmann eventually meandered to an end. 'So I've restated those rights to you and we've talked about them. Do you understand them?'

'Can I ask who is giving me these rights?' Binyam said, stating his question more clearly. 'I mean, is it an organisation?'

'It is published by Military Commission Order Number 1.'

'So it's from your government? Your government is giving me the rights to this or, I mean, where is it coming from? I haven't had that book, so . . .'

'Military Commission Order Number 1 is signed by the Secretary of Defense of the United States.'

'Colin Powell?'

'It's Donald Rumsfeld.'

'See, if it was Colin Powell, I would say that's unreasonable. Rumsfeld, that's reasonable,' Binyam concluded with something close to a sigh. I think it was Carol Rosenberg who snickered. The *Miami Herald* reporter understood Binyam's complex irony. Like many observers of the Bush Administration, Binyam respected Colin Powell as a lone voice and seemingly sensible African-American struggling to resist the extreme tendencies of others in the Cabinet. Binyam considered the military order absurd, so it would have been unreasonable for Powell to author it, but entirely reasonable for someone like Rumsfeld, whom Binyam considered an extremist.

'OK,' Kohlmann said warily, not sure what Binyam meant. 'Any other questions about your rights to counsel?'

'So far, I've got no rights,' Binyam muttered to himself almost inaudibly.

'I did not hear you.'

'The rights that you're talking about, I don't see them as rights,' Binyam said louder.

'OK. Do you desire to be represented by . . . well, let me ask you this. By whom do you wish to be represented in this matter?'

'Is it my desire or is it something you're going to force upon me?' Finally Binyam was making his point in a way that might get through to Kohlmann. The 'right' to counsel was hardly a right if he was forced to have a military officer speak for him when he would rather speak for himself. He was being shackled by these 'rights'.

'Right now, I am asking you who do you wish to be represented by in this matter?'

'In this case here?'

'In this Military Commission case, which we are starting here today. This is our first session here.'

'See, I don't want to be . . .'

'And it's going to go on for some time, I would think.'

Kohlmann was clearly trying to pressure Binyam into making a decision of some sort, though at the time I could not figure out what Kohlmann's game was. The military rules said that the prisoner had to have a military lawyer, whether he wanted one or not. This was a rule the military had concocted because they wanted to keep evidence secret from the prisoner – indeed, even I as the civilian defence lawyer could be barred from seeing some of the classified evidence, despite having a 'SECRET' classification clearance. So whether Binyam wanted Yvonne as his lawyer or not, he was going to have her.

In a normal case, Binyam should be permitted to represent himself. As the US Supreme Court said in recognising this right, 'In the long history of British criminal jurisprudence, there was only one tribunal that ever adopted a practice of forcing counsel upon an unwilling defendant in a criminal proceeding. The tribunal was the Star Chamber.' The Star Chamber was the infamous court in the seventeenth century where Sir Walter Raleigh and many others were tried based on evidence tortured out of prisoners in the Tower of London.

I was not sure what trap Kohlmann was trying to spring, but I was pretty sure he was trying to lure Binyam into saying something in particular. Sitting back in the audience, not able to whisper advice to him, I worried what Binyam would say.

'So when you ask me that I have the right to counsel, I wish no right to counsel,' Binyam said. 'That right came from your government and your government has appointed me as an enemy.

'Take it from our perspective,' Binyam went on, turning his hands towards his own chest, then gesturing towards Yvonne. 'She comes in here, she defends me, I get acquitted, she becomes the enemy of America. I come in here, I get found guilty, she becomes the hero of America. It's my wish: I don't want it. If you are going to impose it, you're going to subject me to having a lawyer here, that's really bad. Even though it's the rule, it's really bad because that's not what a lawyer is. A lawyer doesn't dictate what happens in this room. Like you dictate what happens in your courtroom, I dictate what happens in my case.'

'OK. So ... so when my question is, by whom do you wish to be represented? ...' It seemed that Kohlmann was focused on getting Binyam to say that he did want a lawyer of some sort, since that would take away his right to represent himself.

'I answered that question.'

'... in this case ... you've told me you don't want to be represented by Major Bradley, is that right?'

'I'm going to put it in plain British-English. Maybe American-English you don't understand it, but English-English says, "I ... wish ... no ... representation."'

Kohlmann then embarked on a circuitous effort to get Binyam to say that he did not want Joe and me to help him either. But Binyam immediately saw where Kohlmann was going. 'They're my advisers,' said Binyam. Joe had earlier explained to Binyam that there are over one million lawyers in the US (more lawyers than doctors) and the overwhelming majority never go near a courtroom. The task of a lawyer was more about advice than litigation, so there was nothing inconsistent with Binyam wanting legal help, but at the same time wanting to represent himself. 'And in your rules, there's no rule that says a civilian lawyer has to be inside the room.'

'Actually, there is,' Kohlmann said. I looked at Joe. The rules said that the lawyers had to be in Guantánamo for every hearing, unless excused, but I didn't know any rule that said they had to be in the tribunal room.

'I haven't read it,' said Binyam.

'Well, you're going to have to trust me on this one,' Kohlmann said rather piously.

Suggesting that Binyam should trust someone in the US military after all he had been through was probably not a good choice of words.

'How can I trust you?' Binyam exclaimed. 'Trust is a big thing. Because you stand up there doesn't mean that I trust you.'

'By whom do you wish to be represented in this matter?' Kohlmann wasn't getting into a debate. He wanted to get on with the script.

'Well, she can clarify what the problem is, because I ... I don't speak lawyer language,' Binyam said, taking the sensible way out and turning over the floor to Yvonne. 'And she can try and ... and afterwards you can ask me because I've been advised, I've been told that these laws say the civilian lawyer doesn't have to be in court.'

'OK. Major Bradley?'

'Yes, Your Honour,' she began. Joe and I had worried about her position, appearing in front of a more senior officer acting as a judge. 'In ... in the discussion that I had with Mr Mohamed, I mean, I couldn't name one case where an individual cannot have a legal adviser. I mean, if this court can name a case, I'll be more than happy to ... to take that. I would challenge the court to name one case where an individual does not have a right to have legal advisers.'

Joe and I looked at each other. That was courageous. Yvonne was already taking on the military commission process.

'Major Bradley, we are governed here by commission law, OK, and . . .' Kohlmann interjected impatiently.

'But I . . . I not . . .' Yvonne jumped right in. Interrupting the judge is not something I would normally advise in court, but it was mesmerising to watch someone else try it. 'The problem is I don't understand commission law. I mean, I don't think anyone understands commission law and . . . I have to go by seventeen years of experience of law, of legal cases, of precedents. There is nothing out there, so when you send me back to advise him on something, I can only tell him what has existed, not what is being formulated – created – in these commissions.'

Kohlmann felt he was losing control. Yvonne was only a major and he was a full colonel. We were about to learn that the military takes rank very seriously. He gave Yvonne a strong lecture about the kind of etiquette he wanted observed in his tribunal, with the clear under-lying threat that if she did not shape up, he would be imposing sanctions. Then he turned to Binyam once again

'Now I want to . . . I'm just going to ask you again. Who do you want to represent you in this matter?'

'I can talk right now?' Binyam said, making it clear that he did not understand the ever-shifting rules. I suspected that he was about to launch into another of his perorations. While Kohlmann had been berating Yvonne, Binyam had been writing on a piece of card with a black marker. Nobody else had been paying him attention as Yvonne was being chastised and I could not see what he had written.

'Yes, I'm finished,' said Kohlmann, trying to be clear who was in charge here.

'I don't want to go into offensive like he does,' Binyam began, pointing over to the prosecution table, still irked by the Dracula reference. 'And I've read some of his stories, but I don't consider this place as a commission. So, I mean, I'll call it something else. I've been referring to this place as "the room". I'm happy that she stood up there and said she's confused, and I can understand why she's con-fused about these commissions because this is not a commission, this is a con-mission, is a mission to con the world, and that's what it is, you understand.'

Binyam pulled out the card that he had been drawing. He held it up. It said, 'CON-MISSION' in large letters and he made sure everyone in the room could see it.

'This is a con-mission; it's all it is. Now, if this was a commission, you should understand how to deal with the matter, because she's been in commissions for I think seventeen years. Now, this is a con-mission, which is new to her.' Binyam spoke as if he were sympathetic to Yvonne, trying to defend her. He could see that she was standing up for him, taking a beating from her superior officer.

'It doesn't bother me,' Binyam went on in a disparaging tone. 'You can execute me tomorrow, but don't try and cheat the world of what this really is. This place has got great implications. You start playing around with con-missions, you start here, then tomorrow we have another one in Canada, and then the next day have another in Australia, and the next day have it somewhere, another place, where certain non-citizens have to obey some rule that just got made up.

'There's great implications.' There was no stopping him now. Kohlmann was staring into the headlights of Binyam's speech and could see no way to cut him off. 'That's like the person who built the bomb, the H-bomb. When he built it, he just built it. He didn't know that it was going to be used to kill over 300,000 people in Nagasaki and Hiroshima, right. Now, you're standing there and you're telling me it's moral to be in a commission. Which she doesn't even understand what the heck is a commission, because this looks like a con-mission here. You have a con-administration, which is trying to con the world to get re-elected, and the only way they can do that is to con-vict 500 people in Guantánamo Bay.

'You said ... there is a saying that says preach what you practise,' Binyam said, mangling his aphorisms a little. 'You're preaching something and then practise something else. America preaches democracy and then creates a con-mission because it just wants certain non-citizens to be convicted. I didn't ask for a trial. You can kill me tomorrow; I don't really care. But then I have an obligation to the world that such crap cannot be accepted because of this, I have the right to say it.'

Kohlmann looked ready to interrupt. I assumed he did not like Binyam using the word 'crap' in his tribunal. It was not a word that I would expect to get away with. But Binyam had more to say and was in no mood for stopping.

'If you think your war, you are going to win the war by convicting ten people here, that is very stupid. I am not saying you. I am saying your government.' He paused.

'I'll give you another example. Iran goes around saying, "I have to have a nuclear bomb." America says, "You know what, you can't, because we are stronger than you are." Iran says, "You have a bomb. Why can't I have a bomb?" So tomorrow you are going to have Australia saying, "You know what, you had a con-mission. Why can't I have a con-mission?" When are you going to stop this? This is not the way to deal with this issue.

'That is why I don't want to call this place a courtroom, because I don't think it is a courtroom.

'I am sure you wouldn't agree with it because if you was arrested somewhere in Arabia and bin Laden says, "You know what, you are my enemy but I am going to force you to have a lawyer and I give you some bearded turban person," I don't think you will agree with that. Forget the rules, regulations and crap . . . you wouldn't deal with that. That is where we are. This is a bad place. You are in charge of it. I don't know if you want to be a general. Because I can tell something, if you want to be a general you have to go along with this, but if you want to stay as colonel, like you are, you have to make real big decisions here.'

It was an extraordinary lecture. Binyam finally came to a firm conclusion. 'I am done. You can stop looking at the watch,' he said. He then turned away from Kohlmann, as if to ignore any response. He was holding up his sign, 'CON-MISSION', and waving it to the journalists behind him, just in case they had missed it the first time.

'I am not going to let you put up signs,' Kohlmann eventually said, after surveying the scene for a few moments.

'It is not in the rules,' retorted Binyam.

'Do you understand?' Kohlmann reiterated his position. The law was what he said it was.

'I know but it is . . .' Binyam began, looking at the sign as he waved it again towards the media behind him.

'You need to put that down, or we are going to have to put it away.' Kohlmann sounded like a schoolmistress at this point.

'But it is not in the rules not to put up signs,' said Binyam, unwilling to surrender yet.

'I am telling you that you need to put it down or it is going to be put away.'

'So it is a new rule?' Binyam wanted Kohlmann to admit that these were being made up as we went along.

'Mr Muhammad, there are rules of court, OK?' said Kohlmann, impatience now showing through. 'I can establish additional rules of court for the conduct of these proceedings, OK?'

'OK, so we have a new rule, "No more signs in the court"?' Binyam said. 'Because I want to follow the rules. I don't want to be here and you think, "Oh, look at this idiot." You said I have to obey the rules. I asked about these rules. There is nowhere where it says that I can't have a sign in the court. Now if there is, and if there is not, just tell me, because I will not do it.'

'I am telling you as the Presiding Officer in charge of the proceeding that we are not going to have signs held up.'

'OK, sir, that is a new rule,' Binyam concluded, obediently putting down his sign on the desk, sensing that after waving it around for almost ten minutes he had already won this skirmish.

Binyam turned the conversation to what he would, and would not, be allowed to say, asking Kohlmann to give him some more guidance, since the made-up rules were proving incomplete. Of course, this incompleteness was inevitable. In Britain, lawyers have been arguing about the law for 800 years since the Magna Carta, and they still cannot agree what the rules are. The idea that someone in the Pentagon could create a new legal system out of the whole cloth, publish it on 30 April 2003, and expect there to be no challenges to it was risible.

Kohlmann lectured Binyam on how he would not be allowed to talk in court all the time. The colonel had figured out that his earlier effort to appear accommodating was backfiring, as Binyam was proving far better prepared and more eloquent than the other prisoners who had appeared in earlier commission hearings. Some of them came from Yemen and Saudi Arabia, and barely spoke English. It was hard for them to control a courtroom since they were dependent on translators.

'You are also going to have to be guided by appropriate standards of civility,' Kohlmann said, laying down another rule about the times Binyam could speak in public, 'which, in my view, would not include ... the use of words like "crap" or "shit", OK? That is impolite conduct.'

Joe and I were still sitting in the audience and it was difficult not to smile. Binyam had used the word 'crap' more than once.

'That is impolite,' Binyam repeated out loud, as if he were reflecting over the word. I sensed that he was considering how he had been 'impolitely' tortured for a couple of years.

'And you did all of those things just now and you need to stop doing that. Otherwise, you are not going to be allowed the leave that I have been granting you, OK? I will need to clamp down on that a little bit.'

'Let me have . . .' Binyam began, but Kohlmann was not going to let him back in yet.

'Don't use bad language,' Kohlmann re-emphasised. 'You can make your point, "I think the rules for the proceedings are absurd." OK, that works just as well as "This is crap," OK?'

I almost choked. Here was a quote out of the mouth of the colonel in charge of the tribunal – 'I think the rules for the proceedings are absurd.' Well put, I thought.

'So . . .'

'And you seem like a rather articulate fellow to me and I think you can probably make your points without bad language.'

'Actually, Islam teaches us not to use bad language, but . . .'

'I didn't hear you.'

'Islam teaches us not to use bad language but sometimes I can't control, so it just comes out.'

'OK, well try.'

'I am trying to restrain myself as you are trying to restrain yourself, but I just . . . I want to understand,' said Binyam, thinking he had allowed Kohlmann enough of the talking for a while. 'You say "impolite" and I think it is impolite to have a person tell you that people outside have lawyers who advise them and don't have to have them in the courtroom. And you say, "You know what, I don't care." I think that is impolite. I think you should say, "You know what, I have to go and make an investigation on this."'

'I will give you one minute here.' Kohlmann looked at his wrist. 'Because you are kind of starting up again, all right?'

'I don't need it.' Binyam looked down and started writing something, pointedly ignoring the colonel.

Kohlmann finally got to go back to his script and he kept pressing, kept trying to get Binyam to say he did not want Joe and me as his lawyers. By now Binyam knew where the colonel was going. Eventually he agreed that for today the two of us should come and sit with him at counsel table and we would resolve the issue of our role before the next hearing. It was a stalemate. Kohlmann had not achieved the major objective of his offensive – keeping the irritating civilian lawyers out of the tribunal – but he seemed to consider this a partial victory.

After a pause, Kohlmann turned back to Yvonne, whom he thought he could push around with greater ease. He had decided it was time to give her a lecture on the clothes that her client was wearing. We were in for another surreal discussion of the presumption of innocence. In an American court the prisoner may have been held in jail for months prior to his trial, but the jury is not allowed to see him in prison garb or in shackles, since that is likely to make the jurors think he is dangerous and must already be guilty. Typically, the person on trial is given some kind of civilian clothing to wear instead.

In Guantánamo Bay everyone knew that the real jury was not composed of seven colonels, but of the media. The military wanted the media to think that the prisoners were being treated well, in line with the Pentagon's endless press releases about the Club Med conditions of the prison. Everyone in the military knew that Binyam had come to the commission building in an orange prison uniform, heavily shackled and surrounded by guards, and he would return to his cell that way. Only for the fleeting moment when he was in front of the world press would he be allowed to dress in civilian clothing as part of the military's charade.

Binyam wanted none of that, which is why he had instructed us to get him an orange outfit to wear. Before the hearing we had asked that he remain shackled as well – so that the world could see the truth. That, of course, had been denied.

Despite this, Kohlmann launched into a lecture to Yvonne on the need to preserve appearances by dressing your client in appropriate attire.

'Right now I am asking you, if you all elected to use the ... use this clothing instead of something else despite the fact that someone ...' He paused. He was worried, as all judges worry, that he was about to say something that would make him appear biased. He retreated a phrase. 'Not me . . . but someone might confuse them for prison garb and that might have some impact on the presumption of innocence. Did you think about that?'

'May I say something?' asked Binyam, interrupting.

'No, no you may not.' Kohlmann was not being so polite now.

'This is my uniform.' Binyam said it anyway.

'No, you may not. I have already told you that. You need to remain silent.'

'You said you would give me a chance to speak.'

'Not on this point and not right now. I did not tell you that and you are not going to have that chance.' Kohlmann was petulant. He turned back to Yvonne. 'Do you understand, Major Bradley?'

'With all due respect, going by the rule, it says he should have cultural wear, cultural attire,' replied Yvonne. 'And I don't think, and no disrespect to you, I am trying to be respectful.'

'That is good, you should,' snapped Kohlmann. It was turning nasty.

'No disrespect to you or myself or counsel at the table, there are cultures that we don't understand about, and I would like him to explain the cultural wear that he has on,' Yvonne continued, not letting it lie. Binyam had asked that we pass over the right to speak to him at every opportunity and Yvonne was now doing her part, trying to give Binyam another chance to speak. 'Because you have emphasised to me the rules. It states here cultural attire and obviously either you, or I, or someone is confused about what cultural attire is. Mr Mohamed would like to explain what he has on for the court, at least for the record. I am not able to explain that. In addition, I wanted to also mention that Mr Mohamed made a request to come in here in shackles this morning because he has been shackled for the last two years and the only time he has to come . . .'

'Four!' Binyam corrected softly.

'Four years he has been shackled,' she went on, 'and so now we parade him in here without his shackles. He made that request. I talked to people also about that. I would like him to explain his position, particularly with the cultural wear.'

'OK, that is not necessary or appropriate at this time,' said Kohlmann. He now knew enough not to invite Binyam to talk about why he wanted to be brought into the tribunal in an orange prison uniform and shackles. 'If the defence wishes to raise a motion with regard to any of these issues for some sort of relief, you can do that in accordance with Rule 4-3 and we will litigate it in due course. I have raised the issue of clothing with you. I am doing it for your benefit, and we are done with it. You may resume your seat.'

Kohlmann had got far away from his script. We were now into the afternoon of the hearing, several hours along, and he was still only on page six. He apparently wanted to get to the defence questioning the judge about his impartiality, a process called voir dire.

Normally, in an American criminal trial the lawyers get to question jurors on their qualifications. It is my favourite part of any case, where you can just talk with the potential jurors before either removing them for 'cause' (meaning they are biased), or 'peremptorily' (you can remove a limited number for no reason at all), or accepting them for the jury. It is far more an art than a science. Jurors are unlikely to answer meaningfully in-your-face enquiries such as, 'Are you a racist?' or 'Are you biased against my client?'

Rather, by getting the juror chatting, often you can expose those biases. Ask many southern white jurors what they think of the O. J. Simpson case and you get the same racist diatribe they would give at a cocktail party, because in their community they have never heard anyone disagree with that opinion.

The military apparently allowed a similar procedure with the selection of judges and had imported this to the commission cases. I was told I could ask almost anything of Kohlmann that might be related to his impartiality. Applied to a judge, this was a totally new experience for me, and I salivated at the opportunity to question Kohlmann on his views and how he came to preside on this case.

For example, Bush was Kohlmann's commander-in-chief, and the President had made his views on the guilt of prisoners like Binyam well known. 'These are people picked up off the battlefield in Afghanistan,' Bush had said in 2005, wrapping Binyam in the presumption of guilt, together with all the others held in Guantánamo Bay. 'They weren't wearing uniforms . . . but they were there to kill.'

Kohlmann would have to contradict the President if the theory of a presumption of innocence were to apply in this commission. And it was not just Bush, since various other powerful people in the Pentagon, from then Secretary of Defense Donald Rumsfeld on down, had made similar statements.

'They're among the most dangerous, best-trained, vicious killers on the face of the earth,' Rumsfeld had intoned of Binyam and the others in Guantánamo. All of 'em, according to him, 'were involved in an effort to kill thousands of Americans'.

Naturally, I wanted to ask Kohlmann what he thought of this. Was there any proof whatsoever that Binyam had ever been on a battlefield in Afghanistan? What evidence was there that Binyam was 'there to kill'? If Binyam, who had worked as a janitor at a Muslim heritage centre in Kensington, was one of the best-trained killers on the planet, how did Colonel Kohlmann of the US Marine Corps feel his own troops might compare?

I would get to ask Kohlmann whether this was all rubbish, made up by politicians who would not know the truth about Guantánamo if an Air Force jet spelled it out in skywriting above the White House. There was a serious side to this: President Bush's team had hand-picked the prosecutors and the judges for these commissions and Bush was himself the final appellate authority in each case – all appeals led directly to the Oval Office.

Second, I wanted to ask Kohlmann what he thought about the military prosecutors who had made statements about the commissions being rigged. Were the prosecutors telling the truth when they alleged that Bush had hand-picked colonels such as Kohlmann to convict the prisoners on trial? Or, for some unfathomable reason, had three prosecutors risked their careers to make this up?

Third, I had investigated Kohlmann himself. Baiting the Google hook with the name 'Colonel Ralph Kohlmann, US Marine Corps' we had caught some interesting fish.

The first hit was an 'Ethics and Leadership' programme in North Carolina, held in late 2004, precisely when Kohlmann was under consideration for the job he now held as judge in Binyam's case. The title of the discussion was 'Torture, Terrorism and National Security'. There were various readings set for the seminar, including articles such as 'The Ethics of Torture', 'The Dark Art of Interrogation' and 'The Bomb is ticking; do you OK torture?'. Because Binyam was charged, no matter how dubiously, with the dirty bomb conspiracy, this meant that Kohlmann might have discussed the allegations against Binyam with these students. It was clearly legitimate to ask him how he felt about torture under such circumstances.

Additional investigation into Kohlmann led to other revealing information. He had done some postgraduate work at the Naval War College in 2002, where he decided to write a paper that was critical of the very commissions where he now sat as a judge. Back then, he had argued that it was unwise to use this kind of tribunal in the War on Terror. What was more, his academic adviser had been Colonel Fred Borch, the same man who had later become the chief tribunal prosecutor and who had allegedly assured his junior officers that the system was rigged. I could only imagine the conversations that Kohlmann had had with Borch about the advisability of revising international law to suit the transient needs of the Bush Administration.

There were any number of other questions I wanted to ask Kohlmann, just passing issues that had struck me about the military process. I wanted to ask him whether he planned on violating his oath as a military officer by presiding over this trial. When he joined the US military Kohlmann had been required to swear to uphold the US Constitution. Yet now, taking on the task of presiding over Binyam's trial, he had been given an oath that was Constitution free: 'I, Ralph H. Kohlmann,' he had intoned, 'do solemnly swear to faithfully and properly perform the duties of Presiding Officer in all Military Commissions to which I am so appointed or detailed, so help me God.'

This glaring omission arose because the Bush Administration did not want any constitutional rights to apply to the Guantánamo prisoners. So which oath would Kohlmann follow – the one he took becoming a lawyer and becoming a soldier, or the Constitution-free oath he took for Guantánamo?

The questions could go on, in all likelihood for several days. Whether Kohlmann would respond or not I did not know, but there are some occasions when the question is as important as the answer.

Kohlmann knew this was coming, as I had sent him a sample of 340 questions to be going on with. Indeed, he had filed some written responses, beginning the process of trying to recast some of his earlier statements. One response concerned the paper he had written for Borch, criticising the commission system in which he now served. 'I did make a statement in the paper, however, that I now believe to be incorrect, concerning the Presidential Military Order (PMO) governing the Military Commissions,' he had written.

I thought it likely that Kohlmann would have to be removed from the case when the questioning process was over and when the newspapers finished reporting on it all. I doubted that Kohlmann was looking forward to being put on the spot. He would be trying hard to look for a way out.

Back in the commission hearing, so far, Kohlmann had not resolved the issue of Yvonne's conflict of interest, the problems she had working in the same office as the other prisoners' lawyers. She could not ethically act on Binyam's behalf until it was settled, yet Kohlmann was clearly intent on trying to force us forward.

We had discussed the possibility of this happening, and Yvonne, Joe and I were in a quandary. Questioning Kohlmann was a very important part of the case, yet we could not allow him to ignore Yvonne's conflict by going forward. If we did, Yvonne would be violating her oath as a lawyer. We had to draw a line in the sand.

In the end I tried to intervene politely to point out that until the conflict in her office was resolved, Yvonne was in an impossible position – if the colonel ordered her to proceed, she would face punishment by her civilian bar. If she refused an order by a superior officer, she would face punishment by the military. 'Your Honour, I myself am in a conflict in this,' I interjected, noting that I could hardly represent both Binyam and his military lawyer, Yvonne. 'But my advice to Major Bradley is that she should remain silent.'

'This obviously is a problem here,' said Binyam, coming in as if on cue. 'Fix it. Don't just roll over it.'

'Mr Muhammad,' Kohlmann snapped, still emphasising the wrong pronunciation of Binyam's name. 'You need to remain silent unless I ask you to speak. Do you understand?'

'You are not asking me,' Binyam explained, his voice patient. 'That is the problem. Ask me.'

'No, I will ask you for a comment, or I will provide you an opportunity to speak at appropriate times,' Kohlmann said, trying to turn away from him, back to the script.

'Seriously!' exclaimed Binyam in an undertone with an exasperated shrug.

'We had some of those earlier and we may have some of those in the future,' Kohlmann said, turning back to face the source of this impertinence.

'But we have an issue here,' Binyam said calmly.

'With regard to this matter, it is not appropriate for you to comment at all and you will not. It is as simple as that,' said the colonel, turning to Yvonne. 'Major Bradley, I have already provided you an order to fulfil your duties representing your client. Do you understand that?'

'Your Honour, may I be heard?' I tried to intervene again, so there was at least one line of defence between Yvonne and being locked up in a brig.

'No. Sit down,' he said sternly, turning once again to Yvonne. He singled out the one he outranked. 'Now, Major Bradley, you need to stand up and go to the lectern. I previously provided you with an order to fulfil your assigned duties as Detailed Defense Counsel in this case. And you, I believe you indicated that you understood that order. I think the record demonstrates that.'

Kohlmann was now directly pulling rank. The stakes were dramatically different for Yvonne, compared to Joe and me. The commissions were a farce and everyone in the world but the military seemed to know it. For Yvonne it was very different. Kohlmann was a full colonel. She was a lowly major. If she did not do as she was ordered by a superior officer, she was guilty of a criminal offence. It would not matter that the order was wrong, she still had to obey. She could be locked up for two years and cashiered out of the military, losing years of work towards her hard-earned military retirement.

'And so my question to you is,' Kohlmann continued, pausing again before the punch line: 'Do you wish to ask any additional voir dire questions on behalf of your client at this time?'

Yvonne was alone at the lectern. There was nobody who could help her right now. I knew the feeling. It was like being on the end of a long promontory, stretching out to sea from the safety of a harbour. The waves are crashing around you and there is no lifeline.

'With all due respect,' she said without hesitation, 'I exercise the Fifth Amendment, my Fifth Amendment rights.'

I was very impressed. She took the Fifth, the right to remain silent, the right not to answer a question that could get her locked up. If she refused to comply with Kohlmann's order, she could face heavy sanctions. It took courage for her to invoke her own constitutional rights in this forum. It took courage for her simply to refuse to respond to a superior officer.

'O-k-a-y,' Kohlmann said. He then tried to make out that the defence had chosen not to ask him the hundreds of difficult questions that I had listed for him. I knew I had to intervene again to try to head this off.

'I will note for the record', I said without asking for permission, 'that nowhere in United States jurisprudence for the last two hundred years has it been possible for someone who is accused in a criminal case to knowingly, intelligently and voluntarily waive a legal right merely because his lawyer is taking the Fifth Amendment. Thank you.' I made a short speech about how Binyam would have to rely on the *New York Times*, the *Miami Herald*, and everyone else to investigate the colonel and find out all the interesting things that I had located in my Google search.

'OK . . .' said Kohlmann, once again buying time as he pondered how to chastise this impertinence.

'May I sit down, sir?' I said quickly.

'Yes,' he said reflexively, perhaps reassured that the lawyers were at least still asking his permission to stand up and sit down.

Kohlmann turned back to the task of stamping his authority on Yvonne, while trying to keep Binyam quiet. I had been in her shoes before and it was obvious that he was going to put her in jail for disobeying him. I hated to sit there impotent, unable to defend her. Then an officer came in behind Kohlmann and handed him a yellow note. This was not in the script. He looked at it dispassionately, then looked up. 'OK, we will take a fifteen-minute recess at this time and we will reconvene at 15.30. Court is in recess.'

It was a relief. We could regroup and plan for the next session.

The electric clock behind the judge's seat jerked from one minute to the next. Fifteen minutes went by, then many more. That was the last we heard of Kohlmann until well after five o'clock. As the recess stretched out, there was speculation about what was going on, but the facts did not come until later that evening.

When Kohlmann did finally come back into the tribunal, he was the picture of reason. He stopped threatening Yvonne. He agreed that we should hold a proper hearing on her ethical problems and he put everything else off for three months. It was anticlimactic.

Later we learned what had happened. The Pentagon was real-time monitoring the case and there had been mounting terror at the prospect that Yvonne would end up in the brig. Locking up a military defence lawyer for simply abiding by her oath would have been another public relations disaster. Kohlmann had received a message that he had to calm things down. So much for the independent judiciary.

Normally, we would have expected months of periodic hearings in Binyam's case before we got close to a trial. In the end, there was never even a follow-up to this first one. At the end of June 2006 the US Supreme Court ruled that the military commissions were illegal.

Binyam was returned to anonymity. Perhaps the commission had been a con-mission, but better a kangaroo court than no court at all. For him it had been the first opportunity to speak in public. Maybe no tribunal organised by the Bush Administration in the wake of September 11 would give him much chance of a fair trial, but if the tribunal provided him with a forum in which to tell his story, at least that was something. It also gave him the chance to seize control of his own destiny, so long suffocated in the secret cells of Pakistan, Morocco, Afghanistan and now Guantánamo Bay.

And perhaps even a con-mission trial would have helped us get closer to the truth. I had seen hundreds of pages of discovery from the prosecution. I cannot write about what was in it, because the military rules still forbid it. But if the process had gone forward, perhaps the rest of the world would have seen what I got to see.

Binyam was thrown back into the goldfish bowl of his Guantánamo cell, condemned to swim in aimless circles, silenced once again.

5

COVER STORIES

I had visited Guantánamo several times and there was something nagging at me. I could not work out what left me uniquely unsettled about the place. It was not the depressing environment – few prisons are inspirational. It was not the occasional intimidation.

Eventually it came to me: I could not remember a time in my life when I had been lied to so often and so consistently. I don't mean to be sanctimonious – probably most people indulge in a well-placed fib every now and then – but in Guantánamo lying was a disease that had reached pandemic proportions.

Binyam Mohamed viewed the whole military commission process as a 'con', a lie that was meant to deceive the world. In June 2006 the Supreme Court said the same, in more temperate terms, and struck down the commissions as illegal. The Supreme Court rejected as false Donald Rumsfeld's assurance that the trials would be fair, accusing the Administration of 'jettisoning' long-established legal rights.

The con-missions were just one form of deceit. In Guantánamo the military began with smaller lies and worked upwards.

I was visiting Camp Echo one day and they had messed up the visitation schedule. I had long since given up using the term 'military efficiency' – just as I forswore the phrase 'sober as a judge' in New Orleans, where at least one judge drank vodka out of his coffee cup early each judicial morning. On this particular day in Guantánamo the client whom I was meant to see was not there, although I had sent the schedule for my visits several weeks before. I thought I might as well go ahead and see Shaker Aamer, whom I was not meant to meet until later in the week, but who was being held permanently in Echo. So I asked the SOG (the Sergeant of the Guard, in charge of the camp) whether Shaker was in his normal cell, in which case I would be able to see him without any inconvenience to anyone.

'No, he's not here,' the SOG replied. Ah, well. I settled down for another wasted hour, waiting for the military to bring over someone whom I could see. It was hot even under the umbrella at the 'picnic table' – the area behind one of the cells in Camp Echo where they made lawyers wait. I watched a lizard crawling up the green mesh on the wire fence. For a moment I thought about the spider in Robert the Bruce's cave, continually battling to spin its web and teaching patience to the early Scottish Nationalists. My poor lizard was only trying to escape the prison camp and he wasn't getting very far.

The next day I saw Shaker as originally planned. 'Were you here yesterday?' I asked him.

'Yeah, of course. I've been here for weeks,' he replied, looking at me through his thick, black-rimmed glasses.

So why did the SOG lie to me? He had a panorama of options. He could simply have said, 'Sorry, sir. I am not permitted to speak about that.' He could have said, 'Yes, sir, he is here, but I am afraid we cannot deviate from the schedule.' Instead he looked me in the eye as he spoke and lied. It was unsettling. He had seemed a clean-cut, well-mannered sort of person.

The dissembling disease got worse as time passed. First there was the effort to suppress the truth, with censorship or silence rather than any overt falsehood. Then there was the lie by semantics, where the US military redefined the language in order to provide plausible deniability. Finally, there was the bare-faced lie.

This kind of culture does not germinate in a vacuum. Donald Rumsfeld is responsible for a wholescale reconstitution of the English language. I set about compiling a glossary of the Gitmo-speak. The language was so deceptive that I found it appalling and amusing in equal measure, but the consistent policy of deceit tells its own truths about what was going on.

First there was good, old-fashioned censorship.

In a December 2004 press conference, US Navy Secretary Gordon England tried to defend conditions in Guantánamo by producing the novel argument that the camp was actually rehabilitative: 'People have learned to read and have learned to write, and so it's not just being incarcerated. We do try to get people prepared for a better life.'

Prisoners had some difficulty exercising their newfound abilities. Indeed, contrary to England's statement, prisoners in Guantánamo were certainly not considered 'people' and the guards were not even allowed to call them 'prisoners'. One of the escorts told me that, on pain of punishment, soldiers are required to call them 'detainees'. He wouldn't even say the word 'prisoner' out loud as he explained this, for fear of punishment – he would only mouth it. The Pentagon had come to the conclusion that it sounds better for us to 'detain' someone for several years, given that he has not been offered a trial. To imprison him would be less politic.

Naturally I set about avoiding the word 'detainee' wherever possible.

Meanwhile the authorities exercised rigid control over any information that the prisoners received. Every letter, magazine and book had to go through the censorship process. Each time I went to visit, I would take a suitcase full of reading materials to keep my clients diverted. I maintained a log reflecting the fate of each publication I brought in. Magazines that were awarded the solid stamp 'DENIED' included *National Geographic*, *Scientific American* and *Runner's World*. On one occasion it seemed justified, since that month's *National Geographic* had a front-page story about building an atomic bomb, but the editions about whales and African tribes hardly seemed a threat to national security.

One of the soldiers explained the censorship of *Scientific American* to me – the prisoner might learn about some high-tech weapons system. Banning *Runner's World* was less obvious. Given that the naval base was surrounded on one side by a Cuban minefield and on the other three sides by ocean, *Swimmer's World* would have been more obviously objectionable.

I was surprised – and Shaker Aamer was incensed – that they would not let in *The African-American Slave* by Frederick Douglass. *Uncle Tom's Cabin* was also barred. I dropped off an anthology of World War One poetry for Omar Deghayes that included Wilfred Owen's poem 'Futility', about the ghastly violence of war. It was returned 'DENIED'.

Omar was born in 1969 and was a British refugee from Libya. His father was tortured and killed by Colonel Gaddafi in 1980, and as a teenager Omar moved with his family to Brighton and studied law. He had not completed his law exams, so I brought his books so he could study, ready for his release. Law books, though, were not permitted, least of all a subversive tome about the legal rights of prisoners. Meanwhile, the 'Save Omar' campaign auctioned off an autographed copy of John Pilger's book *Hidden Agendas* to raise funds. The highest bidder donated it back, so I could try to get it in to Omar for him to read. It was written in 1998 and the index had no references to Islamic extremism. The most controversial statement I could see in the book was Pilger's comment that most of the victims of terrorism were Muslims. It never got through.

At this point British political authors began to vie for the status of having a book banned. *New Statesman* editor John Kampfner gave me a signed copy of his book *Blair's Wars* for Omar. Clare Short signed a copy of *An Honourable Deception: New Labour, Iraq and the Misuse of Power*, with a dedication: 'Hope you will be back with us soon, Omar, Best Wishes, Clare Short MP'. George Galloway also wrote a dedication in his book *I'm Not the Only One*: 'Omar, with Maximum Respect, George Galloway, MP'. The Galloway book was perhaps too obvious: the MP had just appeared in the US Senate and no self-respecting military censor would let his rant in to erode the fabric of Guantánamo.

An inverted snobbery began to develop: if your book slipped through the censors, perhaps that would cast doubt on the credibility of your opinions. I worried that Jeremy Paxman would be disappointed that his book *The English* was allowed in. One evening, before an interview on *Newsnight*, I told him that the shelf in Moazzam Begg's Guantánamo cell contained only two books, the Holy Qur'an and *The English*.

'So it's true that they torture people in Guantánamo then?' quipped Peter Marshall, a fellow *Newsnight* reporter.

My clients were not the only ones barred from reading dangerous texts. The only Australian left in Guantánamo, David Hicks, was facing a military con-mission, like Binyam, and his lawyer was banned from giving him Scott Turow's legal thriller *Presumed Innocent*, perhaps because the title gave the wrong impression of how a legal system ought to work. The basis for censoring *The New Dinkum Aussie Dictionary* was less clear.

Perhaps the strangest decision involved four books returned with the notation, 'These Items were not Cleared for Delivery to the Detainee(s)'. They were *Puss in Boots*, *Cinderella*, *Jack and the Beanstalk* and *Beauty and the Beast*, all in Arabic translation. As one FBI agent admonished me, 'You know that Arabic script is full of squiggles, and it can easily hide messages to the prisoners.' Could it be, I wondered, that Cinderella was secretly an enemy combatant?

Eventually the military barred us from bringing books for our clients altogether. So much for education.

Next there was the senseless secrecy.

The censorship blocked information from travelling in two directions, both into Guantánamo and out from it. In order to visit prisoners in Guantánamo I had to have a security clearance. Every word that my clients said to me was deemed classified and I had to get permission from censors to reveal it. I obviously obeyed the rules, because to violate them would be a criminal offence and I could end up in jail, which would make it difficult for me to represent my clients. But to any sensible observer some of the rules must have seemed rather pointless.

Whenever I met with a client in the prison I would take notes, but I could not take them with me when I left. I was obliged to put them into an envelope, seal them with 'SECRET' stickers and then give them to the military escort to mail them to Washington. The notes went by normal mail, which seemed far less secure and much slower than letting me carry them to Washington on a plane personally. Indeed, the first time I visited the base the military lost my notes for weeks.

One thing this procedure did achieve was to prevent the lawyers from revealing the truth about Guantánamo for a long time after any visit. This meant that I would visit Guantánamo, fly back to England, then return to Washington three weeks later to review my own notes. Meanwhile I was forbidden from saying anything to anyone about what my clients had said.

Once the notes arrived in Washington, I would get notice that I could come to the 'Secure Facility' to review them and submit facts for classification review. Even today I cannot repeat some of what my clients told me, but I can say that nothing I learned in Guantánamo would be classified in a sane world. I never saw anything that was in the least bit relevant to US national security, unless it would make the US less secure to admit the truth about torture committed by American personnel.

All this was to enable the Guantánamo authorities to control the flow of bad news out of the prison. From the beginning Joe Margulies, the other civilian lawyer working for Binyam Mohamed, encapsulated the proper response to this: if we could legitimately open up the prison to public inspection, the government would close it down. Eventually the awkward truth about what was happening there would outweigh any perceived benefit of keeping the prison open.

Meanwhile, though, the government wrote the rules. The military censor playing the role of goalkeeper was dogged in defence. It was not his fault; he was merely applying the rules and trying to do it as politely as possible when we met in the secret Washington facility. But when I first visited the prison, nothing could be disclosed that would reveal the government's 'methods of interrogation'. In November 2004, I met Moazzam Begg in Camp Echo. Moazzam was British, from Birmingham, and we talked for hours, and he poured out his desperate experiences. He impressed me from the beginning with his understated eloquence. He had been with his family in Afghanistan working on a charitable project that involved schools and water wells. When he and his family fled the war to Pakistan, he became one of hundreds sold for bounties to the Americans. Later, he ended up in Guantánamo, tarred as a major terrorist. When my notes got back to Washington, in January 2005, I wrote a forty-page memo about how Moazzam Begg had been abused by the US military in Afghanistan. Every word was censored. The way the military had pretended to torture his wife in the next room, even information about American soldiers murdering two prisoners in front of Moazzam, was considered a 'method of interrogation' that could not be revealed.

I sat in the Secure Facility, utterly frustrated. Here were long chapters of evidence about criminal acts committed by American military personnel, yet if I revealed these facts to those who could take action I would go to prison. I was not allowed to reveal how my clients' mental health was crumbling either. Moazzam had been tortured, then held in solitary confinement for eighteen months; he obviously suffered from post-traumatic stress disorder (PTSD), as would anyone in that situation – he had nightmares, flashbacks, all the symptoms. But this, the military said, was a privacy issue – so although I was his lawyer and although he wanted it known to the world, these facts were censored.

As inevitably happens, the effort to suppress this backfired. Had they come out immediately, the facts of Moazzam's abuse would have been one story that would soon have slipped into obscurity. The cover-up ran and ran. I wrote one letter to Prime Minister Tony Blair which began with a title: 'Re: Torture and Abuse of British Citizens in Guantánamo Bay'.

I thought about going for an informal 'Tony' but rejected it: 'Dear Prime Minister'. The next two pages were the highlights of the torture committed against Moazzam and other British citizens. Before signing off, I put in a paragraph saying, 'Anything that has been censored or blacked out in this letter, your close allies in the United States don't think you should be allowed to hear.' I then noted an enclosure and attached the forty-page memo detailing Moazzam's abuse.

What I got back from the censor was extraordinary. Every word about torture was declared to be classified, except the title, but the last sentence made it past the hovering black marker. I ended up with a letter that was more than ninety per cent blacked out. What was left was unclassified, and it was clear that it was about torture. I immediately sent it to the British embassy for transmission to Downing Street and copied it to the media.

I tried to send the same information to various influential US senators, including John McCain. I sent a covering letter to the censors pointing out that surely members of the Senate Intelligence Committee had a far higher security clearance than I did, so they should be able to receive this kind of information. Sure enough, nothing substantive in the letters made it through. With Senator McCain, the paragraph about his torture at the hands of the Vietnamese was left in, but the US torture of my clients was out. I was left with about a dozen letters that had been almost entirely blacked out, perhaps an even more significant story than the actual descriptions of torture the letters contained.

I was only one of several people complaining about this. By now there were perhaps a dozen on our team of volunteer lawyers who had been to the prison to see their clients, and each one was running into similar problems with the censorship regulations. We tried to press the issues systematically, and eventually the government was persuaded to relax the rules. At last we could get information out to prove how the clients had been mistreated, and the memos about Moazzam's mistreatment were cleared. Indeed, with the threat of this evidence of torture making it into the public eye, the pressure on the Bush Administration increased, and at the end of January, Moazzam and the three British prisoners who remained in the prison (Feroz Abbasi, Richard Belmar and Martin Mubanga) were set free. Five others had been released beforehand, but Moazzam and Feroz had been among the six prisoners originally charged in the military commissions, supposedly the very worst terrorists on the base. Their release, and the fact that the British government found no charges to bring against them on their return, illustrated the extent of the American military's delusion.

The same infatuation with censorship permeated the Guantánamo base as well, stretching to matters that were equally hard to justify. The military lawyers who enforce their understanding of the rules were cut off from the real world, so change was harder to come by. To be fair, some of these lawyers have been perfectly professional and pleasant, but there have been remarkable exceptions.

One such problem person I'll call the Commander. I am not allowed to use his real name. This was a man who made the lives of habeas lawyers very difficult. All we were doing was trying to represent the prisoners as best we could, but he seemed to view every step we took as a personal affront to the Stars and Stripes.

I was visiting Guantánamo in August 2005 and on my first day the Commander met me, along with four other habeas lawyers, in Camp Echo. Everyone shook hands, but when it came to me, he exaggerated his refusal. He then turned his back while he spoke to the others, before instructing me to come with him into one of the cells.

Once we were inside, he put on his sunglasses, so I couldn't see his eyes. I was wondering what this was all about.

'I expect you to abide by the court order in your conversations with your clients,' the Commander began in a very hostile tone.

I replied that of course I would. I did not understand what he meant by bringing this up.

'I believe you have already violated the order,' he said aggressively.

I replied that of course this was not true and asked him to tell me what he was talking about.

He said that I was forbidden to tell the prisoners about the London bombings on 7 July 2005, because this was a current political event. That, he said, was forbidden by the court's order. I found his choice of example odd. On my previous visit I had been evacuated from the island on 6 July because of Hurricane Dennis, so I could hardly have told anyone about what happened the next day, which I spent trying to contact my wife who was in London. Besides this, I pointed out that the court's order permits reference to current events that are 'directly related to counsel's representation'. Clearly, given that several of my clients came from London, it was appropriate to talk to them about what had happened. Many of them were seeking asylum in the UK and the bombs made it dramatically less likely that, as accused terrorists, they would receive a favourable hearing from the British immigration authorities.

'Asylum is not relevant to your representation,' the Commander insisted. 'That's solely a political issue. You're here for habeas corpus.'

Wrong again. Of course asylum was part of the litigation. I told him that in the transcript in one prisoner's case, which I had read just the day before, the judge had dealt with nothing but asylum. The prisoner had been asserting his right not to be sent back to China where he would face persecution or death.

The Commander said that talking with prisoners about the London bombs would inflame them and encourage them to think that their al-Qaeda colleagues were hard at work. But by now he seemed ready to drop that one, as even he could see that he was on tenuous ground.

I began to turn to leave, thinking the intimidation was over. I was wrong. He turned to a second allegation, saying that I had planned the prisoners' hunger strike. This was ridiculous. The hunger strikes had been going on from the earliest days of the prison, long before lawyers were allowed near the place. I told him this was false.

'I don't believe you,' he said curtly. 'You violated the order.'

I shrugged. What could I say? Certainly, any lawyer had the right to talk to a client about the conditions of his confinement and try to get the courts to order changes. But I knew he was in no state of mind to accept that, so I said nothing.

With one last expostulation, about how they could take away my security clearance, ban me from the base and even lock me up, he told me that the two clients I was meant to see that day had refused to come to the meeting. They were Jamil el Banna and Bisher al-Rawi, both British residents, neither of whom would ever refuse a visit. I told him so and insisted that they be brought over for the meeting.

'If you sign a request, I can have them forcibly extracted,' the Commander said. I was aghast. I was being asked to have the ERF team burst into their cells, slam their faces into the floor, shackle them and then drag them over to Camp Echo.

'How about, rather, just taking them a message from me, telling them I'm here and asking them to sign it if they don't want to come,' I suggested as an alternative.

I had to wait, sweating partly from the experience of being threatened and partly from being left at the picnic table in Camp Echo for so long. It gave me time to think. It's easy to laugh about these moments later, but at the time it was very intimidating. I was scheduled to stay in Guantánamo for two weeks almost alone, among several thousand soldiers.

Six hours later I gave up and went back over to the leeward side, to sit out the rest of the day in the motel room. The next day I did get to meet Jamil and Bisher, neither of whom had refused a legal visit. Instead, they explained, the soldiers had come for them at three o'clock the previous morning. Because the noise of the guards' boots on the metal floors and the metal-on-metal of the shackles wakes up the entire block, prisoner movement is only supposed to occur after six o'clock, so both men had asked the escorts to come back then – as provided by the camp rules. The military took this as a refusal to meet me.

I didn't bring up the London bombing with my clients, although the Commander was out of line to forbid me. The intimidation worked, as I did not want to provoke the military. But every one of my clients who lived in Britain volunteered what they had heard about London and wondered why I had not brought it up with them. Several of them lived in London and were very worried about people they loved. Of course, they recognised how this would make their return home harder to achieve.

One client described to me how his interrogator discussed the bombing in detail. 'The London bombers left messages saying they did it because of their brothers' hunger strike here in Guantánamo,' the interrogator had said, apparently trying to bait the prisoner. 'You detainees are the cause of those innocent people dying.'

This took a moment to sink in. I realised how it was self-evidently a lie: that hunger strike began on 28 June 2005, but the world outside did not learn of it until almost a month later, long after the 7 July bombings. If the military really believed that the prisoners might be encouraged by the bombers, why was the interrogator telling them that if they missed a few meals this would provoke an angry mob thousands of miles away to start causing mayhem? This was extraordinary folly on the interrogator's part.

Perhaps everyone would be better off if the prisoners were told the truth.

After censorship and the threats, there were the lies, damned lies and semantics. The Administration indulged in a remarkable gerrymandering of the language to facilitate 'the mission'. This allowed the Pentagon PR officers to look the public in the eye and dissemble.

For example, 'enhanced interrogation techniques' were reasonable steps taken to extract critically important information. Not the same as torture at all.

Did 'mild non-injurious physical contact' mean a beating? No, sir!

'Exploiting individual phobias'? An approved interrogation method. No need to explain about the dogs.

There were many other examples of this convoluted language. One of the earliest clues that conditions at Guantánamo did not fit the serene picture painted by the US military was a spate of reports of suicide attempts by the captives. By September 2003 the official estimate of such incidents was thirty-two. The media reported an initial 'ripple of concern at the number of Guantánamo detainees trying to take their own lives'. But then an odd thing happened: the Pentagon announced a radical reduction in the attempted suicide rate, cut effectively to zero. They emphasised the number of prisoners receiving treatment for depression and indicated that the prisoners were receiving medical care equal to that provided to US soldiers, far better than most prisoners were used to getting back home. The implication was that everyone was on Prozac, happy now at Club-Med-in-the-Caribbean.

British journalist David Rose visited Camp Delta and soon detected the semantic deception at work behind these numbers:

> The rate of suicide attempts has declined recently. This, however, has been achieved only because most of the detainees' attempts to

hang themselves have now been reclassified as 'manipulative self-injurious behaviour', or SIB. Many SIBs would previously have been recorded as would-be suicides. They are running at two a week – about the same as the old rate for suicide attempts.

The military had reclassified suicide attempts as SIBs for fear of further negative publicity.

Rose reported that independent psychologists looked askance at the military's refusal to take prisoners' desperation seriously:

> Manipulative self-injurious behaviour 'is not a psychiatric clas-sification' [one forensic psychiatrist insisted], and the Pentagon should not be using it. 'It is dangerous to try to divide "serious" attempts at suicide from mere gestures, and a psychiatrist needs to make a proper diagnosis in each and every case.' At Gitmo ... the 'huge cultural gulf' between camp staff and prisoners makes this difficult, if not impossible.

At this stage, in late 2003, none of us lawyers had been allowed into Guantánamo. The only substitute the prisoners had for legal rights was the persistence of sceptical journalists. More often than not, because the media tours were scripted with increasing care, no evidence came out about further suicide attempts. The most that escaped censorship was the occasional troubling but generalised statement from the International Committee of the Red Cross. Florian Westphal, an ICRC spokesperson, was able only to remark vaguely that the prisoners' uncertainty about their future had led to 'a worrying deterioration in the psychological health of a large number of the internees'.

In January 2005 a military spokesperson publicly admitted that another mass suicide attempt had happened a year and a half before – in other words in mid 2003. The Pentagon blithely dismissed the incident as 'a coordinated effort to disrupt camp operations and challenge a new group of security guards'.

When the lawyers were finally allowed in, we learned a very different story. In March 2006 I was visiting Shaker Aamer. Shaker had lived in London for years, and his wife and children were awaiting his return. He was very worried about Mohammed el Gharani, another of my clients, who was still a teenager after more than four years in prison. Shaker told me that Yusuf, as the kid liked to be called, had twice tried to take his own life since I had last seen him three months before. Yusuf was being held just two doors down from Shaker in Camp Echo.

I had been forced to keep my March visit short because of other commitments and Yusuf was not on the list of prisoners I was scheduled to see. Obviously I would have to change things to fit him in. It should not cause any inconvenience for the military, since Yusuf was already right there in the visitation area.

I wrote to the base commanders that night asking for immediate access to Yusuf to ensure his mental and physical welfare. Two days went by and I heard nothing. I asked again. Again nothing. I e-mailed urgently to the Department of Justice in Washington. No reply.

Clearly, I was going to need a court order, but for this I had to send a 'secure fax' to Washington setting out the (then classified) facts that Shaker had told me. I asked my military escort if I could use the fax machine now.

'They say it's still down,' he said.

'But does that mean it's been down since I was here in January?' I asked, since I had been unable to send a similarly urgent message two months before.

'Yes, that's what I'm told.'

'Is there nowhere else on the base that I can send a fax? Is that something I could ask the lieutenant-commander?' I did not want to vent my frustration on him. 'There are thousands of people with plenty of secrets here on the base. They must have some way to get their secrets up to Washington.'

'I'll ask.'

He later had me speak with his superior.

'There must be a secure fax somewhere else, isn't there?' I asked the lieutenant-commander.

'Yes, there is,' he replied. 'But you don't have authorisation to use it.' Surely he understood how that sounded. I had a client who was talking about suicide.

'How about you?' I suggested. 'Can you do it for me? I don't mind waiving attorney–client privilege on this, I don't care if you read it.'

'No, I don't have authority either.'

'Well, who does?'

'I can't tell you.'

'Well, can you just take what I need to send and have it sent?'

'No, we can't do that.'

So he told me that I would just have to follow the provisions of the court order. That meant I had to put my notes in an envelope, mail them to Washington, go there three weeks later, spend a few days getting it unclassified and bring it to the attention of the judge.

So I wouldn't get to see Yusuf for a couple of months. And if he was dead then, don't worry, no doubt it was just another manipulative SIB by the SOB.

Now we knew when a suicide attempt was not a suicide attempt, but there was also the question of when an imam is not an imam.

The Pentagon constantly tried to peddle the line that the Guantánamo authorities should win awards for their religious sensitivity.

Enter Captain James Yee.

Yee was the son of Chinese immigrants to the United States, a West Point graduate who served with a Patriot Missile battery in the First Gulf War. After that, his career took a less orthodox path. He opted out of the military altogether for a while and spent four years studying Islam and Arabic in Syria, where he married his Palestinian wife, Huda. He then signed back up as one of only twelve Muslims out of over 3,000 military chaplains.

Yee arrived in Guantánamo in November 2002 as the imam, instructed to advise senior officers on religious issues and to provide some spiritual solace to the prisoners – distributing Qur'ans, prayer beads and other reading materials. Tim Golden of the *New York Times* reported how other military officers grew suspicious of Yee because 'he spent an inordinate amount of time speaking with the detainees, took frequent notes during those conversations and seemed to some guards overly sympathetic with the prisoners' plight'.

Resentment at the imam's interactions with detainees led to accusations more than once, but this was not unique to Yee, spilling over to all the ministers.

'Every one of the chaplains was accused of something while I was there,' said Brigadier-General Ric Baccus, a former military commander at the base, dismissing the suspicions as unfounded.

However, Yee fell further into disfavour because he questioned the treatment of prisoners at Guantánamo, particularly when he brought up this complaint among the small number of other Muslims working in the military. 'There was a concern that there was, like, a clique of people who would go off and spend time away from the unit and were not as supportive of the mission as they ought to be,' Air Force prosecutor Lieutenant-Colonel Bryan T. Wheeler told Golden. 'If people want to have a prayer group, that's great. If, on the other hand, you have people complaining about the treatment people are receiving, there are ways to do that. Subverting the mission is not the way to do it.'

Yee was caught in the middle. It is the role of the spiritual adviser to lend a sympathetic ear to the despairing prisoners, but the regime of harsh interrogation does not allow for kindness unless it is woven into a Mutt and Jeff good-cop-bad-cop routine. Yee was made to pay for his rapport with the prisoners.

On 10 September 2003 he flew back to the US mainland on leave and his wife Huda drove to the airport to meet him. She couldn't find him and panicked when he remained missing for ten days. Only when military sources leaked the news of a major espionage case to the papers did she learn that he had been detained on the flight out of Cuba, blindfolded, and placed in manacles and leg irons for the trip to a military brig in South Carolina. There he was held for seventy-six days in solitary confinement and denied access to a lawyer. The military again leaked that he would be charged with spying for Syria, an offence that might result in his execution.

There was some question why Syria would have an interest in spying on Guantánamo. When Yee finally did obtain lawyers, they pointed out that the document he was carrying about Syria was a paper he had been assigned for a graduate class he was taking. Like so many overzealous 'investigations' in the War on Terror, the charges were founded on rumour and petty squabbles rather than solid facts.

For the Pentagon, Yee rapidly devolved from a Syrian spy to a monumental embarrassment and the charges were gradually dismissed. First the espionage allegations were replaced with military charges that involved adultery and the storage of pornography on government computers.

Yee's wife Huda and his four-year-old daughter watched his court-martial hearing, where the evidence focused on his alleged sexual misconduct. Navy Lieutenant Karyn Wallace testified under immunity about the affair she had had with Yee at Guantánamo Bay. Such conduct still remains a criminal offence under US military law, although the same don't-ask-don't-tell policy generally applies to adultery as it does to homosexuality. To be sure, Yee challenged the evidence, and ultimately his punishment was rescinded, but not before he had been publicly embarrassed and humiliated.

With respect to the second offence, concerning the downloaded porn, I was bemused. One of the interrogators at the base had disclosed how some prisoners were allowed to watch porn films as a reward for their cooperation. I noticed that every night the soldiers were served a lengthy helping of porn on Channel 29. The television schedule promised a series of programmes – *The Best Sex Ever (Hearts on Fire)*; *Sex Games (Scents and Sensibilities)*; *Sex Spa II – Body Words*; *Hotel Erotica*; and *Emmanuelle in Space*. I suspect that it is a popular channel among the ninety per cent male military population. For those who joined the Navy because they were promised a woman in every port, it was proving to be a long cruise.

Yet it was difficult not to see the charges against Chaplain Yee as somewhat hypocritical.

Eventually even the reprimand imposed for these minor charges was dismissed by Army General James Hill, but Yee was gagged by the military from speaking publicly about his case. His career ruined, his marriage in jeopardy, Yee resigned his commission in August 2004.

Meanwhile, back on the base a different farce was playing itself out. After Yee was hauled off in shackles, the Guantánamo authorities assured the world that the spiritual interests of the prisoners were well cared for by another spiritual adviser. Who might this be? And would he or she be intimidated by Yee's fate?

Journalist David Rose interviewed the man now fulfilling Yee's role as minister to the Muslim prisoners' spiritual needs. Colonel Steve Feehan announced himself a devout Christian, 'from the conservative strand of the Southern Baptist Church'.

Rose asked whether he was a fundamentalist.

'I believe the Bible is literally true, yes,' said Feehan. 'The world *was* created in seven days.'

What about those who don't share the Christian faith?

'Without believing in and accepting Christ, without faith, you cannot be redeemed,' he said, matter of fact. 'It's impossible.'

The military's message was clear, at least: if a prisoner wished to get into heaven, he must renounce his faith and recognise Jesus Christ as his Lord and Saviour.

Rose's revelations proved embarrassing to the Bush Administration. Undaunted, they announced that a new Muslim imam had been brought to Guantánamo. What they failed to note was that the imam was no longer permitted to meet with the prisoners. His role was limited to holding Friday prayer with the dwindling number of free Muslims on the base and teaching 'religious sensitivity' to American soldiers.

The catalogue of deceit unfolded apace, but one of the most callous examples of lying with semantics involved our gradual understanding of the military's interpretation of the term 'juvenile'.

In April 2003 US authorities confirmed that they were holding children as young as thirteen years of age at the base. This drew sharp criticism.

'Despite their age these are very, very dangerous people,' the Chairman of the Joint Chiefs of Staff argued. 'They may be juveniles, but they're not on a little-league team anywhere; they're on a major-league team, and it's a terrorist team.'

These youths were certainly in a major-league prison – until 2004, when mounting international pressure led the United States to 'determine' that three young Afghan suspects, aged between eleven and fifteen, 'no longer posed a threat' and could be released.

Jon Manel, a journalist with BBC Radio 4's *Today* programme, followed up on the release of the juveniles from the base on 29 January 2004.

'We don't plan on … er … detaining … um … juveniles at Guantánamo further,' the Pentagon spokesperson, Lieutenant-Commander Barbara Burfeind, assured Manel, leaning into his microphone. 'Er … I can't say in terms of the future of anywhere else.'

'Why not at Guantánamo any more?' Manel asked.

'Um … they just, I've just been told that they are not planning on having juveniles at Guantánamo,' she replied.

This did not leave much room for wriggling. There would be no juveniles in the prison. The definition of 'juvenile' under both US and international law was clear: a person accused of a crime that took place when he was under eighteen. This was the rule in the Optional Protocol to the Convention on the Rights of the Child, which the US has signed and which specifically addressed child soldiers. This was the rule of the US Supreme Court. Indeed, the court had recently banned the death penalty for juveniles – those under eighteen at the time of the original offence. The philosophy behind this rule was simple: a person was to be punished for his crime regardless of how long it took to bring him to trial. If the crime was committed when he was underage, perhaps under the influence of his elders, he was deemed less able to understand the full consequences of his actions.

Lieutenant-Commander Burfeind's promise should have been very encouraging news for Omar Khadr, a Canadian. He had been just fifteen at the time he was captured in Afghanistan. Omar grew up in a family where radicalism had been preached at most meals. His father had been killed in Afghanistan and one older brother, Abdurahman, was one of the earliest prisoners released from Guantánamo, reportedly because he had been living in a safe house in Kabul for nine months, working as a CIA informant.

Presumably, if what Lieutenant-Commander Burfeind said was true, Omar would soon be going home. The months passed by. On 6 March 2006, more than two years later, I met Omar in the visitation cell in Camp Five. By now he was nineteen years old. He was still in Guantánamo. Indeed, he had been charged with a 'war crime' – killing an American soldier. He strongly denied the allegation that he had thrown a grenade at US forces, but he had plenty of proof that he had been badly injured himself. The skin on his neck was rippled with scars from the shrapnel wounds when he was blown unconscious by an American grenade.

If Rumsfeld really meant it when he said that the prisoners in Guantánamo were 'the worst of the worst', presumably the tiny number, just ten out of hundreds who had been selected for military commissions, were the worst of the worst of the worst. People die in war and I obviously do not mean to ignore the tragedy of an American soldier losing his life, but it is hard to believe that the Nuremberg tribunals would have included a fifteen-year-old grenade thrower in the Major War Criminals trial, no matter what the strength of the prosecution's case.

It was an indisputable fact that Omar Khadr was a juvenile

according to law, so what was he doing in Guantánamo, let alone on trial? Gradually the media pressed the Pentagon officials to reconcile the promise made by Lieutenant-Commander Burfeind with Omar's continued detention. The charge sheet against Omar had the dates in clear black ink: he was born on 19 September 1986 and was seized by the US on 22 July 2002, the day he allegedly committed his crime. So he was fifteen years, ten months and eight days old at that time.

Eventually Colonel David McWilliams, a military spokesman in Miami, said 'that of the remaining 525 or so detainees, there was no one at Guantánamo who was not at least sixteen when he arrived'. In order to provide Lieutenant-Commander Burfeind with a licence to look Jon Manel in the eye and declare that there were no juveniles at the base, the military had simply redefined the term 'juvenile' to mean someone currently under sixteen. According to them, as Omar was already over sixteen he had already passed out of their newly defined category of juvenile.

This dishonesty had been clear to me for many months. Omar was not even the youngest person left in the prison. Mohammed el Gharani, the kid who went by his nickname Yusuf, had been only fourteen when he was seized in Pakistan. I was collecting data on other juveniles still on the base to make out the case for treating this group more appropriately.

This was complicated by the fact that the military did not seem to know how old some of the prisoners were. The guards at Guantánamo genuinely thought Yusuf was in his mid twenties.

'Boy, but you're right, he sure does look young,' one soldier said. We were sitting at the picnic table in Camp Echo and I was waiting to see Yusuf. The kid would get frustrated when he thought he was being treated unfairly and would shout every swear word he had learned while in American custody. I wanted to help him to remain calm and encouraged the soldiers to show Yusuf more understanding, given his youth.

Yusuf was technically a citizen of Chad, but he was born in Medina, in Saudi Arabia, and had lived his whole life there. The US military could have got his birth certificate from their Saudi allies with a telephone call. It was a little more difficult for me, but I got it and it showed he was born in November 1986. After four years of intensive interrogation, far from securing a rich harvest of 'enormously valuable intelligence' (General Geoffrey Miller's words), the military could not even work out Yusuf's age, just as they could not spell Binyam Mohamed's name after years of torture in Morocco and Afghanistan.

As Shaker had warned me, Yusuf was suffering and his mental state was fragile. In addition to the two suicide attempts Yusuf had made in January 2006, he showed me the scars on his arms that he said came from an interrogator burning him with cigarettes. I could not verify his story, of course, but unfortunately it seemed credible. Cigarette burns are very distinctive; the prisoners were not allowed to smoke, so he could not have done it to himself.

Much of Yusuf's history could be corroborated by other witnesses, including his family in Saudi Arabia and two cousins who later visited London.

'I was born in Medina,' he told me. 'I grew up and was brought up by my family. I was happy. I was taught reading and writing at home.'

'What did you . . . do you want to do with your life?' I asked him.

'My dearest wish?' He thought for a moment. 'To become a medical doctor. However, it was not possible for me to realise my dream because of the Saudi laws. People born in Saudi Arabia of foreign parents are not considered as Saudis. They are foreigners and do not have the same rights as the nationals, such as the right to a normal education. Even if I was to complete successfully my studies, because I am a foreigner, I can't pursue studies at university. In my case, I did not even achieve secondary school. I started work at nine years of age, to help support my family.'

'What sort of work did you do at that age?' I asked, thinking of what I was doing at nine: playing cricket at school. My father used to chastise us as children for being immature, pointing out that at the age of sixteen he was flying with the RAF bombing the Axis in the Second World War, but he would have paused before sending out a child to work at nine.

Yusuf sold bottles of water at the crossroads, all day long, to people driving by. As he got older, he branched out. The best time of year was the annual haj, when millions of pilgrims would come to Medina.

'One day during the pilgrimage, while I was working . . .' he began, thinking through the words he would use. Partial proof of Yusuf's remarkable intelligence was the way he had picked up English. Before leaving Medina he had never travelled abroad. I was part gratified, part sad, when he told me that I was the first white person he had ever met who had been kind to him. Every word of English he had learned in custody, starting with the word 'nigger', used on him by American soldiers when he was first seized.

'My job consisted in selling taglias,' he said, referring to the Muslim skullcap. 'Also I sold rosaries, rings, carpets for the prayer and other like religious things. I worked not less than fourteen hours per day. I had a friend who was Pakistani. He thought I was too young to be there working. He thought that my place should have been at school. He believed that if I studied, I would be able to get a better job.'

Yusuf's friend gave him the name of a contact in Karachi, a man who could teach Yusuf how to fix computers for a modest price. Yusuf had been saving, and the Saudi riyal would go a long way in Pakistan. Computers were now common in Saudi Arabia, but there were few who could service them. It seemed very practical – Yusuf could return home, borrow money and start his own business. 'The rain starts with a drop,' encouraged his friend.

'As he was saying these words, sometimes I was laughing, sometimes I thought he was making a fool of me,' said Yusuf, a broad smile on his face as he remembered the conversation. It seemed a long time ago. 'And other times I thought he might be right. As he was finishing his speech, I told him, "It is a beautiful dream if it comes true." And I shook hands with him. I told him then that I had to go back working, and that such a dream was nice before going to bed. I said goodbye to him.

'As I went back to work, I thought of my friend's story. I thought it was funny and that made me smile. I thought that my friend had a big heart; he had kind thoughts for the others. All the same, I found him a bit crazy.'

Two days later, when the sun was at its height, and Yusuf sweated at his work, he thought of working in an air-conditioned shop, drinking coffee. The idea grew in his mind. He went to the souk, and saw that the computer shops offered little follow-up to their customers – broken machines had to be shipped to a man in Jeddah.

'I then remembered the phone number my Pakistani friend had given me. I started laughing and went to see him. There and then, I told him that I found his idea a very good idea. He told me then that we should start on it right away.'

'Pack your belongings. I will help you as best as I can,' the friend said. Yusuf had 7,000 riyals saved up. He began with a passport, but he had to get a friend at the Chad embassy to alter his date of birth, as a fourteen-year-old could not travel alone, no matter what the size of his dream. He got a visa for Pakistan and booked his first ever flight on an aeroplane, about four hours to Karachi.

Naturally, for a Muslim on the move, Yusuf went to a mosque when he arrived. He was oblivious to the drama around him, and had made no connection between the recent dramatic events of September 11, far away in America, and the fact that he was in Pakistan to learn about computers.

'Explain to me how you came to get seized?' I asked.

'I was praying in the mosque alongside my new friends,' he said. The Pakistani army arrived. They surrounded it. They told us not to move and to not show any resistance. Each one of us came out of the mosque with the hands up. They were talking to us in Arabic. We went out. They took us to prison where interrogations and torture started.'

Yusuf explained how his interrogation quickly descended into farce. Early in his captivity the US agents questioned him with the assistance of a translator who used a dialect of Arabic in which the word *zalat* means money; in Yusuf's Saudi dialect it means salad, or tomato. Yusuf reconstructed the interrogation as best he could remember it.

'When you left Saudi Arabia for Pakistan, what *zalat* did you take with you?' demanded the translator, suspecting that the money must have come from al-Qaeda sources.

'What? I didn't have any *zalat* when I went to Pakistan.' The fourteen-year-old was confused. He had been through a difficult time since his seizure by the Pakistanis. He was prepared for any trick the Americans might spring on him, but all this talk about tomatoes was beyond him.

'Of course you had *zalat*. What do you take me for? An idiot!' The translator flared into hostility.

'I didn't! Why would I?'

'Of course you did. Now tell me, where did you get the *zalat* you took with you?'

'I didn't take any *zalat* with me. I didn't!'

'Aha! So you got *zalat* in Pakistan when you arrived?'

'Well, yes, what *zalat* I wanted, I could get there. That's natural.' Yusuf was trying to be conciliatory, though the conversation continued along this strange line.

The translator seemed suddenly excited. 'Where could you get *zalat* in Pakistan, then? I want a list of places. Details. Descriptions, places. Details.'

Yusuf wanted to keep him in a good humour. Trying to remember Karachi, he began to discuss places in the market where one might buy salad. With each description of a market stall the translator turned to the American interrogator, who took careful notes.

That evening Yusuf was returned to the cage where he was being held. He was a very muddled adolescent. He talked through his bizarre interrogation with other prisoners, turning over each of his recollections.

Finally one of the older prisoners solved the puzzle: 'You were talking about tomatoes. They were talking about money. That's what it must have been.'

Four years later the US had given up on the idea that Yusuf was an al-Qaeda financier, but they still hadn't yet worked out his real age. According to the unclassified allegations still pending against him in 2005, Yusuf had been 'identified as belonging to a London, United Kingdom cell led by Abu Qatada al-Masari, circa 1998'. Abu Qatada may have become well known later, when the British government detained him in Belmarsh for his allegedly extremist views, but at the time Yusuf had never heard of him. In 1998 Yusuf would have been eleven and he must have been beamed over to the al-Qaeda cell meetings by the Starship Enterprise, since he had never left Saudi Arabia by conventional means.

Another client – Sami al-Haj, who was an al-Jazeera journalist held in the prison – wanted to act as a witness in Yusuf's case. He had compiled a list of juveniles in Guantánamo and he identified forty-five kids. I had often found Sami to be reliable, but I still doubted him. Surely the military would not have denied that there were any juveniles in Guantánamo when so many of the prisoners were kids when they were seized?

Still, cross-referencing Sami's list with other juveniles identified by the Red Cross, there were additional names. For example, the Red Cross had pointed out how the military had one prisoner's birth date as 29 November 1968, when it should have been 1986 – they had transposed the last two numbers. Instead of being thirty-seven, he was still a teenager.

Verifying Sami's list was difficult. For over four years the military had refused to reveal who was actually held in Guantánamo Bay. Finally, on 15 May 2006 the military complied with a court order and released a complete list of all 759 prisoners who had been in the prison, along with the best estimate of their dates of birth. Now I could cross-reference Sami's list against the military's. He had done a good job, but he had underestimated the total number of kids. There were as many as sixty-four prisoners who might qualify as juveniles. I could not be sure with a number of prisoners, because the military recorded their dates of birth as 1 January 1986. Apparently the prisoners did not know the day and month when they were born under the Gregorian calendar, so as many as thirty-seven might have been either seventeen or just eighteen when they were captured. But there were twenty-seven prisoners who were confirmed juveniles by the military, including nineteen who were still in Guantánamo as of mid 2006.

Other juvenile prisoners had similar stories to Yusuf's, sometimes even worse. Sami had thought that Hassan bin Attash was seventeen when he was seized by the US military. The Pentagon records suggested he had actually been sixteen. Hassan was rendered to Jordan for sixteen months of torture because the government wanted information about his older brother, Tawfiq.

At the other end of the scale the Pentagon records revealed that the oldest prisoner on the base had been Mohamed Sadiq, an Afghani born in 1913. He was ninety-three years old at his release, which mercifully came before I learned about his ordeal.

Most reasonable people would think that a prisoner's age would have been a relatively simple objective issue, where it would be difficult for the military to dissemble. The question of a prisoner's guilt or innocence would prove a rather more flexible concept.

Prior to 28 June 2004, assessing guilt had been easy. President Bush had conclusively determined that all the prisoners were 'bad people' and designated them as enemy combatants. The military did not give them any opportunity at all to contest their status. They had all, we were told, been 'through multiple layers of review' before they reached Guantánamo and everyone had been captured on the battlefield. What more did anyone want?

The Supreme Court then intervened and insisted that each prisoner be allowed some form of tribunal. In a rush, the military created two new bodies – the CSRT, or Combatant Status Review Tribunal, and the ARB, or Annual Review Board.

These are not the full military commissions faced by Binyam Mohamed, those denounced by British Lord Justice Johan Steyn as 'kangaroo courts'. The CSRT is the diminutive cousin of the commission. The prisoner has even fewer rights – there are no formal charges; he is presumed 'guilty' of being an enemy combatant, even though there is no clear definition of what that means; a panel of three military officers serves as judge and jury; the prisoner is allowed no lawyer, only a 'Personal Representative' from the military who reports everything the prisoner says back to his superiors; the prisoner is not allowed to know what the classified evidence is against him and so forth. Indeed, none of my clients was ever allowed a witness at his CSRT, as such luxuries were only permitted if the military deemed the person 'reasonably available'. Because the CSRT provides even less due process than the military commissions, Lord Steyn might well have dubbed it the 'wallaby court' of Guantánamo. My clients did not hold out much hope that they would be found innocent at a CSRT.

If the prisoner fell at this hurdle and was found guilty of being an enemy combatant, each year he would be given an ARB hearing, a 'joey court', which would provide even fewer rights if that were possible. It took me some time to explain this nomenclature to Hisham Sliti, who was from Tunisia and who had to put up with laborious explanations of my weak English jokes in my still weaker French. I began by realising that it would take half an hour to get him to understand the derivation of the idiom 'kangaroo court' (where the judge bounds from the charges to the verdict, without bothering with facts or legal niceties). Then I had to look up the French for wallaby and joey in the dictionary. Finally Hisham got the general idea, though he also probably concluded that his lawyer was an imbecile.

In December 2004 US Navy Secretary Gordon England appeared at a Pentagon press conference and described these CSRT determinations to the media. 'It's an up or down decision,' he explained. 'You are or are not an enemy combatant. If you are an enemy combatant, then you go to the Annual Review Board. If you're not an enemy combatant, you go home.'

On 29 March 2005 Secretary England announced the Department of Defense (DOD) had finished with the CSRTs for everyone in the Guantánamo facility. For most prisoners the kangaroo had bounded with alacrity to the verdict long since reached by President Bush. However, the military announced that thirty-eight detainees were found to be innocent, about seven per cent of the prisoners at the time. They were therefore considered 'not enemy combatants' (rapidly reduced to the latest military acronym, NECs). These men were innocent and presumably, given what Secretary England had promised, they would rapidly be sent home, or to a safe location of their choosing. Perhaps the US officials would even apologise to the men they had wrongly imprisoned for years.

I was representing more than one such fortunate prisoner at the time, including a man called Sami al-Laithi. He was an Egyptian who had left his country almost twenty years before. Every time I saw him he would bang on and on about democracy in a way that would make President George W. Bush proud.

Sami had been fighting for democracy since the Eighties, when he first went to vote in Egypt. He told me the story, as indignant today as he was two decades earlier.

'Why did you come all this way on such a hot day?' an Egyptian election official asked him. 'We have already voted for you, so you needn't have bothered.'

Hosni Mubarak's cronies had borrowed the vote of the wrong person. Sami was unforgiving. He left Egypt for Pakistan soon afterwards and vowed never to return so long as the country was in the thrall of such a crook. He worked his way up as a professor of English and Arabic, and he minded his own business. Sami was a hermit, satisfied with a small room that held nothing but the great writers of Britain, France, Germany, Russia. Later, in Guantánamo, he impatiently refused to discuss his legal case, dismissing any question I might have with the simple assertion that he was innocent. But he asked me to bring everything from Kant to Kierkegaard for him to read.

The only thing that would bring the hermit out of his cave was Sami's improbable infatuation with football. He had been a dedicated centre forward, playing each week on teams made up of his students.

Sami spoke, and taught, very precise English, but had never visited the birthplace of the language. He decided he would like to take a trip from Pakistan to Britain to improve his accent and pursue his academic ambitions. He had not travelled for many years and he had to get his passport renewed. The Egyptian embassy stonewalled. They did not recognise that, no matter how annoyingly bureaucratic they might be, Sami could out-obstinate them all. They made him come to the embassy every day for a month on end and forced him to sit there for hours each day. Typically, Sami fought back and spent his time in the embassy waiting room loudly proclaiming the corruption of the Mubarak regime to the assembled crowd of expatriate Egyptians.

Finally they announced that he would only be allowed a visa for a one-way trip back home to Egypt, where he would find repayment in full for his free speech. As he left the embassy for the last time, livid, he noticed that he was being followed. Two other Egyptians had recently turned up dead and Sami was spooked. He turned sharply off the road into a crowded market and never went back to his one-room den. He left the city and stopped briefly in Peshawar, before being warned that strangers were still looking for him. Eventually he was advised to go to Kabul until the Egyptians lost interest in him again. He wrote to a student to send on his precious books.

Sami was very well qualified and well liked, so he soon found a job as the only foreigner in his department at Kabul University. He respected his students as adults. If they wanted to learn they would show up and if they did not that was their loss. Aside from his continuing role as centre forward, he lived only for his books. He remained quietly in Afghanistan for six years, minding his own business unless provoked. This happened only once and his refusal to remain silent nearly got him into trouble again. He despised the Taliban for their repressive and undemocratic ways, and when some government enforcers were harassing a young man for failing to grow a proper beard, Sami intervened loudly. The local bullies seemed to recognise the irrepressible force they were up against and abandoned their victim.

The American forces were not so easily put off. First they dropped bombs on Kabul and Sami was injured when one fell near him. He decided to try his luck in Pakistan again until the war was over. He reached the border safely, but then became a victim of the bounty programme. The locals were selling suspicious foreigners to the US for $5,000.

From the beginning of his captivity, Sami loudly and incessantly insisted on his innocence to everyone who would listen. He said the same to me when I finally got to visit him on 29 April 2005. The US military had held his CSRT in November 2004, but they had not bothered to tell either Sami, or me, that they had in fact found him to be innocent, an NEC. They waited until the Tuesday after my visit to tell Sami, so he could not pass on the news to his lawyer. At the time he was in Camp Five, the worst part of Guantánamo where prisoners were segregated into small, individual concrete cells.

Despite this good news, there would be no more football for Sami; he would be lucky if he ever walked again. During his confinement, he had fallen victim to another Guantánamo acronym – he had been ERFed. Sami's preliminary encounter with the Emergency Reaction Force came when he was told to go to the shower – he refused because he had been suffering fainting spells and worried that he would collapse there. The ERF team first beat him to force him to do as he was told. Then, because he had been beaten, the Camp Five guards wanted to take him to the hospital. Sami refused again, as the prison hospital had a reputation among the prisoners for taking people who had minor injuries and injuring them permanently through botched treatment. The prisoners are not permitted the word 'no' in response to an order, so they ERFed him again and forcibly dragged him to the hospital.

As Sami was waiting, shackled, someone called out the number 264. He didn't respond, as his number was 287. Later he remembered that 264 had been his old Kandahar number and worked out that they must have been reading it off his medical chart. But because he hadn't responded fast enough, the ERF team assumed it was more gratuitous disobedience. They grabbed him, lifted him up in the air several times and slammed him down on the ground. This time Sami resisted, bewildered by what they were doing to him. The ERF team responded by grabbing his testicles as they kept on slamming him down.

Sami had come to the hospital with scrapes and bruises, and now had two fractured vertebrae. The medics immediately told the soldiers that his back might be broken. Radiography later confirmed that it was. Sami had to stay in hospital for over a month while they worked out what to do with him. A young doctor wanted to operate, but Sami was afraid that he would be permanently paralysed and refused the surgery. This was still more insubordination and for it he was taken back to Camp Five.

Clearly, Sami needed physiotherapy if he was ever to stand again. Even without help from the authorities, he could have worked on it with the aid of other prisoners. But now he was wheelchair-bound, held in total isolation.

I only learned that Sami had been found innocent on my next visit, two months later on 3 July, now eight months after his CSRT. During our meeting Sami heaped scorn on his captors, telling me how they had come to his cell with the good news. Because of his previous 'non-compliance' they were holding him in an orange uniform, without any of the 'comfort items' that the Pentagon boasted were available to the prisoners.

'So when I was found innocent, what did the US military do?' he demanded, his voice becoming shrill, almost hysterical. 'They came to Camp Five and offered me a white uniform instead of the orange one. They gave me a water bottle and a comb for two days, and then they took them away again. That is what it meant to be innocent. I refused their white uniform. To me innocence means more than this. It means freedom.'

He was an NEC and, according to Navy Secretary England's promise, he deserved immediate release. Yet even when Sami told me what had happened I could not at once proclaim his right to be sent home. According to the security rules, his status as an NEC was classified.

When I was eventually able to petition a court for his release, the Administration's response was bizarre: first their lawyers refused to 'admit or deny' that he had won his CSRT. Next they said that Sami was not an NEC, as that designation had now been changed. He and the other thirty-seven who had miraculously won their CSRTs were not NECs, but had been redesignated as NLECs – 'no *longer* enemy combatants'. In other words President Bush had been correct to designate Sami as an enemy combatant, but the US had generously decided that he had changed his wicked ways. Under the law, we were told, Sami had no right to release, as an enemy combatant could still be held for the duration of the conflict, even if he was no longer dangerous.

In August I complained loudly to the court about Sami, as he was still being held in Camp Five. So the military moved him to Camp Iguana, which had originally been constructed for the three Afghani juveniles, where conditions were far better. I was relieved that at least he was in a better place.

Sami was released from Guantánamo to Egypt on 30 September 2005, a year after the CSRT cleared him, and I talked to him on the telephone. It was only then that I learned the truth. The military had apparently moved him to Camp Iguana so they could represent that he had been transferred to better conditions. But a few hours later he had been moved back to Camp Five, where he remained until he was released.

The Pentagon contorted the language to mislead the media: Christian fundamentalists became Muslim imams, juveniles became adults, the innocent became the no longer guilty. Wrong became right.

I struggled to understand why so many well-trained, generally civil people had become incapable of telling simple truths. It was tempting to assume that a contagion had taken over the prison base.

I developed a theory about why all this went on: it began with the Navy axiom about loose lips sinking ships and developed from there to the point where soldiers started to think they were all James Bond. Those on the ground in Guantánamo, following directives from far above in the Pentagon, did not believe they were telling lies at all; they had been trained to use 'cover stories'.

In his early cinema appearances, even when SMERSH had the circular saw inching towards his crotch, James Bond generally denied that he was a British secret agent. He said he worked for Universal Imports. This kind of cover story was expected of someone in his position; if Bond admitted he was a secret agent his agency would hardly be secret.

In Guantánamo several thousand soldiers who had a weekend's training in SEC-OPS were now indoctrinated to believe that to tell the truth might spell the end of Western democracy. Thus eventually the 'cover' took over the entire story.

6

BAD MEN

It's trite to say that we're human, therefore we occasionally make mistakes. It's also probably an understatement. It would be more accurate to say that a lot of human beings are hard-wired to make mistakes all the time. Our prejudices and preconceptions inevitably lead us in one direction, often the wrong one. In an open system such mistakes are common, but at least they are made in public view and can be mitigated. In a secret, closed system the mistakes are even more common and less likely to be identified or corrected.

Sami al Laithi's case had been a rare one. He was one of just thirty-eight men to have been found innocent at a CSRT(or, at least, no longer guilty). This left more than ninety per cent of the prisoners in Guantánamo as 'guilty' according to the wallaby courts that the military had established. At the core of the debate regarding the truth of what was going on in Guantánamo was whether the Bush Administration had accurately identified the prisoners as enemy combatants. Gradually it has become clear that Guantánamo was the mother of all mistakes – an analysis of the allegations against the prisoners reflected that fifty-five per cent are not even alleged to have ever taken part in hostilities.

From the beginning I had my doubts – not because I mistrusted the military's motives, but because I doubted their ability to work out who among the billion Muslims in the world were the real terrorists. Osama bin Laden would be easy to identify if only they could catch him, since he kept making appearances on television. With others it would not be so simple.

Britain and the United States are open societies where secrecy is the exception, yet even open societies have their flaws. There is an intellectual disconnect that increasingly disturbed me as I defended death penalty cases in the Deep South: how could one group of people (the defence team) gather all the evidence available and be sure of a prisoner's innocence while others (the jurors), with far less evidence, deemed him guilty *beyond a reasonable doubt* and sent him to Death Row?

I defended capital cases for a decade in New Orleans, where thirty-seven prisoners had been sentenced to death since the reintroduction of capital punishment in 1973. Six, including three whom I represented, were subsequently released from prison when new evidence proved their innocence. These are only the mistakes that have already been uncovered. If I were generous I would estimate that the New Orleans justice system wrongly decided who should die about sixteen per cent of the time (six in thirty-seven).

It is hard to argue that such an error rate, in an open legal system, comes close to being acceptable. To put it in perspective, the British railway system boasts that 83.6 per cent of trains arrive on time (a similar sixteen per cent error rate). The consequences when they make a 'mistake' – defined as the train being more than five minutes late – are relatively inconsequential, yet many British travellers think that privatisation was an expensive calamity, and pine for the good old days of British Rail. The Royal Mail delivers a letter to the wrong address fewer than one time in a thousand. If it had the same error rate as New Orleans capital trials, and 160 letters out of a thousand arrived in the wrong place, the government would probably be voted out of office.

Somehow American society is willing to accept a much higher error rate for matters of life and death than it would for trains or postcards.

It is obviously important to understand why these mistakes happen. Unfortunately nobody seems very interested.

One part of the problem is the psychology of those who choose to prosecute. Consider the profile of the career prosecutor. It would be a very strange person who spent his working hours prosecuting people whom he thought innocent. Instead, career prosecutors protect their sense of personal integrity by constructing an almost unshakeable faith in the police and a tenacious belief in the guilt of the defendant. My client Ryan Matthews was an African-American juvenile convicted on a white woman's testimony that he had shot the owner of a convenience store just outside New Orleans. Originally she had been uncertain of her identification, but she became aware that she was the lynchpin of the prosecution case, and if she wavered a 'dangerous criminal' could go free. She eventually testified with complete certainty.

There was DNA on the balaclava worn by the killer that was found at the scene. It did not match Ryan, but the prosecutor found that easy to explain away: Ryan could have borrowed the mask from some mentor in gangland. Various witnesses said that the killer dived into the getaway car through the passenger window. Although the electric window in the vehicle Ryan was arrested in was jammed closed, the prosecutor told the jury to consider whether the window motor gave out after the crime. The jurors returned a verdict of guilty beyond a reasonable doubt and sentenced Ryan to death.

We took up Ryan's case for appeal soon after the trial was over. Ryan cried the first time I saw him up on Death Row. We soon learned that another man, Rondell Love, was bragging about committing the murder.

'Ryan Matthews is my duck!' Rondell said of the kid who had been sent to Death Row for his crime.

We collected half a dozen witnesses to Rondell's confessions. Meanwhile Rondell had been charged with another murder and we checked the file in that case. There was a DNA test and his results matched the DNA on the mask.

What were the chances of unrelated people fingering a suspect whose DNA just happens to match the DNA at the scene of the crime? That was not just a reasonable doubt of guilt; it was proof of innocence, with virtually no room for doubt remaining. Surely it was game, set and match?

Instead, the ball inevitably bounced around the court for months to come. The prosecutor was immovable. He was having a very hard time accepting the fact that he was responsible for a miscarriage of justice that sent a kid to Death Row. As court hearings came and went, he would do everything to avoid talking to us about the case. He slipped in the side door and sat stolidly on the opposite side of the courtroom, staring at the judge until our case was called. Then he asked for more time to do more forensic tests. Initially we encouraged him to conduct as many other tests as he wanted. As months went by, we tried to set deadlines to reach a final resolution.

Six DNA tests later the evidence pointed at Rondell Love, not

Ryan. Ryan finally walked free, but the prosecutor – still perplexed – continued to insist that he must be guilty. Prosecutors' faith in the reliability of police investigation is often remarkable but it is normally sincere. Never once has a prosecutor admitted that an individual who I have helped exonerate was innocent. The prosecutor in Ryan's case was not a bad man; he was simply someone whose comfort with certainties predisposed him to become a prosecutor. Indeed, in a legal system with career prosecutors, lawyers self-select for the task, opting for that professional path because they believe in it so strongly. While some people would give their fellow travellers the benefit of almost any doubt, the prosecutorial mentality tends not to.

Some might say that the system is badly constructed, that the 'fittest' people for the job of prosecutor are not 'surviving' the selection process. Yet the problem is that people disagree on the goal of the presecution function. American career prosecutors are uniquely 'fit' for the purpose of ensuring that people get locked up; they are just not so good at ensuring that the right person gets locked up or, equally important, that mistakes get rectified. Lawyers quote the aphorism, 'Better that a hundred guilty go free than one innocent person is imprisoned.' If we truly meant it, we would structure the system very differently and press a person who is less comfortable with certainties into service as a prosecutor.

This flaw permeates every step of the American criminal justice system. Wishy-washy former social workers rarely become police officers. Those who doubt their ability to pass judgement on a fellow human do not angle for judicial office.

The same is true of jurors. When faced with the awesome task of sitting on a jury, someone who feels inadequate is given plenty of opportunity under the American legal system to slide out of the courtroom. As a result, those who end up on the jury tend to be confident in their ability to condemn. Every time a Death Row prisoner has been exonerated – well over a hundred in the thirty years since America reinstituted capital punishment – twelve jurors have conferred and decided he was guilty beyond a reasonable doubt, before going even further: deciding he should die.

Sometimes defenders of the system point to the exonerations and argue that they are proof that the process works. This is an illusion. I have clients whom I have represented, as well as I could, who have been convicted, although I am as certain as I can possibly be that they are innocent. The true test of the system is whether innocent people continue to sit in prison cells and death chambers across America.

When I arrived in Guantánamo, after twenty years of defending capital cases, I knew that an open legal system would routinely make mistakes even though the government was required to file clear charges against the accused, presume him innocent and disclose the evidence to a jury carefully selected for its impartiality. I knew that in such an open system a defence lawyer could put up the best case possible for the prisoner and the jurors could still get it wrong.

Guantánamo Bay, the least secret of America's secret prisons, represents one aspect of the closed legal system that has been created by the Bush Administration in the wake of September 11. It would take a true optimist to think that the US military could show up in Pakistan, deal with people who speak only Urdu and Arabic, offer the locals twenty years' salary for every Arab they turn in, abuse the prisoner into confessing, refuse to tell him the charges against him, deny him a lawyer, presume him guilty, have the allegations reviewed by military officers with no legal experience and expect to do better than New Orleans.

The prisoners in Guantánamo were described by Donald Rumsfeld as the worst of the worst terrorists in the world, justifying their detention in the legal black hole. From the beginning it was difficult to assess whether Rumsfeld was right. By the end of 2006, of the original Guantánamo prisoners only ten, including Binyam Mohamed, had ever been formally charged in the military commissions. The rest, 98 or 99 per cent of them, were held solely on the military's assurance that military review accurately established their status as enemy combatants.

Should we believe the Bush Administration when it assures us that no mistakes have been made and that even people like Sami al Laithi were only NLECs – guilty combatants who had now seen the error of their ways?

Despite my initial misgivings, I never believed the military would get it as wrong as they have. When I began visiting clients in Guantánamo Bay, I expected to learn that most had been seized in Afghanistan. Perhaps some would have an innocent explanation for being there, like Sami al-Laithi, but others surely would not.

Instead, the overwhelming majority of the men I spoke to insisted that they had been seized outside Afghanistan in the first place. Bisher al-Rawi and Jamil el Banna, both British residents, had been grabbed in the Gambia in West Africa. This was rather further away from the Afghan battlefield than London. Yet my experience was only anecdotal and from a small group of clients. The full picture took a long time to emerge.

For four years, for the most part the military successfully refused to disclose the names of the prisoners, let alone the basis for their detention. As various people – lawyers and journalists – sued and convinced the federal courts to order the release of documents about Guantánamo Bay, our legal team divided them up for analysis. Professor Mark Denbaugh, at Seton Hall University Law School, had his students analyse the allegations made against the prisoners in their CSRTs. These represented the best case the military could make against each prisoner and revealed that ninety-five per cent had not been taken into custody by US troops – they had been turned over by the Pakistanis and the anti-Taliban Northern Alliance, usually in exchange for large bounties. Ninety-two per cent were not even accused of being al-Qaeda fighters, let alone proven guilty.

Gradually American officials began to admit in public that the prisoners were not all superterrorists.

'Only like ten per cent of the people at Guantánamo are really dangerous, [and] should be there, and the rest are people that don't have anything to do with it,' said a CIA operative, speaking anonymously to a PBS television station in April 2004. They don't even understand what they're doing here.' He had spent a year working at the base when he reached this conclusion.

'There are a large number of people at Guantánamo who shouldn't be there,' said another former interrogator to the *Wisconsin State Journal* in August 2004. 'They have no meaningful connection to al-Qaeda or the Taliban.'

'Sometimes we just didn't get the right folks,' said Major-General Jay Hood. This time it was the commander at Guantánamo acknowledging the possibility of error to the *Wall Street Journal* in January 2005.

What was the reason those 'folks' were still in Guantánamo months and years later?

'Nobody wants to be the one to sign the release papers,' Hood said. 'There's no muscle in the system.' The Administration rapidly distanced itself from Hood's comments, but other people closely connected to the process kept on saying the same thing.

Eric Saar was an army linguist who participated in many Guantánamo interrogations. He wrote a book about his experiences and was interviewed on CBS television in May 2005. He was asked how many of the prisoners had any connection with terrorism.

'At best, I would say there were a few dozen,' he replied.

In total, by the autumn of 2006, of the 'bad men' who had been held at the prison, 201 prisoners had been freed before the Supreme Court forced the military to institute review tribunals in the summer of 2004. Another 180 prisoners had been released after the Supreme Court's intervention and perhaps seventy more prisoners had been cleared for repatriation, although they remained in custody months later. Thus the Pentagon admitted that well over half of the original total were more or less innocent, albeit under a definition of innocence that continued its metamorphosis.

What about the three hundred or so who remained, supposedly all dangerous enemies who had gone through 'multiple levels of review' by the military proving their guilt? One of them was my client, identified at one time by the military as among the biggest and baddest terrorists held in the camp. His name was Ahmed Errachidi.

Ahmed had never been charged with a formal crime, but the Pentagon's informants said they spotted him at the notorious Khaldan training camp in Afghanistan run by al-Qaeda in July 2001. Once he got to Guantánamo the military determined that Ahmed was leading the prisoners in their opposition to the camp rules. They challenged him directly when he demanded better treatment for the other men.

'You have to get off the stage,' said one senior officer angrily. 'You put yourself on a place so high that you've got a long way to fall.'

Ahmed was so high that he had been dubbed 'The General' by the US military. Colonel Mike Bumgarner, the senior officer running the camp, implied in the media that Ahmed was the head of the military wing of al-Qaeda in Guantánamo.

Here, surely, was the hardest case for the defence, the man whose existence justified Guantánamo. It would be simply naïve to suggest that Ahmed should be set free – to release the military leader of al-Qaeda would be the equivalent, in the words of Karl Marx, of capitalists selling their class enemies the rope with which to hang them. We would be lynched with our own liberties.

It was easy enough to maintain this fantasy about Ahmed so long as there were no defence lawyers around.

The truth was rather different.

Ahmed was no general. He had lived in London for eighteen years, working as a chef. He was chest-puffing proud of his cooking. When I first met him in Camp Echo, Ahmed was unstoppable in his anecdotes.

'A customer came to the kitchen one night,' he said in his murmuring Moroccan accent, 'and said my fish was the best he had ever tasted!' Ahmed started writing out recipes for me, until I pointed out to him that the Washington censors would never let them through. They would puzzle over them, convinced that The General was sending out coded instructions for the manufacture of a dirty bomb.

I checked out his story. Ahmed came to London in the early 1980s and began working his way up through the London restaurants. In the early days he was a grill chef at the Hard Rock Café and he did two years at Joe Allen's. From 1988 he worked as a sous-chef at Rudland & Stubbs followed by Turnmills, the Highgate Brasserie and finally for two more years at the St John's Café in St John's Wood. Promotion came when he was made head chef at Centuria, through to September 1999, when he moved on to the Julius Restaurant. In 2001 he worked at the Westbury Hotel, before being taken on as head chef at Café Loco in Muswell Hill. I met his employer and she told me how the restaurant had been going through a refit, so she and Ahmed spent some of August debating the menu and place settings.

Throughout his years of cooking, life was not easy for Ahmed. As he struggled to help his family in Morocco, he suffered from mental illness, manic depression. Ahmed talked openly about his affliction, without any of the shame that embarrasses many people. His first major breakdown came in 1992, when his father died. The stress was too much and he was sectioned in St Anne's Hospital in London.

The medical records from the time reflect an 'acute manic episode' that took place in a newsagent's. 'Whenever he saw something of the colour black it meant he was God,' wrote the psychiatrist. 'God has given him special powers. He has the cure for AIDS.'

The British doctors placed Ahmed on medication, but by 1997 he had stopped taking it. Unsurprisingly, given the abuse meted out to him by the US military, Ahmed suffered further mental breakdowns in Guantánamo. He became psychotic during February and March 2004, and was prescribed anti-psychotic drugs, including Haldol. The military kept a green book of observations of him in Guantánamo. Other people, both guards and prisoners, later described what he had been doing and saying. Once, he stripped naked in front of the soldiers. Around 2 February he felt that there was a big snowball that would envelop the earth, and told the soldiers to call their families and warn them. Troublingly, the military continued to interrogate him during his psychosis. Ahmed boasted that in addition to his being Jesus Christ, Osama bin Laden was his student.

Because he spoke English fluently and very loudly, he was identified as a leader in the prison. The General was promoted from cooking to command, not by al-Qaeda but by the US military. Yet after years of intelligence gathering, the US military made only one allegation about Ahmed's role as a violent 'enemy combatant' – his July 2001 visit to the terrorist training camp in Afghanistan.

Ahmed assured them that this was false, because he was working in London at the time. Yet how could he prove it, locked up in his prison cell? Presumably the British government could have confirmed his story, had their American allies asked, but nobody seemed very interested.

Once Ahmed was allowed a lawyer, four years in, it was simple enough to verify what he had been saying. We dug up the documents and witnesses in no time. Ahmed worked hard in London to support his two young sons, Mohammed and Imran. He could not have been in Afghanistan in July 2001, as he was cooking at the Westbury Hotel, just as he had insisted. In August 2001 he learned that Imran had a heart condition that required an operation costing several thousand pounds. Ahmed concocted a plan to make some quick money.

'I know that in July, August and early September 2001 Ahmed was definitely here in London as I saw him routinely during that time,' said Abderrazzak Sakim, a friend. 'Ahmed was in England when 9/11 happened and I remember him condemning it, saying that acts like this do not benefit Islam. He left as a result of his son's heart condition. He said business in London as a chef was too slow for him to be able to pay for Imran's health needs. I personally took Ahmed to the airport when he flew to Morocco in 2001.'

Work records and the Royal Maroc Airlines tickets backed up this story. His British immigration lawyers confirmed that the Home Office had required him to surrender his passport in June 2001. It had only been returned to him shortly before he travelled in September. He could not have left the country when the US military said he had.

'Ahmed's son Imran had a serious heart complaint,' confirmed Mohammed Rabi, another friend in London. 'I know this required surgery. Being from Morocco I can tell you that medical treatment is expensive. Ahmed is a very proud man and would never have asked anyone else for financial help. Ahmed had an idea to raise money for the operation. This was to use his savings to travel to Pakistan and buy silver jewellery with a view to then selling this in Morocco. I firmly believe that Ahmed, a more moderate Muslim even than myself, was in the wrong place at the wrong time.'

This was not the first of Ahmed's ideas to go awry after a moment of inspiration. An earlier bakery business foundered in Morocco. This time, pictures on CNN derailed Ahmed's original intentions. He was sitting in his motel room in Pakistan planning his silver purchases when the bombing began. His reaction was instinctive.

'I entered Afghanistan to help the poor children and the women, and to partake in their calamity, to taste what they taste and to fear just as they fear, and to be hungry just as they are hungry,' he said formally, almost biblically. 'I am not in prison because of a crime or drugs or robbery. I am in prison because I wanted to wipe away the tear of a little boy who lost his parents, who has been terrified, I was so moved by his plight. And an infant who has lost its mother and her milk – he stole my heart.'

When he saw the pictures of bombs cascading down on innocent children, he leapt on a bus and crossed the border into Afghanistan to fulfil his Muslim duty of *zakat*, charity towards the families and children in need. But he soon learned that there was little he could do to help these innocents. He described the clear blue sky to me, the US bombers 12,000 metres above him, dropping death on anything suspicious below. He told his story with the clarity of intense emotion: how a bomb arced through the air towards a bus, how it struck, how the explosion threw the bodies of children in small, fleshy parts across the ground. He described how he ran down to help, only to find a woman's brain oozing out of her skull. After less than a week he decided he was more of a burden than a support to the people of Afghanistan and returned across the border, planning to go back to his own children in Morocco.

Before he could return the Pakistanis intervened.

'I was not "captured",' he said scathingly. 'I was in a car going to Lahore so I could get a plane out. We were stopped by the Pakistanis. I asked to be allowed to make a call to my family. But we were taken to the police station.'

He was sold.

'There were seven of us people in Islamabad. There was an American who was speaking English, which I understood,' Ahmed said. 'They were talking about the prisoners. The Pakistani had a small case and I heard them counting out money. Imagine the feeling of being *sold*, and becoming *his*! Later an Arab-American military policeman in Bagram told me that I had cost them five thousand dollars. I am a hostage and traded commodity.'

When he reached Bagram Air Force Base in Afghanistan the abuse began in earnest. The sign on the door of the interrogation room read '*Janaham*', meaning 'Hell' in Arabic. Ahmed spent the next twenty-six days being tortured and interrogated in his own hell. A source still kept secret from Ahmed apparently placed him at the Khaldan training camp. The American interrogators wanted him to 'tell the truth'. Inevitably, under torture he would agree with whatever they wanted. If he recanted, they told him that he was lying again and they ratcheted up the violence a notch.

The British Home Secretary could have been one of a dozen witnesses to prove that the evidence placing Ahmed at a training camp in July 2001 was worthless: the British government was holding his passport while he tried to regularise his immigration status. I submitted all this evidence to the US military prosecutors and yet, just as with prisoners on Death Row, they remain zealously committed to their original story.

'The cook has become the general,' Ahmed said with the kind of smile that came to him with decreasing frequency. 'In the minds of the Americans, the crack of an egg has become the explosion of a bomb.'

Ahmed was once a big-chested, hearty laugh of a man. Four years of imprisonment had taken their toll and as we talked his reddish beard obscured now hollow cheeks. Every now and then there was a boom of the former humour, but for the most part Ahmed remained in the same gear, frustrated and angry.

In five years, the US military offered no evidence – nor even a suggestion – that Ahmed took part in any fighting in Afghanistan, or planned to. But Afghanistan was wrapped in the smoke of war and where there was smoke the military intelligence officers inevitably knew there had to be fire, probably from a Russian-made AK-47. How likely was it, five years later, that the military would admit their mistake?

Unfortunately Ahmed's experience was not uncommon. The secret nature of the prison base inevitably enhanced the chance of errors. But another of the key ingredients to the multitude of mistakes was the reliance on bounties. In September 2006, Pakistan's self-appointed president, General Pervez Musharraf, published his memoirs, *In the Line of Fire*. He went to America, partly to meet with President Bush and partly to promote his book on the talk shows.

Musharraf did some kissing and telling. He described how the US threatened to bomb Pakistan immediately post-September 11 if his government did not cooperate in the War on Terror.

'Be prepared to go back to the Stone Age!' exclaimed then US Deputy Secretary of State Richard Armitage to a Pakistani counterpart, according to Musharraf's book.

Musharraf spilled various classified beans about his country's nuclear deterrent. But one of the most interesting nuggets involved Pakistan's sale of hundreds of stray Arabs to the Americans, for shipment to Bagram Air Force Base and on to Guantánamo Bay.

Many of my clients in Cuba had insisted that, far from being captured on the battlefield of Afghanistan, they had been seized in Pakistan and flogged to the Americans like slaves at auction. Predictably enough, for five years the Bush Administration remained very silent on the issue. Musharraf's book shed new light on the bounty payments.

'Many members of al-Qaeda fled Afghanistan and crossed the border into Pakistan,' Musharraf wrote. 'We have played cat and mouse with them. We have captured 689 and handed over 369 to the United States. We have earned bounties totaling millions of dollars. Those who habitually accuse us of "not doing enough" in the war on terror should simply ask the CIA how much prize money it has paid to the Government of Pakistan.'

His revelations set people to arguing and more truths came tumbling out. Rather than denying or condemning the bounty programme, the US Department of Justice complained about who received the loot. 'We didn't know about this,' said a DOJ official. 'It should not happen. These bounty payments are for private individuals who help to trace terrorists on the FBI's most-wanted list, not foreign governments.'

Musharraf backed away from what he had written, agreeing that the money was given directly to individuals rather than the government. That made it OK to sell Arabs for a few pieces of silver, then.

The payment of bounties helps us to understand why so many innocent prisoners ended up in Guantánamo Bay. Musharraf wrote that 'millions' were paid for 369 prisoners – the minimum rate was apparently $5,000. This may not sound a lot, but in Pakistan the per capita annual income is $720, so it represented about seven years' salary. That would be the equivalent of almost a quarter of a million dollars in Britain, enough to tempt anyone to shop an Arab to the Americans, gift-wrapped with a story that he was up to no good in Afghanistan.

Just like Ahmed Errachidi, at the start of his interrogation the prisoner would deny he had anything to do with the fighting. His US captors would expect no less of him. The American authorities would then get to work. Donald Rumsfeld had authorised 'enhanced interrogation techniques', and after a few days of 'mild non-injurious physical contact' (e.g., water-boarding) and 'exploiting individual phobias' (setting on the dogs), the prisoner would inevitably confess to whatever was asked of him – generally confirming the story fabricated by the Pakistani bounty hunter. The US agents felt that they were only extracting the truth and this 'truth' was worth a ticket to Cuba. Once there, the prisoner's coerced confession would also earn him the label 'enemy combatant' at a Combatant Status Review Tribunal.

If you go into the market place to buy everything that glitters, you will end up with very little gold but a whole lot of iron pyrites.

7

ASSAULT ON AL-JAZEERA

Contrary to popular misconception, the European national sport is not football. It is bashing America – a simple pastime that many Europeans seem to enjoy. One irony of this snobbery is that the British chastise American excesses, but their government – particularly Tony Blair's – almost invariably copies the worst extremes of American social experimentation, from privatising medicine, to imposing student loans, to abolishing various legal freedoms.

Sadly, Europeans tend to ignore America's strengths, rather than emulate them. In 1789 the US cobbled together a Constitution that has, to date, defined and preserved rights more effectively than anything Europe has achieved in the intervening two centuries. Even today in the UK, free speech is an undervalued human right, yet it was enshrined in the First Amendment to the US Constitution when the British were still chasing Napoleon around Europe.

Nowhere is free speech more important than in a prison. As the American courts have ruled, the need for media access to prisons is 'buttressed by the invisibility of prisons to the ... public'. The less transparent the prison, the greater the need for the media to have access in order to be able to expose any injustice.

Unfortunately the Bush Administration has jettisoned this American commitment and skirmished with free speech while waging its War on Terror.

Traditionally, the military and the media make uncomfortable bedfellows, and historically the free press has been banned from the battlefield. The US military originally considered the Armed Forces Network to be a perfectly satisfactory substitute, where carefully controlled propaganda can be churned out by military journalists. However, more recently the military have come to see the disadvantages of this in an age of aggressive journalism: closed out, the civilian media were presumptively hostile, seeking out the reasons for their exclusion.

Thus the word 'embedded', as journalists were billeted side by side with soldiers on the battlefield. The American strategy of embedding journalists in Afghanistan and Iraq was an unqualified success. Partly, it drew the media on to the 'team': it was harder for journalists to be critical when they were facing the same danger as the soldiers and witnessing daily the courage of the men around them. They were also experiencing the dehumanisation of the enemy that is critical if soldiers are to become effective killing machines. Perhaps the media also respected the relative openness with which the military allowed them to report.

But the task of taming the press proved more difficult in Guantánamo. The military set about it with an overt and senseless system of censorship, not just for the prisoners and the lawyers, but for the media as well. I encountered the first category of censorship – military propaganda – on an early visit when I was travelling back across the bay with some journalists on the ferry.

It had been a rough day. I had visited two particularly depressed clients; the sense of helplessness that I had when leaving them alone in their solitary cells at Camp Echo affected me profoundly.

One of the journalists, a Frenchwoman, had been on the standard media tour and asked me kindly how the day had been.

'Horrible,' I said. 'How was your propaganda tour?'

She shrugged. I did not mean to be rude, but she obviously saw I was in no mood for a chat.

Moments later her older male associate hurtled up to me and pulled my shoulder, turning me round. 'It may be propaganda to you, but it is not propaganda to me!' he shouted at me in excitable French. He expounded angrily on his journalistic objectivity. He was, he said, never affected by propaganda, as he always saw through to the truth with his own eyes.

I was totally taken aback, both because I could not understand what got him so upset and because he had just been on a tour that was patently a propaganda exercise. But I had had enough confrontation for one day, so I apologised and went off to lick my wounds alone on the other side of the boat.

Two days later, the colonel from the staff judge advocate's office, a decent man doing an unenviable job, came to Camp Echo during one of my visits and asked me to come out of the cell where I was meeting a client. Such calls make me worried, as they often mean that I have to leave early due to some opaque military security concern. This time my use of the word 'propaganda' had, it seemed, gone to the top ranks, and the general had instructed the colonel to tell me that I was a guest at the facility and was not to use such terms. The colonel asked for my reply.

My normal response would have been to laugh. I was hardly a guest, generously invited by the US military. We had spent three years persuading the United States Supreme Court to order access for lawyers. However, I bit my tongue. I liked the colonel and he was obviously worried that escalation was in the air. So I told him to express my apologies to the general.

Some months later I was in Guantánamo for New Year's Eve in 2005, bored, with nothing to do. I ran across the officer who was then in charge of public relations. He seemed to have consumed his entire quota of alcohol for the upcoming year and poured out the frustrations of his hopeless job.

By then the name Guantánamo had become an international byword for injustice and to persuade the world otherwise would have been to push the Mississippi river back to its source. Yet whatever job he was assigned, he wanted to do well and was struggling valiantly in the face of fatuous rules imposed by the Pentagon. He described how, despite the promise of openness, journalists were forbidden from taking photographs of certain perspectives of the base. He had no idea why these prohibitions existed. 'It makes us look so bad!' he said, slurring each word. 'So I went online and in less than fifteen minutes I found pictures of every single view that is banned. I printed them off and showed them to the people in charge down here.' He snorted. 'They just told me that nothing could be changed without authority from Washington.' The bureaucratic imperative.

No matter what the limitations, he had ensured that the media tour was carefully scripted and as persuasive as possible. There was a show block in Camp Four, where conditions were better than elsewhere. There was a show interrogation cell in Camp Five, designed to make solitary confinement look like a private suite. It had a refrigerator, a television, a VCR, and a comfortable chair – everything but the popcorn. Various military personnel were wheeled out for interviews about one humanitarian highlight of the prison or another. Whenever an inconvenient question might arise, they could shelter politely behind the barricade of institutional security.

The experience laid on for elected officials was similar. President Bush challenged any member of Congress with doubts about the mission to visit the base. Their tour might have come out of a Peter Sellers movie. Legislators, including one clad in a pith helmet, were ushered about with careful choreography. At the end, they received gift packs – Guantánamo Bay hats, a flag that had flown over the base, and a souvenir DVD of their visit

The military's pitch worked. 'It would be hard to imagine any better treatment that this country could provide for those kind of people,' said one politician, duly impressed. 'They are treated humanely and respectfully.'

On one of my visits I was back in my Guantánamo motel room after seeing my client Sami al-Haj, the al-Jazeera cameraman who had been arrested on 15 December 2001, and had arrived in Guantánamo a few months later. Sami is tall and thin. He had a knee injury that set his right leg askew, suffered when he was beaten by soldiers at Bagram Air Force Base in Afghanistan. First the tendon on the outside of his right knee had gone. This would not have caused great discomfort had the security forces allowed Sami to follow the doctor's orders and use a knee support. Security outranked the doctors and the tiny rods in an elastic support that would keep his knee straight were deemed a threat to the soldiers' lives, so Sami had to go without.

Sami then suffered a fall and a second tendon running down the kneecap also went. Now he could barely walk.

Somehow Sami managed to smile incessantly. There was virtually nothing that could dampen his optimism. When his brother Asim came to London for a conference Reprieve held, I recognised that this was a genetic trait. I bought Asim an astoundingly crass woolly cap with 'England' emblazoned across the front and he stood in his new hat in the rain on the corner of the Strand beaming as if he had won the lottery.

Sami had been in a white uniform for most of his time in Guantánamo. The colour meant that he was HC, or 'high compliant'. The only time Sami ever got into trouble was when he protested over the desecration of the Qur'an. Otherwise he kept his nose clean.

Sami was a prisoner in the Bush Administration's assault on al-Jazeera.

Sami was detained at the border between Pakistan and Afghanistan. The CSRT allegations in 2004 established him as an 'enemy combatant': Sami had 'attempt[ed] to re-enter Afghanistan in December 2001 ...'

This sounded very suspicious, of course. What had he been doing, trying to go into Afghanistan *again* while war raged? Clearly, he must have been up to no good.

In the allegations against him the military had failed to mention that Sami worked for al-Jazeera, or note that on both trips to Afghanistan he was on assignment with a valid visa. He had been sent there as a cameraman and his team operated out of the same house as CNN.

On Sami's first tour in Afghanistan his correspondent had been Yousef al-Shouly. I met Yousef in 2005 when I went to the al-Jazeera headquarters in Qatar, and he described how Sami alternated between solid good sense and rash acts of bravery. Two days after the al-Jazeera crew had arrived in Kandahar in October 2001 a bomb landed very close to their house. Yousef was doing a piece to camera for CNN at the time and Sami caught the explosion on film.

The anchor in Atlanta was watching all this and shouted at them to get to safety: 'Go!'

'Sami and I dived into a ditch to avoid getting killed,' Yousef recalled. 'Then I told Sami to get up and take pictures of the flames.'

'Are you insane?' Sami shouted in his face. 'I'm not going to do that to get a crazy picture!' Sami had presumably remembered that he had a wife and infant child back in Qatar.

'But Sami was no coward,' said Yousef wryly, remembering. 'In this house where we stayed there was a garden at the back and we dug a ditch. Most of the people slept there, but Sami wouldn't. He slept indoors. He said that if he had to die, he might as well die while sleeping in a bed, rather than a ditch.'

Yousef recalled Sami as a man who liked to sleep and eat a lot. He, too, had noted Sami's eternal smile. Sami had saved some stills on his camera, one of his son Mohammed, then less than a year old; a second of his son and wife; and a third of the whole family together. Sami would show them to anyone who would look, with the same grin on his face that I had seen during my visits to him in Guantánamo. He was not, Yousef insisted, the kind of person who could be drawn into extremism.

CNN had asked al-Jazeera to vacate their shared house, worried that al-Jazeera's presence might be drawing fire on the rest of them. Now Sami wonders whether the American crew had been warned off in some way by the US military, but at the time the al-Jazeera crew moved without complaint.

The crew did some interviews with Taliban commanders – that is, when the Taliban were not trying to arrest them.

'Sami and I got arrested or accused of spying about twenty times by the Taliban in just the time we were in Afghanistan,' said Yousef, estimating that they spent no more than thirty days there while the war was raging. 'We would be taken to jail and it would take an hour, sometimes as many as four, for us to track down a senior Taliban officer who would get us released.'

The Taliban accused Yousef and Sami of sending pictures to the United States showing the Taliban in a weak position. 'There were not really any "military positions" that we could shoot,' said Yousef. 'The Taliban only had foot soldiers and trucks with machine guns or anti-aircraft guns on them. But Sami had some courage and took pictures of these things anyway. He took some risks doing it, put the camera under his jacket and did what we call "stealing" the pictures.'

Yousef explained how they would be driving along and he would try to distract their Taliban driver, getting him to drive slower on the pretext that the road was too bumpy, when actually he was buying Sami the chance to take pictures that were banned.

They were arrested for other crimes, in addition to spying. Some-times it was just for filming human beings. According to the Taliban's extreme interpretation of Islam, it was inappropriate to take pictures of any living being – whether human, animal or bird.

At the end of November 2001 the war had already peaked and Sami went with the crew back to Pakistan. Yousef was recalled to Qatar, but the station asked Sami to consider returning to Afghanistan with a new correspondent, Abdulhat Sadah. This time Sami never made it past the border.

It is not clear why he was initially stopped by the Pakistanis, although piecing it together from his interrogations, the US authorities seem to have requested his detention, thinking he had filmed an al-Jazeera interview with Osama bin Laden. Presumably they hoped that if they interrogated him they would learn clues as to bin Laden's whereabouts. If this was true there would have been a simple expedient: they could have asked politely to speak with Sami, in which case he would have agreed, and they would have learned of their mistake. The bin Laden interview had been done by another crew.

Instead, Sami ended up in Guantánamo Bay.

I first met Sami in early 2005. He had been friends with Jamal Kiyemba, one of the British residents then held in Guantánamo, and Jamal asked me to represent Sami. Fortunately Sami spoke good English.

His position as an al-Jazeera employee in the prison was ironic. Journalists who visited Guantánamo constantly complained that they were not allowed to speak with prisoners. Of all the media outlets in the world, only one had daily access to large numbers of prisoners: al-Jazeera, the station most hated by the Pentagon. When I asked him to help on my case, Sami would assemble important facts on almost any topic in the prison relying on the incredible prisoner bush telegraph – I still have no idea how so much information gets around the prison, though the guards seem to spread most of it. He could then give me what he wrote, and when the censors legitimately processed it out, the information could be published. By mid 2005 the lawyers still had to put everything through the censorship process, but three to six weeks later much of it came out the other side if it had a legitimate link to the lawyers' job of representing the client.

Sami wrote reports about his treatment, the conditions at the prison and the pattern of his interminable interrogations. Perhaps two-thirds of these eventually made it through the censors, the others being held up for reasons that seemed little related to US security. Al-Jazeera would then broadcast each one to millions of viewers, read by someone else but with a picture of Sami. Some were broadcast on television; others on their website.

It seemed to me that the military could be persuaded to set Sami free without too much trouble. He was no terrorist and he was a liability so long as he was dispatching embarrassing stories from his prison cell. This was clearly the most effective strategy that I could take as his lawyer to secure his freedom.

But the military proved obstinate. I had underestimated the venom with which the Bush Administration hated al-Jazeera. This was paradoxical. Prior to September 11, the US lauded al-Jazeera as the only beacon of free speech in the Middle East. Many of the station's journalists had previously worked for the BBC, but were made redundant in 1995 when Saudi Arabian censorship severely curtailed the BBC's Middle Eastern programming. When these journalists were hired on to al-Jazeera, they tried to follow the BBC model of objectivity.

The early praise they received from the US was hard-earned. In just two weeks, in early 2000, for example, Colonel Gaddafi withdrew the Libyan ambassador to Qatar, the station's home, because al-Jazeera was giving airtime to a member of the exiled opposition. Kuwait complained that the station was biased in favour of Iraq, while Saddam Hussein's government condemned al-Jazeera for a report on his lavish birthday celebrations. Tunisia criticised a story about its human rights violations. A conservative Iranian newspaper railed that the station was 'attributing false news to the esteemed leader of the revolution', Ayatollah Khamenei. Every despot in the Middle East hated al-Jazeera. For the most part, the station was everything that the US should admire.

By 2006, anti-democratic governments were no happier with al-Jazeera's aggressive journalism. Bahrain had banned al-Jazeera for having a 'suspicious' relationship with Israel, and the station's offices have been closed from time to time in Algeria, Jordan, Kuwait, Iran, Iraq, Palestine and Sudan for broadcasting material that upset each respective regime.

The difference, six years on, was President Bush's new alliance with these repressive governments. Now the US was irritated by al-Jazeera's exercise of free speech, as some inconvenient truths were being broadcast. Bush's most celebrated excess was his chat with Tony Blair, where he mooted the idea of bombing the al-Jazeera headquarters in Qatar. Bush's spin doctors said he was only joking. The employees of al-Jazeera failed to see the humour.

There was significant circumstantial evidence that the Administration was waging a broad offensive against the television station, challenging the journalists' freedom of expression. Four times the US authorities had searched the al-Jazeera offices or hacked the website because of its criticism of the Iraq war. Three al-Jazeera journalists were arrested by US forces.

Al-Jazeera offices were bombed in both Afghanistan and Iraq, resulting, in Baghdad, in the death of one of their correspondents, Tareq Ayyoub. I met his widow, Dima, when I was in Jordan. She showed me the picture of their young child and told me her dead husband's story. Tareq was a Palestinian from Kuwait who lived in Amman. He had an MA in English Literature, and spoke both English and French fluently. He had worked with the Associated Press in Jordan, before becoming a reporter for al-Jazeera's economic news bulletin.

Far from being an opponent of the US, Tareq had worked with various American news organisations. When he was with Associated Press, he had been arrested by Iraqi intelligence for filming an illegal demonstration. The American ambassador had intervened to secure his release. Tareq had recently been given a scholarship by the British Council in Jordan to obtain a degree in journalism. He had not been able to take it up at once, as he had only just gone to work for al-Jazeera. However, his dream was to earn a PhD and go on to teach at university.

Al-Jazeera assigned Tareq to cover various aspects of the Iraq war and he travelled frequently from his family home in Amman as the war began. He drove to Baghdad early in the morning when it was least likely that the Americans would be bombing the road. Dima was very worried, but Tareq assured her a hundred times that he would be all right. 'The Americans aren't stupid enough to target reporters and media personnel,' he said. 'We're just neutral eyewitness.'

Tareq should have been right. al-Jazeera had delivered a letter to Pentagon spokesperson Victoria Clarke giving precise coordinates for its Baghdad bureau. A Pentagon spokesman, Ramzi Khouri, assured the station director that he had nothing to worry about.

Meanwhile, Tareq reached Baghdad safely and soon broadcast his first report. Seeing him in a bulletproof jacket, alive and well, gave Dima some solace. She and her family slept in shifts, with someone awake for each news bulletin to make sure Tareq was all right. Dima saw his last live piece, then she woke her mother to take over. Soon after she had gone to sleep her mother came into her room, crying and shouting.

It was 7.45 a.m. on 8 April 2003. Tareq was on the roof of the al-Jazeera headquarters with a cameraman, filming the arrival of two American tanks crossing the strategic al-Jurnhuriya bridge not far from the al-Jazeera headquarters. The cameraman was cutting back and forth from the scene below to Tareq for his report.

There was gunfire below. Suddenly this was drowned out as an American fighter came low across the cityscape. It banked, turning straight for where they were standing. 'The plane was flying so low that those of us downstairs thought it would land on the roof,' Tareq's al-Jazeera colleague, Maher Abdullah, later told the *Independent*.

Inside the bureau Tareq's other colleagues heard the initial sound as the pilot launched the missile. There was a high-pitched whine, followed by the thunderous roar of an explosion. 'It was a direct hit, the missile actually exploded against our electrical generator,' Abdullah recalled.

Tareq was killed, probably instantly, although the continuous gunfire prevented anyone from getting to his body for an hour. Finally Jaber Obaied, a senior reporter from the Abu Dhabi channel, managed to get up to the roof to where he lay.

The missile seemed to have targeted the electric generator on the roof to stop al-Jazeera from broadcasting. Whether this was true or not, the US military certainly knew that this was al-Jazeera's building.

Speaking for the Pentagon, Victoria Clarke was unchastened. 'Our forces came under fire,' she insisted, suggesting that the US military simply 'exercised their inherent right to self-defence . . . Baghdad is not a safe place, you should not be there.'

*

Against the background of this campaign against al-Jazeera, what I learned about Sami's ongoing interrogation in Guantánamo was disturbing. In the first hundred-plus sessions the US military never posed a question about the allegations against him, as they were only interested in turning him into an informant against al-Jazeera. He had to ask them to interrogate him about what he was supposed to have done wrong. Sami learned that when he was on assignment in Afghanistan his telephone calls to his wife were monitored by the CIA. Extrapolating from the experience of a lowly cameraman like Sami, it did not seem implausible that the phone of every al-Jazeera journalist was being tapped.

Meanwhile, anything Sami said to me had to go through the censors. Osama bin Laden, on the other hand, could speak to the world whenever he felt like it, without limitation. He generally sent his videotaped messages to the Qatari station, which always put them on air. This, in the eyes of the US military, was proof that al-Jazeera was in league with al-Qaeda. Everyone at the station was presumably an 'enemy combatant'.

Our team of volunteer lawyers had been in court in Washington before Federal Judge Joyce Hens Green on 1 December 2004, on our habeas challenge. The issue at stake was the legality of the government's detention of our clients in Guantánamo and that revolved around the adequacy of the military's hearings on whether each prisoner was an 'enemy combatant'. One issue was the vagueness of the term: nobody seemed to understand what it meant.

Judge Green was grilling the government lawyer, Brian Boyle, about the definition of an 'enemy combatant' – someone who would be liable to detention in Guantánamo Bay. She had posed various hypothetical examples, asking Boyle whether a little old lady in Switzerland might qualify as an 'enemy combatant' if she sent money to charity in Afghanistan, not knowing that it ended up in the hands of al-Qaeda. Because she was supporting terrorists, Boyle did not hesitate in agreeing that the definition would include her.

Judge Green reached her final hypothetical. She looked over Boyle's head towards the journalists in the courtroom. She had a kindly, patrician manner, and she was not trying to trip Boyle up. She genuinely wanted to know what the boundaries were to the military's sense of its own power. 'What about a *Wall Street Journal* reporter, working in Afghanistan, who knows the exact location of Osama bin Laden, but does not reveal it to the United States Government in order to protect her source?'

'Well,' Boyle began cautiously, 'I think that's a tougher case to make, to say that that reporter is supporting al-Qaeda forces simply by reason of declining to reveal a source.'

'So according to the rules and regulations, she would not be construed as an enemy combatant?' she asked, pressing him.

'I'm saying it's a tougher case,' he said, refusing to rule it out.

'Yes, I know,' she said, urging him on.

'I'm saying it's a tougher case to make that the reporter is subject to the definition that the CSRTs are operating under as defined by the Deputy Secretary of Defense,' he said, waffling to try to avoid answering her.

'But you can't rule it out?'

'At the same time I can't say, and I won't say, that the power to detain such an individual pursuant to the exercise of military force is categorically beyond the President's commander-in-chief powers.'

At last he had brought himself to say it. A journalist could be locked up in Guantánamo as an enemy combatant simply for refusing to volunteer the location of an interview with bin Laden.

The only reason bin Laden sent his tapes to al-Jazeera rather than anyone else was that the station had by far the largest audience in the Islamic world, and was not in the control of a repressive government that would censor them. It seemed obvious to me that any television journalist in the world would leap at a bin Laden scoop, as he was such a big story.

Bizarrely, Osama bin Laden, who could speak without censorship, decided to come to Sami's defence in one of his tapes. Bin Laden seemed rather put out by the 'amazing' fact that some Guantánamo prisoners 'oppose al-Qaeda's methodology of calling for war with America'. These people had no business being locked up. Specifically, he singled out 'those working in the media, like Sami al-Haj . . .'

It was the kiss of death for Sami, of course. If bin Laden had identified Sami as a member of al-Qaeda, the US military would have viewed it as conclusive proof that Sami was guilty. As it was, the fact that bin Laden asserted that Sami had nothing to do with al-Qaeda was almost certainly viewed as ... conclusive proof that Sami was guilty. Why else would bin Laden say such a thing?

8

ASYMMETRIC WARFARE

It was mid 2005. The Guantánamo *Titanic* was steaming towards the iceberg, with no lifeboats on board. Unfortunately, the captain of this ship – actually, at the time a general was in charge – was an amateur at this particular job. Few recognised the impending disaster, as official censorship disguised the ship's perilous course.

The generals and admirals of Guantánamo would be justifiably insulted if they were labelled as amateurs. None was an amateur military man; but each one was an amateur when it came to running a prison. Rear-admiral, major-general or brigadier-general, they had one thing in common: none had any real experience in penology. Brigadier-General Michael R. Lehnert of the US Marine Corps became the first commander of the Guantánamo prison when it opened in January 2002. He was an engineer whose most public prior role had been supervising the handover of the Panama Canal in 1999.

After just two months, Lehnert was succeeded by Army Brigadier-General Ric Baccus, an infantry officer. Baccus's career had been mainly in army logistics, but at least he had nine months' experience running a military police brigade in Rhode Island. Perhaps this gave him some sense of how a prison should be run. If so, it was experience that did not suit the architects of Guantánamo Bay: his Guantánamo tenure was just seven months and Pentagon sources told the *Washington Times* that he was sacked because he was too soft on detainees.

The infamous Major-General Geoffrey D. Miller took charge in November 2002. He joined the Army in 1972 as a field artillery officer. He had no previous experience running a prison, but Donald Rumsfeld seems to have decided he was a natural. Miller went on from Guantánamo to bring his newfound knowledge to Iraq – to 'Gitmo-ise' the prisons there. The commander at Abu Ghraib, Brigadier-General Janis Karpinski, has claimed that Miller told her to treat prisoners 'like dogs'. 'If you allow them to believe at any point that they are more than a dog,' Miller allegedly opined, 'then you've lost control of them.'

Army Brigadier-General Jay W. Hood replaced Miller on 24 March 2004. He was another artillery officer. From March 2006, Navy Rear-Admiral Harry B. Harris took charge. He had a distinguished career on ships.

It would have been a difficult task for a seasoned prison administrator to run the prison in Guantánamo, but the sailors, engineers and artillery officers had no chance. Each approached his job with an experimental eagerness, keen to charge up the hill to victory. Each faltered, inevitably, before the first slope was scaled.

Towards the end of 2005 the home page of the Guantánamo Joint Task Force website was trumpeting the special meals being developed in observance of Ramadan. The cheerful PR photo of salads being prepared for prisoners stood in grim contrast to the Ramadan reality inside the camp, where some prisoners had been on hunger strike for five months.

Some prisoners did not feel they were giving up much by going on hunger strike. 'The food is very, very terrible,' said Sami al-Laithi, my Egyptian client, wrinkling his nose. 'I would prefer to eat grass.'

I used to taste the food that each man had for lunch during our legal meetings. Used to the food of an English public school, I consider myself an expert on bad institutional meals. One Guantánamo lunch was slimy boiled tinned okra, dry undercooked rice and some rancid fish. Another consisted of boiled tinned potatoes served with inedible mushy carrots that had a bitter aftertaste. One day, with Bisher al-Rawi, I tried the mashed tinned potatoes, tinned peas and kidney beans, washed down with iced tea. It was revolting.

'This is about once a week and is considered one of the best meals,' Bisher explained with a wry smile. Like me, he had also been to an English public school, Millfield.

Whatever the flaws with the food, these were comparatively superficial complaints. My clients told me of daily abuses, invasions of their cells and beatings by the ERF team. Later, some similar stories surfaced in a sworn statement by Sergeant Heather Cerveny, of the US Marine Corps. She was working for Lieutenant-Colonel Colby Vokey, a burly military lawyer who had brought his aggressive attitude to the defence of a prisoner in the military commissions. Cerveny had been relaxing in a Guantánamo bar. Given the leashed testosterone on the base, various guards had boasted to this stray female about their tough treatment of the prisoners. One told Cerveny that he had beaten several of his charges, slamming the head of one prisoner into a cell door. Other men described how they punched prisoners in the face, denied them water and arbitrarily removed their privileges.

This was just the beginning of the story, a brief conversation over a beer. In common with anything that reflected badly on the operation at Guantánamo it would be suppressed. The guards stopped boasting when they found out Cerveny worked for the defence. Colonel Vokey took his complaint to the media but his supervisor, Colonel Carol Joyce, gagged him 'pending her review of the facts'. There was a suggestion that he might be speaking out of school when he revealed this abuse. The military would prefer it to remain classified. For some weeks, Vokey was told to stay silent, or face punishment. The military promised an investigation. Its conclusion was depressing, recommending that Cerveny was investigated for filing an allegedly false report.

I found Cerveny's credible report, but it was only the most recent one. The UN had already concluded that the mistreatment of the prisoners at the base amounted to torture.

Colonel Mike Bumgarner, who was in charge of the day-to-day running of the camp in 2005 and the first half of 2006, under the direction of General Hood, found himself accused of supervising a concentration camp. 'Sir, most of all, I look at it ... with disappointment,' he told a television interviewer. 'I'll relate to you a story just from my kids. They called me up one time, they called some other officers, other families, and they said, "Dad, what are you all doing down there?" And you're just really disappointed that the truth is not coming out.'

'So your own kids asked you if you were torturing people?'

'Yes, sir, they did. They did. But when you look at the American media, what's presented, you would think we're the most horrible people in the world.' Bumgarner sounded deeply disturbed at this. 'But we're professionals, we're Americans, we're the guys that live right next door to you. We grew up on the same football fields and softball fields. We're Americans and we do what's right.'

So how could there be such a gap between the military's view of Guantánamo and the evolving perspective in the outside world that it was a torture camp? And if the prison was being run by professionals, how could it all be going so wrong?

Part of the explanation was the circle of fear that was created by the guards' training. A prosecutor enters a public courtroom with strongly held views and a soldier comes to his military base the same way. Before arriving at the Guantánamo job, each guard was indoctrinated with the danger presented by these prisoners. The guards' fear translated into violence whenever they perceived a threat; the prisoners resented the abuse; and language barriers enhanced any misunderstanding.

Yet even if the guards had complied with every standard in the American Correctional Association handbook, the prison would still have been doomed. A cultural gulf that was broader than language separated the prisoners from the base personnel. Harsh punishment is the rule in the United States and sentences of natural life in prison are handed down rather casually. In Louisiana there are 4,000 prisoners serving life without the possibility of parole. There are only about twenty-five prisoners in Britain who are serving whole life tariffs, with no real hope for release. The population of Louisiana is 4.47 million; Britain just topped sixty million. To match Louisiana's per capita rate of true-life sentences, Britain would have to have more than 53,000 people locked up for ever – two thousand times the current number, two-thirds of the entire British prison population.

When the US military boasted that Camp Five was a 'state-of-the-art maximum-security prison', they believed what they were saying. Visiting dignitaries and journalists taking the tour were impressed. The prisoner had his own cell, quite large by prison standards – a triangle eight feet in one direction, twelve in the others. There was privacy; there was air conditioning. Some of the military were perplexed by prisoners' horror of the place.

Meanwhile, indefinite solitary confinement without a trial was driving some of the prisoners insane. All they could see was a void, with no chance of a fair hearing, no meaningful contact with their families and no definition to their future. There was nothing to do, nothing to distract them from their daily hopelessness, not even a television or the chance to expend energy on a football field. Cosmetic alterations to the prison regime – 'comfort items' awarded to those who behaved well – were not going to change this.

The very term 'comfort item' was another of the military's Orwellian forays. These derisory rewards were meant to sweeten an intolerable existence. A high-compliant prisoner might receive an extra pair of underpants. The compliant prisoner would be given a short toothbrush, smaller than the one his four-year-old might use at home. If he behaved badly, he would be downgraded to a brush that would fit on his forefinger like a ring, and that would be taken from him each day after the allotted five minutes. If the guards didn't like him he might not see a toothbrush of any kind for weeks.

For reasons common to any secret interrogation facility, Guantánamo was not going to be shored up by additional access to toothpaste. The guards in Guantánamo Bay faced a problem: their task was impossible.

Hunger strikes had been a part of prisoners' ongoing struggle in Guantánamo for most of the prison's history, though the military authorities laboured hard to keep the details from the public. The first coordinated hunger strike began on 27 February 2002 and ran until the last man was fed through a tube in his nose after a seventy-one-day fast. The military did ultimately admit that some prisoners had been refusing food, but conceded that it was because of their 'murky future' and 'the fact that they don't know what is happening to them'. But they did not accept that the terrible conditions at the prison played a role.

Even in the early days of Guantánamo, journalist David Rose reported an astonishing attitude on the part of the medical personnel who were meant to be treating the prisoners. He described an exchange with one of the camp doctors: in the camp's acute ward a young man lay chained to his bed, being fed protein-and-vitamin mush through a tube inserted in his nostril. 'He's refused to eat 148 consecutive meals,' said Dr Louis Louk, a naval surgeon from Florida. 'In my opinion he's a spoiled brat, like a small child who stomps his feet when he doesn't get his way.'

Some of the PR statements emanating from the Pentagon reflected a similar approach. Donald Rumsfeld said the hunger strikers were 'on a diet' to get press attention. When not disparaging the strike itself, the military argued that the protest was further proof, if proof were required, of the evil nature of these men. They referred to the Manchester Document, supposedly an al-Qaeda manual found during a search in England that instructed captured terrorists to go on hunger strike. Ergo, if anyone engaged in such a strike, this was proof that he was a member of al-Qaeda. When I read this latest theory I snorted at the idea that a non-violent protest such as this was proof positive that a prisoner was an al-Qaeda terrorist. The ghosts of the suffragettes and Mahatma Gandhi must have been surprised to learn that they were in league with bin Laden.

Inevitably, as the prisoners became increasingly hopeless the number of 'spoiled brats' spiralled. On a trip to the base in late June 2005 I found my clients dispirited. By then, most had been locked up for over three years and conditions were getting worse rather than improving. The Supreme Court had recognised their rights a year before, yet no court had ordered the release of a single prisoner. We lawyers seemed to have achieved nothing.

The prisoners announced to the authorities that they had endured enough and planned to embark on the biggest hunger strike to date. Their demand to General Hood: either set them free, or put them on trial, but end this lawless limbo. Set in perspective, this was not an unreasonable position, since almost everyone but President Bush – world leaders from Tony Blair to Fidel Castro – now echoed their claim. But I was immediately concerned that they were writing their own epitaph. 'Live Free or Die' is the motto on the New Hampshire licence plate, derived from the revolutionary war slogan used by those who challenged the British. It is a dangerous gambit. The local military command in Guantánamo did not have the authority to make a fundamental shift in policy and the prisoners were likely to end up dead rather than free.

I did not want to find corpses on my next visit, so when the men brought up their plans to starve themselves to death, I tried to talk them into being more realistic. I suggested legal steps that we could take to improve their conditions. Other lawyers similarly tried to calm their clients. In the end the strikers elaborated their demands into three tiers, which would allow both sides room for manoeuvre, and hopefully help them reach a resolution. The top tier remained the same: the hundreds of prisoners should get a fair trial. The second tier involved the most serious complaints about the camp: the continued desecration of the Qur'an must stop (much earlier it had been thrown into the toilet, and the soldiers still routinely mistreated the prisoners' holy book during searches), those who had been found 'innocent' by the CSRT process had to be released at once, and juvenile prisoners should no longer be punished with solitary confinement. The third tier was essentially a checklist of violations of the Geneva Conventions, such as the yellow, unsanitary water, and the inedible food. The prisoners wanted an end to the different levels of treatment, where the most compliant among them wore white uniforms, while others wore brown and orange ones.

Presumably, if the demands were more limited, two reasonable parties would be able to compromise, and nobody would starve to death. The emphasis was on the qualifying adjective: would the military prove to be reasonable? Was it realistic to expect that five hundred prisoners, long mistreated, would ever trust the military long enough for any solution to work?

One of the leaders of the hungerstrike was Shaker Aamer, one of my clients. Born in Saudi Arabia, Shaker had lived in London for several years, where he had worked as a translator for various lawyers, married and had four children He was close friends with Moazzam Begg, one of the British citizens released from Guantánamo in January 2005. Their lives ran parallel in almost every respect. Both Shaker and Moazzam were married to English women. Both had four British children. They had decided to travel to Afghanistan together, with their families, in early 2001 to spend several months as part of their religious duty of *zakat*, or charity. Moazzam had provided the ideas behind the trip – the first, to create a school that would have facilities for girls as well as boys and the second to help drill wells in the dry parts of the country. The Aamer and Begg families shared a house in Kabul. When they arrived, there were some low-level hostilities between the Taliban and the Northern Alliance outside the city, but it seemed safe enough.

Then the clouds of an impending American invasion skidded across the sky. Shaker and Moazzam tried to leave the country with their families. Crossing the border to Pakistan was easier for women and children than for men, but Moazzam eventually made it to Pakistan to rejoin his family and they prepared to wait out the hostilities. Shaker was unlucky and was seized as he left Afghanistan. It did not take long for Moazzam's path to converge again with Shaker's; he, too, was grabbed by the Pakistanis and sold to the United States. Both men ended up in Guantánamo.

The salient distinction between the two men was the British passport that Moazzam had in his pocket: for Moazzam, as eventually for all nine of the British citizens held in the prison, intense British diplomatic pressure would bring him home. For Shaker, a British resident rather than a British citizen, the British political ear would prove deaf. Moazzam spent eighteen months in isolation in Camp Echo; two years after Moazzam arrived home, Shaker was still there.

For a long time Shaker's wife told the kids that their father was away at a school. She gave me pictures of Shaker in happier days in England. He had weighed more than eighteen stone, smiling into the camera with a child on each muscled arm. When I first met him in early 2005, Shaker still had the broad smile on his face. His thick dark hair was tied back behind his head. His eyes were lively, when they were not obscured by the glasses he had been given in Guantánamo – strange things that looked like black swimming goggles with an elastic band to hold them on.

Now Shaker pulled up his shirt to show me how thin he was. He still tried to keep fit. After weeks without solid food, he did a hundred push-ups and several hundred sit-ups every morning, just to show the guards he could. But the Guantánamo hunger strike threatened to dissolve him beyond recognition.

I did not see Shaker until the strike was well under way. It was not easy to get him to talk about it. More than my other clients, Shaker had never been sure whether he could trust me. I heard snippets from other prisoners of what he had suffered in a dark cell in Afghanistan, but he never volunteered all the details. He worried that if he identified the torture he had feared most, he would face it again. He dressed up his mistrust as kindly as he could.

'You know, Clive, maybe you are with the CIA,' he would say with an enigmatic smile. It was never a matter of joking; he simply wanted to dull the sharper edge on his words. Honour and politeness were everything. 'Maybe you're the latest devious plot the Americans have come up with. But then maybe you're not with the CIA. Maybe you don't even know that you're being used by them. They let you in here, they listen in to what we discuss and bingo, they learn how to manipulate me.'

Shaker couldn't fully trust me, but it was a combination of loneliness and civility that made him keep on coming out to meet with me.

He told me about the big hunger strike that began in early July 2005. He had been promoted to play an important role in the protest, partially by the military and partly by the other prisoners, because he spoke fluent and eloquent English. He had been dubbed 'The Professor' by the guards. They seemed to respect him.

'We began the hunger strike in Camp Five because of our ill treatment there,' Shaker told me. He had been in the solitary cells in the new concrete prison. 'Prisoners would be moved from one place to another and the news soon spread. Our brothers heard in Camp Delta and Camp Four and they stood up in solidarity. When the number reached 250, the medics could not help those who fell every day. However, as usual the Americans showed indifference to the very fact of our deaths. They said to us, "Do you think the world will ever learn of your hunger strike? We will never let them know. We care nothing if one of you dies."'

Colonel Mike Bumgarner was the military's point man who would have to deal with the hunger strike. He was forty-seven years old, six foot two and still – as Shaker had been once – nineteen stone. His balding head was generally covered by a military cap and he wore the new US camouflage uniform, with its Rorschach test of grey-green blotches. He was originally from Kings Mountain in North Carolina, not far from where I went to university, and he was North Carolina to the core, talking non-stop about NASCAR racing. His glory days had been on his high school football squad, where he had fought to replace a student a year older for the position of quarterback, the leader of the team. He had once dreamed of being a secret service agent, or a football coach, but he ended up joining the military. He married his first love and they had two kids.

Gradually his dream changed. 'Every year I've been in the Army is the year I was getting out,' he reminisced to the Charlotte *Observer*, the local newspaper. 'All I wanted was to get back to North Carolina and be a cop.'

In 2005 his future got put on hold again. On 5 April he received a call from General Rod Johnson asking him whether he would be interested in the job at Guantánamo Bay. He accepted on the spot, only later talking to his wife. It would mean another year away from home.

Bumgarner loved the idea of working at Guantánamo, where he would command over a thousand soldiers and be on the front lines of the War on Terror. With such a large force, he thought guarding the prisoners would be easy. His nickname on the base was 'Rawhide', borrowed from the name used by the Secret Service for former President Ronald Reagan, a man Bumgarner worshipped. He was proud of the prison's slogan, 'Honor Bound to Defend Freedom'.

'Honor Bound, sir!' each soldier would salute him, passing.

'Honor Bound!' he saluted back. Constant use meant they were shortening the motto.

He was more likely to shout 'hoo-rah' in parting than 'goodbye'.

I hoped that Bumgarner might be the best solution to the prison's problems. Unlike his superior officers, he actually had some experience in running a prison. He had almost a quarter-century as a military police officer and before going to Guantánamo he had taught corrections at the Military Police School at Fort Leonard Wood, Missouri.

But Bumgarner was deceived if he thought his job would be simple. And I might well be wrong if I thought he could make a difference.

Bumgarner came to recognise that the military must make concessions if there was any hope of running the prison. He heard that this man Shaker Aamer was very respected by the other prisoners and might be the key to a solution. He went to see Shaker and ended up holding long sessions squatting outside Shaker's cell, talking through the metal mesh, trying to fashion some kind of compromise. Meanwhile Shaker had little to go on but his instinct for judging character. His information came exclusively from the Guantánamo goldfish bowl, but he decided that Bumgarner was a man whom he could trust.

The colonel listened to Shaker's complaints about the prisoners' treatment and talked about the possibility of change. In late July 2005 Shaker had been on strike for almost four weeks. In his most recent strike he had dropped thirty-five pounds and in his four years in American custody he had lost half his body weight. Now he weighed in at just over nine stone. As a personal demonstration of his own faith in Bumgarner, Shaker began eating again.

Shaker was moved to the main hospital, and at the colonel's request he tried to persuade the other men there to give up their own hunger strike to allow the military a chance to demonstrate that they were committed to change. Bumgarner assured Shaker that he would personally look into all the complaints and try to fashion responses, but to date he had made no concrete proposals. The other strikers thought it was all talk. They had come a long way in their protest and it was going to take more than a handful of second-hand assurances to persuade them now. They rejected Shaker's suggestion. On the contrary, in solidarity with each other a number of prisoners pulled out their IV needles and prepared to allow their lives to slip away.

The situation was desperate. Without water, death can be quite rapid and some of the weaker prisoners might last only days. Later, when we met, Shaker described the dispute between the doctors. One was willing to feed the prisoners against their will while the other was not, citing his ethical obligations. Dating back to 1975, the Declaration of Tokyo made it quite clear that a doctor may not force-feed a mentally competent hunger striker: 'Where a prisoner refuses nourishment and is considered by the physician as capable of forming an unimpaired and rational judgement concerning the consequences of such a voluntary refusal of nourishment, he or she shall not be fed artificially,' the World Medical Association had declared. 'The decision as to the capacity of the prisoner to form such a judgement should be confirmed by at least one other independent physician. The consequences of the refusal of nourishment shall be explained by the physician to the prisoner.'

To Shaker it appeared that both doctors wanted to avoid personal responsibility for the prisoners' deaths.

'I was a witness to the doctor in charge as he took verbal statements from dying prisoners refusing resuscitation efforts if they lapsed into coma,' Shaker said. The doctor went from bed to bed, tape recorder running as he told the prisoners what would happen to them and securing their consent to withhold medical assistance when they lost consciousness.

It was now a game of higher stakes. At that time, the military apparently had neither the medical resources nor the plan to deal with a mass protest like this. This time Bumgarner's promises were much more specific. Shaker later told me how the negotiations had gone. 'We have permission from Secretary of Defense Donald Rumsfeld himself to change the camp, consistent with the Geneva Conventions,' Bumgarner assured him. 'First, then, I can agree to do away with the level system, make everyone level one.' Eliminating the different colour of uniforms and the disparate number of inconsequential 'comfort items' might seem a minor victory. Because the Geneva Conventions forbade any kind of punishment without proper procedures, the compliance levels – the orange, grey and white uniforms – were illegal anyway. But the petty rules that went with the levels, such as the daily indignity of having to hand in a single thin blanket to the guards at six o'clock in the morning, and beg for toothpaste, grated among prisoners.

'Second, I can agree to allow input from the prisoners so that the food can be improved, be made more agreeable to the tastes of the detainees,' Bumgarner went on. This might begin with small gains, such as a sachet of hot sauce, but finally the food would have some taste. 'And I can agree that three bottles of water will be allowed to each prisoner each day, to replace the water from the camp's taps that has been the subject of complaints.'

More significantly, Bumgarner agreed that a prisoner council would be permitted, effective immediately, allowing the prisoners to present united requests for further changes. There were some concessions Bumgarner could not make. It was never realistic that he would promise fair trials for all. Shaker also asked the colonel to close the hated Camp Five, but millions of dollars had been spent building the place and this was again above Bumgarner's pay grade.

'I can't agree that Camp Five will be closed,' was Bumgarner's verdict. 'But we can discuss the conditions there and nothing is off the table.' Optimistic, Shaker hoped that the prisoners might ultimately prevail even on this issue.

Shaker recognised that the hunger strikes were a powerful form of non-violent protest. He had taken part in this strike for weeks, and he respected the individual commitment and opinions of his fellow strikers who were determined to go on. He was half convinced that he should have continued himself, as he knew the history of Bobby Sands, the Irishman who starved himself to death in 1980: Sands's sacrifice had helped secure better treatment from the British government for his fellow IRA members. Yet after praying for guidance he felt he owed it to Bumgarner, so Shaker pressed the other men to give the authorities a chance.

Over the next two days Shaker engaged in shuttle diplomacy, as the Henry Kissinger of the prison. He insisted he would not do this in his despised shackles. Bumgarner initially baulked, then gave way, allowing Shaker the run of the prison with nothing more than handcuffs. Shaker went camp by camp, block by block, and sometimes prisoner by prisoner, convincing them that this man Bumgarner was to be trusted.

Shaker was respected. He had built a reputation around the prison as a man who had suffered more than most for his faith in the American detention centres. Typically, those who spoke English were identified by the Americans as leaders, and subjected to harsher treatment. Eventually the strikers agreed that Colonel Bumgarner's specific promises bound the military and on 28 June 2005 they suspended their self-destruction for two weeks to permit the military to prove their bona fides.

The military now had a breathing space until 11 August.

I had left on 6 July, before all this drama took place, and my next visit began on 5 August. I learned of the concessions. None seemed very radical, as all were required by the Geneva Conventions. Donald Rumsfeld had repeatedly told the world that the prisoners were being treated 'consistent' with the Conventions and the very fact that thirty men came within hours of death to secure these promises was proof that Rumsfeld was not telling the truth. Yet I found a new atmosphere of hope among the prisoners. Perhaps they thought the military had finally turned the corner towards a new, more humane process for resolving some of the injustices of Guantánamo Bay.

As good as his word, Bumgarner had immediately addressed an array of relatively small problems. The quality of the food improved. The call to prayer no longer included the wrong Arabic words. The prisoners were no longer to be moved from their cells between 10 p.m. and 6 a.m.

Bumgarner also fulfilled his promise on other more substantial issues. There was a prisoners' council, just as Article 79 of the Geneva Conventions required: 'In all places where there are prisoners of war ... the prisoners shall freely elect by secret ballot ... prisoners' representatives entrusted with representing them before the military authorities.'

Shaker was one of the six members of the committee. He had been designated secretary and spokesman. As required by Article 81, the committee was allowed to hold meetings and canvass their fellow prisoners to resolve grievances.

'We held meetings,' he told me later when I saw him. They had us in a room where we could talk.'

Colonel Bumgarner promised that there might be even more radical changes. What would they be? And how long would the changes last?

The iceberg was still clearly visible, but the *Titanic* had lost its head of steam. The colonel had negotiated his way past the immediate danger of prisoners starving themselves to death. But while Bumgarner had some experience running a prison, the man ultimately in charge was General Hood, the artillery officer who was dabbling in corrections for the first time. After four years of mistreatment, the prisoners still mistrusted the soldiers and the soldiers still feared the prisoners.

Soon it became clear why Shaker's negotiations with Bumgarner were doomed to disaster.

At the best of times there is a strong, and not always constructive, rivalry between the US Army, Navy, Marines and Air Force. There is always a naval officer who is technically in command of the

Guantánamo Naval base. He is a captain and is outranked by the generals and admirals who have been the commanders of JTF-GTMO (the joint taskforce running the prison operation). On one of my early trips to the base a soldier gossiped gleefully about the rivalry of the moment – whether the base captain or the JTF general should get the best house.

Yet the main problem was not the tension between the naval base and the prison, but forces within the prison itself. While the JTF commander had undisputed control there, his mission was schizophrenic – to keep the prison under control and to obtain the 'actionable intelligence' that was the *raison d'être* of the place. When General Miller took command, Rumsfeld had transferred ultimate authority over the prison to the Military Intelligence Team.

Running a maximum-security prison is not easy when the warden's only goal is the management of the prisoners. Whether Colonel Bumgarner was sincere in his efforts to parley with Shaker or not, he was not in charge of the intelligence work and he had no control over it. *New York Times* reporter Tim Golden spent weeks researching a piece about Shaker and the hunger strikes, and he reported that the Joint Intelligence Group 'were furious' about Bumgarner's concessions to the prisoners. Later some of the officers told me the same thing. There were only a small number of privileges to give out at Guantánamo (the 'comfort items') and interrogators wanted to dispense them in return for cooperation. The prisoners reported that even medical care was withheld from people who would not talk.

Bumgarner may have been struggling honestly to calm the crisis, but there were others who believed that adding to the prisoners' stress helped the interrogations. Bumgarner might order his guards to treat a prisoner with respect, but the next moment an intelligence officer would be wanting to apply one of Rumsfeld's 'enhanced interrogation techniques'.

Often the people doing the interrogation were no more experienced than the people running the prison. Bill Tierney was a contract interpreter at Guantánamo with Worldwide Language Resources. He was also a military intelligence veteran. Back in his Florida home, he discussed the early days of the prison with Associated Press. 'The whole thing was a mess,' he said.

The interrogation was amateurish. There were few interrogators who understood Arabic. Those who did were trained in classical Arabic rather than the fifty dialects used by prisoners. They were often young, with only rudimentary training. Tierney spent two months there in 2002 before being ordered to leave. The military said he was meddling with the interrogation process. He said that he simply told an interrogator that Karachi was in Pakistan.

Others joined in the criticism. Professor Richard Kohn, former chief Air Force historian at the Pentagon, taught military issues at the University of North Carolina at Chapel Hill. He spoke to Associated Press about the military's confused mission, half-jail and half-inter-rogation, no part respect. The military was essentially the jailer down there,' he said. 'And that's not the intelligence gathering business. It's not the cultural sensitivity business.'

From day to day, even hour to hour, there was confusion in each part of the military as to which business it was in.

On the day I arrived for my August visit, just six days into Bumgarner's new regime, the détente began to disintegrate.

Coincidentally, it was another of my clients, Hisham Sliti, who was at the heart of the first controversy, although it was one that he tried to avoid. Hisham came from Tunisia. He was a short man, his oblong face coming to a point at the chin, with a straggling goatee that made him look a little Chinese. He spoke no English, so we muddled along in French. I complained to him that my French was much more fluent after a couple of glasses of red wine, but the guards would not let me bring a bottle into Camp Echo. With some of my clients, I could not joke about alcohol, but Hisham laughed at anything. He had been no angel himself, and had done time in both Italy and Belgium for drug offences. He spoke Italian as well, so we threw in some of that. For the most part he humoured my mélange of languages.

'My dream is to marry a good woman and live quietly away from the big city,' he told me. 'In the countryside somewhere, without many people.' He had hoped to find a wife in Afghanistan. When he had travelled there, he found that he disliked the Taliban, who were intolerant of an unmarried foreign man.

'The Americans say I am an extremist,' he said with a shrug. 'How could that be? I have not been good. It's true, I did deal drugs. I had a problem for a long time.'

Now he found himself in another prison.

'Ah, this, it is not *la dolce vita*. Not like Italy,' he reminisced, mixing his French and Italian. 'In Italy the prison was wide open for six hours a day. You could have anything in your room – I had a little *fornello*, a gas cooker. Can you imagine the Americans allowing that? Here, we call a plastic spoon a "Camp Delta Kalashnikov", as the soldiers think we're going to attack them with it – they're terrified we might hide one away. Maybe they even think we'd build bombs out of toilet paper and that's why we're limited to fifteen pieces a day. But in Italy I'd only use the *fornello* for coffee and mocha. The cooks were the prisoners and they were all Italian. The guards played no role in the food, they just looked on.

'My cell in Italy was not much bigger than this, but the toilet was separate, not in your room. He waved around the cell, wrinkling his nose as he pointed to the metal toilet beside the bed. 'I had three cupboards for my clothes and things, I had a television. There was an open window, for fresh air.

'The Belgian prisons are not quite as good as the Italian ones, though I was only in them for a couple of months, in Saint Gil,' he said. 'Even the Arab prisons. They'll abuse you for six months before your trial, maybe, but then you'll be in a normal prison. Nothing like this place.'

Hisham was emphatic that the military had no idea how to run a proper institution.

'The punishments and rewards the Americans do are meaningless. Look –' he said, pinching the fabric of the orange uniform that he was wearing, the colour denoting his lack of 'compliance' with the prison rules. 'The prison clothes are made of the same material, whether they are white, brown or orange. If you were colour blind, you would know no difference.

'A prison is not about the walls, it's about the people who run it,' he said sagely. 'Partly it's the relationship between the guards and the prisoners, and there's none here. But here, there's worse. In Italy, your cell is the only limit. It, alone, is your desolation. But here, everything is desolation.'

Hisham's problem on 5 August 2005 came in the form of King Kong, a civilian intelligence officer. The prisoners were not allowed to know his real name, but this man had earned a reputation and a nickname to go with it. On this occasion King Kong brought an Arabic interpreter, a skinny man with a mousy beard and glasses, who always wore a hat. Almost four years in, the prisoners had nothing more to say. For the past few days the prisoner council had been working with Colonel Bumgarner to regularise these pointless interrogation sessions, but no agreement had been reached yet.

King Kong forced Hisham to sit on a chair, his ankles chained to the floor, his wrists shackled. Hisham told the interpreter, politely, that he had a lawyer and he did not intend to make any statement.

King Kong responded by shouting. The gist needed little translation, but the interpreter explained to Hisham that he would have to answer questions, or they would force him to. That meant, in Rumsfeld's terms, a little 'mild non-injurious physical contact'; in plain English, Hisham could look forward to a beating.

'He'd come to cause problems,' Hisham explained to me.

King Kong shouted again, and the interpreter explained to Hisham that King Kong knew that Hisham spoke English. It was not true. The only word Hisham did pick up was the word 'bitch'. King Kong started wagging his finger in front of Hisham's nose.

King Kong's version, later, was that Hisham bit his finger. Hisham told me that he might have been tempted to, but it would have been impossible. 'What he said was not true,' Hisham told me. 'But I did spit at him. I had enough of telling him I wasn't going to talk, enough of being shouted at.'

Unencumbered by shackles himself, King Kong could do more than spit. He picked up a small refrigerator, and threw it at Hisham.

'It was unplugged, empty and mostly made of plastic, so it didn't hurt much,' said Hisham. 'I spat at him again.'

This time King Kong picked up a chair and swung it, catching Hisham with one leg. Now Hisham was bleeding from a gash above his right eye, and I witnessed the scar when the military finally let me see him, three months later. The ERF team had already been summoned and they finished the job, beating Hisham up and dragging him back to his cell, where the soldiers messed with his Qur'an again for good measure.

The bush telegraph of the prison spread the news around within hours. It became clear that Hisham was not the only prisoner abused by the interrogation officers on that one day. A Saudi called Sa'ad had been taken off for five hours of interrogation by a woman; the session involved sexual humiliation. Omar Khadr, the kid from Canada, was violently ERFed. There was no way to know whether the intelligence branch of the military was intentionally undermining Colonel Bumgarner, or simply singing its favourite song. My guess would be it was some of both. Either way it had the same effect.

The unravelling of the peace accord was inevitable. The last meeting of the prisoners' council took place on the next day, 6 August. The council discussed the three incidents that had taken place.

'They had us in a room where we could talk. But we had problems immediately. They insisted on listening in,' Shaker told me later. The discussion was in Arabic, so the military wanted two translators to be present, along with a tape recorder. 'We said no, we had to have an open debate before presenting our conclusions to the military. They said no, we might be plotting something. So we started writing notes around the room to each other. They came in and wanted to seize the notes.'

Shaker smiled, but by now his smile was wan. 'So we ate the bits of paper.'

The prisoners won a point, but the game soon went against them. Colonel Bumgarner ended the council's meeting. General Hood told Bumgarner that this experimenting was over. The next day Sa'ad was ERFed, with his face pushed into his toilet, when he refused to go for more interrogation. Another respected prisoner, Abdulsalaam al-Hayla from Yemen, was taken for 'interrogation' for five hours. He had to sit in a chilled cell and nobody ever came to question him.

The prisoners saw the military as a monolith, and could not see the difference between the prison and intelligence functions. They could only interpret these abuses as an intentional resumption of hostilities. Word spread that the hunger strike was to begin again on 11 August.

Shaker was still willing to negotiate, but he never had the chance. The military retreated into its comfort zone. The prisoners' council was forcibly disbanded, the six members immediately separated to dissolve their leadership influence. Shaker was taken to Camp Echo, which would soon become his permanent home. The other Saudi Arabian, Ghassan Oteibi, had been one of the most steadfast strikers and he was removed to the hospital. A third member of the council, Sheikh Saba, an Islamic scholar from Bosnia, was taken to Camp Romeo. One Egyptian, Abdurrahman, was taken to Camp Five, while the second, Sheikh Ala, had long since been found innocent at his CSRT and was moved to Iguana. The treatment there was better, there were only two other NECs, so his isolation from all the rest of the camp was virtually complete. The sixth and final member, Zaif, the former Taliban ambassador to Pakistan, was immediately shipped home, released under political pressure from the Karzai government. This was another illustration of the purely political nature of the whole process, as he was by far the most senior Taliban leader in Guantánamo, yet he went home months before the small fry.

The military withdrew many of the other concessions that Bumgarner had made, despite being legally required by the Geneva Conventions. The white, brown and orange uniforms were back in vogue.

Although the strike restarted on 11 August 2005, as far as the outside world was concerned, nothing was happening. When Bobby Sands and nine other members of the IRA starved themselves to death, almost every moment of their decline was broadcast live; nothing could come out of Guantánamo unless it was cleared by the censors. I left the base with a clear picture of what was happening, but I was gagged and had to sit silent. I could speak to nobody for now, and it was a lonely and worrying experience. The military, true to their word, told the media nothing about the resumption of the strike

Along with the other lawyers, I was desperate to avoid the death of any of my clients. Each lawyer visiting the base learned the latest news, and would make a concerted effort to unclassify as much information about the strike as quickly as possible. We needed to press the men's cases in court, and we hoped that if the true facts were known, the military would return to the negotiating table.

I had used an urgent mechanism at the base (which rarely worked) to send a fax of my interview notes to the Secure Facility in Washington, so it was only two weeks before I got a complete statement from Shaker through the censorship process, dated 11 August, the first day of the resumed strike. 'There must be a third party,' he had written. 'We wish to have an intermediary to hold the US to its word, as the military has sadly betrayed its word on every occasion a promise has been made.'

It was not clear what the endgame of this would be, but the best chance for reconciliation had passed.

Our clients could also write to us in Washington, though it was a slow process. A month later I found a letter from Bisher al-Rawi waiting for me at the Secure Facility. Bisher was an emphatically polite man. When his parents fled Saddam Hussein, he came to Britain and acquired a capacity for understatement. He never took up a British passport, as he hoped one day that the Iraqi people would throw off Saddam in favour of democracy.

Now he was on strike himself. 'I am taking this opportunity, whenever I can, to write to you,' the letter said.

> These are very difficult times, and my emotions are shifting and changing rapidly. I am thinking about anything and everything. The evenings and nights are no longer times for sleep for me. I am always wide awake going through memories, some happy, some sad. It all flows back to this dismal and depressing reality. (I really don't wish to sound so down, I am sorry.) This new reality, this new existence, is the food strike. It has made me live in the shadows, where one can't feel quite alive, but one does not die. A very strange existence.
>
> I think it is only now that I can claim that I've moved a step closer to understanding the feelings and emotions of the poor and millions of human beings who are starving through the world. Pictures in my mind of the starving men, women and children, which I have seen through the years, now all make sense. Now I understand what deprivation really means, why people fight and kill each other over food. Despite my weakness and the helplessness that I feel during the days, I am determined to survive this and think this is my biggest struggle in this jail. I hope I'll further discover myself. Just like this whole experience has been a self-discovery full of pain and sadness, full of desperation and hope. I pray to God that this last episode will not break me, but

will help me be the best I can both here and when I get out. It'll be a valid and precious asset that will always be at my side.

As the hunger strike went on, I was glad to learn that Bisher had given up the strike for the month of Ramadan. I respected the prisoners' right to peaceful protest, but I'd rather they were not suffering. The prisoners had apparently agreed to designate a small number to carry the torch forward. While the military trumpeted the fact that there were only between twenty and thirty strikers left, these were a core, steeled to continue.

The next time I was back at Guantánamo it was 2 November 2005, and Ramadan was coming to a close. Shaker had also suspended his strike for the holy month. Now, he told me, he was going back to the test of wills and he had additional personal reasons for his commitment. He had asked repeatedly to speak with Colonel Bumgarner about the rapid descent in prison morale. He felt betrayed that Bumgarner had refused to meet with him. He had not seen the man since 6 August.

Shaker decided that he had to make a concerted effort to persuade Bumgarner back into negotiations before prisoners came to further harm. He told the guards in Camp Echo that he wanted to see the colonel. Nothing happened. So he took a step that he knew would bring them running. He hung his shorts over the camera in his cell. The spherical eye would watch him twenty-four hours a day – whether praying, asleep, or on the toilet. Covering it was a violation of the camp rules. Immediately the panicked guards came over to his cell and ordered him to take them down. He refused. They called the ERF team.

'I refused to come out when they arrived,' said Shaker, smiling. He had endured the struggle and, after being alone in the cell for several months now, I was his first audience.

'I sat quietly on the floor as they came in. There were five of them. They threw me down on my face and took me out of the cell while they searched everywhere.' Shaker told them that he simply wanted to talk to Colonel Bumgarner, or another senior officer. The members of the ERF team were not interested; they took his shorts with them as they left. When they were out of sight, Shaker waited long enough for them to take off their Darth Vader uniforms. He then took his shaving soap and covered up the camera again. Fifteen minutes later the ERF team was back, lurking menacingly outside his cell while the guards ordered him to clear the camera.

'I told them they had done this too often and there was nothing left to search, or to watch on the camera. What was I doing that needed this constant surveillance? It was just a way to invade my privacy. So I refused to come out again.'

He told them, once more, that all he wanted was a meeting with a senior officer. They ignored him. This time the female soldier in the ERF team was the one they designated to search around his groin, as part of the ritual humiliation. After working him over, the ERF team departed with all of his personal items. There was going to be no more shaving soap for him to use on the camera, or anywhere else.

Shaker found that the ERF team had left a nail hidden in his cell, to give them something to search for next time. This was Shaker's home, now, and he tended to it with exaggerated care. If they came in and found the nail, such 'contraband' would justify punishing Shaker some more. He immediately called the guards to turn over the nail. They might ERF him, but he was not going to let them do it on their terms.

His sweep of the cell completed, Shaker sat on the thin isomat – the half-inch exercise mat that served as a mattress for those in isolation – to ponder his next move. His cell was stripped of everything but the thin clothes he was wearing. Even the blanket was now gone. He knew he had only one option. As he described it to me, he grimaced at the memory.

He took his own faeces and smeared them over the camera, once more closing out the peeping Toms in Camp Echo central control.

The guards were immediately back at his door. This time they did not seem too keen on coming into the cell to get their wandering eye to work again.

'I only want to be treated with respect,' said Shaker, explaining that he wanted to talk with Colonel Bumgarner. 'Do you think I like doing this? Do you think I want you to come in and beat me up each time?'

The soldiers eventually said they would stop the incessant searches of his cell if he cleaned off his own camera. Respect was a two-way street and Shaker did not want to force the cleaning on a soldier, so he agreed.

This was a small victory in a very long battle, but he still did not get his meeting. His momentary success was followed by more isolation.

What Shaker said next he asked me to write down and submit to the US military censors.

'I am dying here every day,' he began. 'Mentally and physically, this is happening to all of us. We have been ignored, locked up in the middle of this ocean for four years. Rather than humiliate myself, having to beg for water here in Camp Echo, I have decided to hurry up a process that is going to happen anyway.'

He paused, searching for the right words. 'It is a matter of personal dignity.' He stopped as if something were wrong. 'No . . . It is a matter of religious belief and personal dignity. I have got kidney problems from the filthy yellow water. I have lung problems from the chemicals they spread all over the floor. I am already arthritic at forty because I sleep on a steel bed and they use freezing air conditioning as part of the interrogation process. I have eyes that are ruined from the permanent, twenty-four-hours-a-day fluorescent lights. I have tinnitus in my ears from the perpetual noise. I have skin diseases from chemicals and never being allowed out to see the sun. I have ulcers and almost permanent constipation from the food.

'I have been made paranoid, so that I can trust nobody.' He looked up at me intently. There was no smile there. 'Even my lawyer. Because the Americans play with my mind.'

He paused again. 'I would like to die quietly, by myself. I was once more than eighteen stone. I dropped to just nine stone in the hunger strike. In respect for Ramadan, I suspended my protest, but on 4 November I must begin again. I want to join my brothers. I want to make it easy on everyone. I want no feeding. No forced tubes. No "help". No "intensified assisted feeding". This is my legal right.'

I felt as though I was taking down his epitaph. Shaker read over what I had written and satisfied himself that they were really his words. He signed it. The date was 2 November 2005.

He then asked me to write a short note to Prime Minister Tony Blair. 'The British government refuses to help me. What is the point of my wife and children being British? I thought Britain stood for justice and human rights, but they helped the British citizens and then abandoned the rest of us. People who have lived in Britain for years, and who have British wives and children. I hold the British government responsible for my death, as I do the Americans.'

Again, Shaker read the words through and signed them.

It is always a dismal moment when one leaves a client in prison, but in twenty-five years I have never been as anxious – never felt the dread – that I did when I left that day. If Shaker became ill, I knew that I would be one of the last people the US military would tell. They would do everything they could to hide it, knowing that he would have supporters in Britain who would be outraged. Normally I can try to protect my clients from the harshest aspects of prison. Here I knew I could achieve little for him if he sickened towards death.

By now, two dozen prisoners had been on strike for twenty days more than the longest of the IRA hunger strikers in 1980. Drinking water, a fit person should be able to survive without food for at least forty days. Some of the IRA lasted seventy days before they died. But nobody could survive ninety days.

So what was going on? And what did Shaker mean in his statement by 'intensified assisted feeding'?

Dr John Edmondson was a captain in the US Navy. He was the doctor in charge of the Guantánamo hospital. He knew all about the Tokyo declaration's prohibition against forcefeeding prisoners. Edmondson took umbrage when British doctor David Nicholl accused him of behaving unethically. He got into an e-mail debate with his medical colleague.

'In actuality I am not currently force-feeding any detainees,' Dr Edmondson wrote to Dr Nicholl. 'I am providing nutritional supplementation on a voluntary basis to detainees who wish to protest their confinement by not taking oral nourishment.'

Dr Edmondson also swore an affidavit that was filed in court, seeking to refute allegations made by the lawyers concerning the treatment of prisoners. 'The actual feeding process, both at the detention hospital and on the cell block, is very voluntary,' he swore. 'Detainees retain a large measure of control over the administration of the nutrition.' The phrase 'very voluntary' was odd. Just how voluntary was 'very voluntary'?

Did he mean that there was no forced feeding? If this was true, it meant that all the prisoners were trying to put one over on the world, happily hooking up to the IV each day and pretending to be starving themselves to death. Did he mean that Donald Rumsfeld was right: this was just a publicity stunt by some trained al-Qaeda operatives trying to get attention. Indeed, Edmondson insisted that the strike was in rapid decline by the end of 2005. By then, the military did admit that the prisoners were experiencing 'assisted feeding' and one official referred to 'intensified assisted feeding'. What was really happening?

I had asked Shaker to keep a diary, in which he would identify the numbers of all the guards who took action against him, so that we could hold them to account for what was happening. Shaker described what the guards did to him to make him accept his nutrition each day, and he gave me the diary on my next visit.

'November 21, 2005,' he wrote.

> I am in day 18 of my hunger strike so far. I have lost a lot of weight, but they refuse to take me to hospital. It seems they are scared to let me talk to my brothers, so they brought the Ensure to my cell. They do everything here in my cell to avoid me going to the hospital. So far I have been isolated here in Echo for 58 days. I have been out to rec only two times. I have only the most basic items in my cell. They try to do their best to destroy me mentally to stop my hunger strike. They try to keep me awake all night long by coming in and out so many times and making so much noise. They come to clean the cell in the middle of the night and make strange noises just outside my cell door. This is all in the name of 'checking up on me' and 'making sure I am all right'. I swear I have never seen such a devilish way of thinking as they seem to have. Sometimes I really stop to wonder whether they are human beings.

Shaker finally got to meet a more senior officer. It was not Colonel Bumgarner and the man had not come to negotiate.

> November 23, 2005. They came to weigh me. They tried to get me to do it, but there was an ERF team there of six people, Colonel

[CENSORED] and others – a total of 15 people. Most left when they started beating me. The colonel said, 'We will weigh you.' I said, 'You won't do it by force.' The ERF team came in and threw me in the air, and then on to the scale. They twisted my arms and did some kind of permanent injury to my left ankle. The SOG [Sergeant of the Guard] was the one who twisted my left ankle. I started screaming at that point. They put the loud noise maker on to drown this out. I had bruises all over my hands and my legs, and cuts on my ankles from the shackles. They refused to get a doctor. They could not weigh me so they strapped me on an orange board and put that on the scale. But I wiggled around all the time so they could not get a reading. This went on for about 35 minutes according to the clock in the cell. Finally, the colonel said, 'You're right, we cannot weigh you.'

The weighing was all about checking up on the strikers. Partly it had a medical pretext, to see how the prisoners were doing, but the more important purpose was to expose the secret strikers. Some prisoners would pretend to accept their food, and then flush it down the toilet. Large numbers had apparently hoped to get well into the strike before the military figured it out.

Shaker made no secret of his strike. Ultimately there would be different ways of feeding the prisoners. The first was with an IV, generally into the arm. That would drip different nutrients into the striker. On 23 November, they fed Shaker with an IV for the first time. A lieutenant, an Asian doctor, did it to him.

> November 25, 2005. An MP Commander admitted in front of me for the first time that the interrogator [King Kong] beat Hisham Sliti in the interrogation room. He said the interrogator was punished for this. Today I finished 75 days in which only three times I have been out in the sun.

On 1 December 2005, they threatened to ERF him again. 'They threatened to strap me down if I refused to take the IV. The doctor came and I told him that I refused their food. But they said they would do it by force so I went along with it so I wouldn't get hurt by the ERF team. They gave me two IVs and one banana bag.' The banana bag was the name that the prisoners gave to the plastic bag of liquid administered after the first type of nutrient. Shaker told me how he regretted letting them feed him without the ERF team, as he knew this meant that the military would claim he was taking nutrients 'voluntarily'. But he just could not face more violence at that time.

On 6 December 2005, finally Shaker got a real meeting with a senior officer. General Hood himself came to the cell. They spoke for one hour about how the prison could be improved. General Hood said that allowing Shaker and the other members of the Prisoners' Council to speak freely before had been very dangerous, as they had demanded rights.

'He said he could keep me in Camp Echo until he was sure that I would not cause him trouble in the camp,' said Shaker.

On 9 December they tried to weigh Shaker by force again. He was beaten, and they forcibly took blood from him. They tried an IV in his right arm five times and twice in his left. The eighth time it finally worked. They left it in for ten hours. It was extremely painful, because it felt like it was next to the bone, and Shaker asked the male nurse repeatedly to take it out, but he refused.

'Even if the general gave me an order I would not take it out,' the man said, spitefully.

Finally, Shaker managed to pull it out himself. He bled badly, so he dipped his right forefinger in his own blood and smeared words on his cell wall: 'Justice Must be Restored!' The male nurse freaked out and taped up his bleeding arm.

The message stayed there, as nobody would come in to clean it. Later General Hood came in and saw it, and sent a team in to clean his cell.

Prisoners had pulled IVs out before, and the military decided it was time for a new regime to deal with people who resisted feeding. On 11 December 2005, they came for the first time with the nose feeding tube. This would go into the nostril and down to the stomach. One type of liquid food, generally a couple of cans of Ensure, would be chased with the banana bags of liquid nutrients.

Shaker refused to accept the tube. He had a copy of the Tokyo declaration, informing the military that it was his voluntary decision to take no food. This was, he argued, his legal right.

'This is a competition,' the doctor said, refusing to give a name. 'I will not let you fast. Now you are going to be isolated because of your hunger strike.'

Shaker had been isolated for four months already. The nurse, an anonymous lieutenant-commander, forced a tube into him. Shaker asked each of the medical staff for their identification numbers so he could report them.

'You can call me Double-O-Seven,' the doctor said, laughing at his own joke. Licensed to kill, Shaker thought to himself. They forced the tube up his nose, painfully. They blew a syringe full of air into his stomach and listened with a stethoscope to determine how deep the tube had gone. This gave him diarrhoea. The medical staff told the personnel to give him ten hours of the banana bag in addition to cans of Ensure liquid supplement.

While he was lying alone with his banana bag, Shaker scraped off the label. He later gave it to me and I submitted it to the censors so I could determine what was being used on him. The liquid in the bags was 'Dextrose 5% in 0.45% Sodium 1,000 ml, with Potassium Chloride 20 MEQ, Magnesium Sulphate 500 MG, Folic Acid 1MG'.

Along with the nose tube, the military had a programme of punishing the hunger strikers. Shaker got a copy of the Camp Echo Detainee Rules, which I again submitted to the censors. 'While on hunger strike,' the rules instructed, 'you are not allowed to go to recreation with other detainees. If you come off the hunger strike, you may conduct recreation with one other detainee. However, that detainee must also be off the hunger strike.'

In addition to threatening punishment, the rules made clear that the prisoner was required to keep his feeding tube up his nose and was not allowed to remove it. 'At no time will you cover your head so as the guard force cannot see where the ambulatory tube is. The re-feeding tube will be draped over your shoulder or wrapped around your ear so the guard can see it.'

If the senior doctor, Captain Edmondson, denied that the prisoners were being force-fed, these rules were hardly consistent with his claim: 'You will receive re-feeding in accordance with your feeding schedule. You MUST take your re-feeding when instructed to do so.'

The military was using twenty-four-hour lighting on the prisoners: 'At no time will all the lights in your cell be completely off. While you are sleeping, you may have your lights dimmed to a comfortable level in accordance with your current Detainee level.' In other words if you were an HC ('high compliant') you would have your lights at the dimmest level. Of course, the hunger strikers were all, by definition, non-compliant and therefore on the most punitive level – segregation. So the 'comfortable level' of lighting would be the brightest allowed by the military, which generally meant a constant state of neon brilliance.

The military had raised the stakes with the use of the tubes and the punishment regime. The number of prisoners on strike was falling, with only seventeen prisoners still being fed through nasal tubes. The hunger strike was, the military insisted, now no big deal.

I next saw Shaker on 5 January 2006, two months later. He was still being held in Camp Echo. Up to this point, most of the striking prisoners had been held at the hospital camp, within sight of the other prisoners. Sami al-Haj, my al-Jazeera client, had watched the ERF team going into the hospital where the prisoners were being force-fed during Ramadan and reported what he saw. The ERF team would arrive each morning before dawn and leave after three hours. They would return at sunset and remain for two hours more. It did not take a genius to deduce that the prisoners were undergoing 'intensive assisted feeding' with the looming presence of the ERF team.

Now Camp Echo held all the long-term hunger strikers, where they were safe from prying eyes, as well as isolated from each other in the solitary cells. The gravel paths were gone, replaced by concrete, so that when a weakened skeletal hunger striker was allowed out into the Camp Echo 'recreation cage' for sunlight, his walker or his wheelchair moved more easily. The camp had the air of a geriatric home, with the inmates shuffled around by their military minders.

As I came into his cell, I was nervous. Shaker smiled. It was more of a scowl, as his face tried to accommodate the plastic tube that came out of his right nostril, curving up over his ear.

'I thought it might be you,' he said and immediately began to pull the tube out of his nose. It was painful just to watch him. The off-white plastic tube inched out of his right nostril and he grimaced each time he pulled it. Pausing part-way through, he pulled the medical tape off his neck, leaving a harsh red blot on his skin. Finally, forty-three inches later, the end of the tube emerged, stained a deep red.

He passed it across the table to me, so I could note down the details.

It was a 'Corpak Viasys Medsystems tube #20-5431'. Watching Shaker pull out the tube, and now holding the tube in my hands, brought home the reality of this 'intensified assisted feeding'.

'For the record, Shaker,' I said. 'I just need to ask you this: is your decision to take liquid up the nose a voluntary one?'

Shaker grinned at me. Of course not. I was clearly an imbecile.

I was an external observer to the battle of wills between the military and the prisoners. This latest sight – Shaker showing total resolve when in great pain – made it even more obvious that there was going to be an unhappy ending, unhappy for both sides, if the struggle continued to escalate. I was angry at the military, which responded at each turn by more extreme treatment of the prisoners. Did they not see how the prisoners had valid complaints, complaints that were not going to be dissolved in a can of Ensure forced up a prisoner's nose? At the same time the military were not acting out of wanton sadism for the sake of it. They were afraid that a prisoner was going to die in Guantánamo Bay and they knew it would be a PR disaster, hardly consistent with the image they were trying to project. They were like deer in the headlights, not knowing which way to turn.

If the forced feeding had been hard on the prisoners all along, it was about to evolve to a new level of cruelty. Having a tube up your nose for a week at a time seemed painful enough. When I had come into the room and seen it projecting out of Shaker's right nostril, I wondered what could be worse. It was a perpetual irritant and Shaker had sucked gratefully on the throat lozenges that I had brought for my own festering flu. (Later the military would ban lawyers from bringing in throat lozenges.)

However unpleasant this had been, Shaker told me that a more painful regime had recently begun for other prisoners. The military had decided to launch a new counter-offensive.

A month before, in early December 2005, the base had taken delivery of mobile restraint chairs, such as are sometimes used in maximum-security prisons for violent mentally ill prisoners. I looked them up on the Internet and they looked rather like an updated electric chair, with two small tyres at the back so they could be wheeled in when needed. The normal version had straps for the prisoner's arms and legs, but the Guantánamo chairs had been modified to add two additional straps for the head and the chest. The manufacturer had an advertisement for the chair that exclaimed, 'It's like a padded cell on wheels!'

The prisoners immediately dubbed it the torture chair.

Under the new regime the military strapped down the prisoners for feeding, but they were no longer leaving the tube in. Prior to each feeding they would force the tube in and afterwards they would pull it back out. With the prisoner strapped into the chair, unable to move, a soldier would take hold of the tube and walk away, pulling it until all forty-three inches came out. Twice a day.

Persistent reports about the chairs prompted the military to admit to the *New York Times* that tactics had changed: 'General Craddock said he had reviewed the use of the restraint chairs, as had senior officials at the Department of Defense, and they concluded that the practice was "not inhumane". General Craddock left no doubt, however, that commanders had decided to try to make life less comfortable for the hunger strikers, and that the measures were seen as successful.'

When the torture chair operations began, there were roughly two dozen prisoners who had been on strike for five months, who were being subjected to 'intensified assisted feeding' with the tube. Within days the number dropped to six.

'Pretty soon it wasn't convenient, and they decided it wasn't worth it,' General Craddock said of the hunger strikers, seeming to gloat at the success of the new strategy. 'A lot of the detainees said, "I don't want to put up with this. This is too much of a hassle."'

Life was not 'less comfortable' for the prisoners – it was excruciating. While the prisoners had previously agreed among themselves that thirty would remain on strike, the torture chair meant that only those with the strongest will could continue. I worried that Shaker would be among the few to keep up the protest. It was another two months before my next visit, and I was glad to discover that he was not one of those who had volunteered for this task.

By early 2006, many of the strikers had capitulated, at least for now, but it had always seemed obvious to me that the military could not ultimately break the hunger strike by force, any more than the United States would win the War on Terror by high-altitude indiscriminate bombing. If a prisoner was willing to kill himself for a cause, slowly starving to death under torturous circumstances, it was naïve to think that he would not take his own life by a quicker method if that became the only available alternative. Meanwhile the military's strategy of abusing the strikers only glued the rest of the prisoners together more firmly.

Yet the most obvious precipitant of the Guantánamo hunger strike was the hypocrisy and deceit with which the Bush Administration dealt with the prisoners' complaints. This attitude was tilting world opinion inexorably in the prisoners' favour, no matter who they were or what they might have done.

As the Guantánamo hunger strike began in July 2005, Bush's White House spokesman Scott McClellan issued a press release in support of Akbar Ganji, an imprisoned Iranian journalist. Ganji had originally been a supporter of the 1979 revolution and joined the Islamic Revolutionary Guards Corps. He later became disillusioned and criticised the regime. He was given a six-year sentence in 2000, mainly because of some investigative journalism he had done linking some of the country's officials to the 1998 'serial murders' of dissident intellectuals.

Ganji had himself resorted to a hunger strike to protest against his unfair trial. Now Bush was championing his cause against Iran, a member state of the Axis of Evil. He called upon Iran to release Ganji 'immediately and unconditionally'.

'Mr Ganji is sadly only one victim of a wave of repression and human rights violations engaged in by the Iranian regime. His calls for freedom deserve to be heard. His valiant efforts should not go in vain,' McClellan said, reading the President's statement. 'The President calls on all supporters of human rights and freedom, and the United Nations, to take up Ganji's case and the overall human rights situation in Iran.

'Mr Ganji, please know that as you stand for your own liberty, America stands with you . . .' McClellan continued. 'Through his now month-long hunger strike, Mr Ganji is demonstrating that he is willing to die for his right to express his opinion. President Bush is saddened by recent reports that Mr Ganji's health has been failing and deeply concerned that the Iranian government has denied him access to his family, medical treatment and legal representation.'

Ganji should certainly have received support, and I was glad when he was set free by Iran on 18 March 2006. But Ganji had refused food for one month; by then, the Guantánamo prisoners had starved themselves for nine. No doubt Ganji's trial had been rigged, but the Guantánamo prisoners had no trial at all – half of them had never seen a lawyer. The Guantánamo prisoners had not seen their families for close to five years – Shaker had never met his youngest child Faris, who had been born after his capture. Their 'medical care' consisted of doctors violating international ethical rules and soldiers using nose tubes to inflict terrible pain.

Upon his release, Ganji visited the United States, and was invited to the White House to discuss the future of democracy in Iran. He refused to go. Apparently, he, too, thought Bush a hypocrite for pitching the Middle East into chaos with the Iraq war.

Meanwhile, in Guantánamo, it seemed likely that the latest escalation would lead to the ultimate tragedy – the death of one of the prisoners.

'Blizzard,' came the radio call from Camp One, soon after midnight on 10 June 2006. This was the code for prisoners making simultaneous suicide attempts.

That morning, England had won its opening game of the World Cup campaign. I had watched on a television screen in Atlanta as they played out an unconvincing victory over Paraguay. I had then caught a plane to Washington. I was due to fly from Andrews Air Force Base, in Maryland, to Guantánamo for the second hearing in Binyam Mohamed's case.

I learned that Binyam's hearing had been cancelled as I arrived in DC. Three men had committed suicide at Guantánamo. I received the news with the sinking feeling of inevitability, chased immediately by panic: was anyone I had been representing among the three? They could be anyone. Indeed, it struck me as unlikely that any of the front-line strikers would be among the dead, as they would be monitored too closely.

True to form, the Pentagon would not name any of suicides, so I could not know whether Shaker was among them. Unable to travel to Guantánamo, where I might have learned the truth, I scoured the news reports for the next twenty-four hours, looking for clues as they seeped out. Meanwhile, the Reprieve office were receiving frantic calls from our clients' families.

The first information was that two of the dead men were Saudis and one a Yemeni. I only had one Saudi client – Shaker. I was increasingly worried about him.

Eventually the three dead men were identified. I felt guilty to be glad that Shaker was not among them. Yasser al-Zahrani was the first named. I looked for him on the list of prisoners that we had finally extracted from the Pentagon just a month before. Yasser had been born on 22 September 1984 in Yanbo, Saudi Arabia. That meant he would have been just seventeen when he was originally seized by the United States. I wanted to learn more about each of the people who had died, more than merely a date of birth and serial number, so I contacted Tarek Dergoul, one of the British clients who had been released from Guantánamo Bay in 2004. Tarek seemed to have met almost everyone in the prison during his time there and remembered them all.

'Yasser, I got to know him very well while at Guantánamo,' said Tarek. 'He was an optimistic man, very defiant in a sense that he wasn't the type of person to give up.'

The second dead prisoner was Mana al-Otaibi, thirty years old, from al-Qarara in Saudi Arabia. 'He was about five foot eleven, slim build,' said Tarek. 'He was well liked by all at Guantánamo. He was well versed in the Holy Qur'an and was well known for reciting beautiful poetry. At one time I spent three weeks in the adjoining cell, where he taught me Tajweed and we shared a lot of our innermost thoughts.' Tajweed was a term used to describe the proper method for reciting the Holy Qur'an.

The third man was Ali Abdullah Ahmed, twenty-nine, from the city of Ib in Yemen. He was one of the few prisoners whom Tarek did not remember.

There was a painful footnote to Yasser's story. The previous week some Saudis had been released and Yasser's father had talked to the media. 'We are extremely happy about the release of the men, whom I also consider my sons,' Talal al-Zahrani told Arab News, saying that this release augured well for getting his own son back. 'I am very optimistic and have faith in God that my son and the rest will be released.'

His son was now dead.

Rear Admiral Harry Harris, who had recently taken charge of

the Guantánamo base from General Hood, immediately labelled the suicides an 'asymmetrical act of war'. This was possibly the most offensive thing the military had said to date. Asymmetrical warfare refers to the kind of subversive tactics that an out-manned or out-gunned opponent uses in battle, including the suicide bomber. But the comparison with suicide bombers was silly – no suicide bomber kills himself but makes no effort to harm his enemy.

The Pentagon PR machine took over from Harris, who was new on the job and clearly an amateur when it came to the media. The Pentagon experts claimed that the military was being 'culturally sensitive' in its response to the tragedy.

'Taking their own lives was not necessary,' said Colleen P. Graffy in an interview with the BBC. 'But –' Here she paused. She should simply have stopped. '– this certainly is a good PR move to draw attention.'

Graffy, whose title was PR Spokesperson for the Secretary of State for Public Diplomacy, was calling three suicides a good PR move. She seemed to be trying to outdo Harris with her sensitivity.

The Middle East was already effervescing with mistrust. 'We strongly doubt the US account and call for an independent investigation to establish the cause of their deaths,' said Khalid al-Odah in one paper. He suggested the three might have died of wounds sustained during a clash with guards the previous month.

Khalid's son had been held on the base for four years. Khalid was one of the most level-headed people I had met in the Middle East, a former fighter pilot with the Kuwaiti Royal Air Force who had come to both Bahrain and Yemen and helped translate for me as I had met with the family members of prisoners. If Khalid was calling this murder, there was little chance that the US military would convince the Arab world otherwise.

Next, the Pentagon pushed forward their own imam, Navy Lieutenant Abuhena M. Saifulislam, to tell the world that the washing, shrouding and praying over the bodies would be done after a pathologist completed autopsies. The idea that they were conducting an autopsy surprised me. It is common enough in the West, but many traditional Muslims would not accept it.

Once the autopsies were over, the military would be faced with another intolerable dilemma: what to do with the bodies. These were three long-term hunger strikers, emaciated from their protest, and if pictures of the dead men ever surfaced it would be Abu Ghraib all over again.

Desperate to counter worldwide condemnation of these deaths, the military went on their next misguided PR campaign. At the time the prisoners died the Charlotte *Observer* happened to have reporters on the base to do a fluff piece about Colonel Bumgarner, native son of North Carolina. Bumgarner had found them friendly and unthreatening, and decided to let them listen in at a planning meeting as the military set about trying to re-establish control. They were not allowed into the room, as 'classified' pictures were being viewed; instead, the journalists were told to lurk just outside the door, listening to what was being said and reporting it.

'Sir, I'm sure you have this under control,' one of the junior soldiers said to the colonel sycophantically.

'Trust me,' Bumgarner interrupted. 'We do not have this under control. If we did, none of this would ever have happened.' He collected his thoughts. 'Right now, we are at ground zero,' he continued, drawing on a metaphor directly from September 11. 'The trust level is gone. They have shown time and time again that we can't trust them any farther than we can throw them. There is not a trustworthy son of a bitch in the entire bunch.'

The solution Bumgarner proposed was to crack down on the prisoners, to make sure that nobody could kill himself in future. He ordered the officers to cut back on prisoner clothing, meals and recreation time, and to keep the lights on. He ordered more frequent patrols in the cell blocks. He said rules must be enforced to the maximum.

'If a brother covers up a window with a sheet or blanket, you give him an order and then you go get him,' Bumgarner said, using the term 'brother' derisorily.

The prisoners were asking what happened to their 'brothers', one officer noted. What should they be told?

'Acknowledge nothing,' Bumgarner said emphatically. 'Tell them it's none of their damn business.'

Anyone who looked likely to hang himself should be put in a suicide blanket, a smock that is made of tightly wound material that's hard to rip, hard to fashion into a cloth rope. Bumgarner ordered suicide blankets for various prisoners.

'Sir,' one of the officers said, 'we're going to run out of smocks.'

'Order some more,' Bumgarner instructed. 'I want them in the next seventy-two hours if I have to put you on a jet to get them.'

Later in the day, with the journalists still listening in, Senior Petty Officer Mac King walked into the colonel's office to discuss how to handle The General. The two military men thought they could safely speak in a code that nobody reading the Charlotte *Observer* would understand, but I knew who The General was – my client Ahmed Errachidi, the erstwhile chef from London's Westbury Hotel.

Officer King said The General had refused to exchange his brown uniform for an orange one, downgrading him to 'segregation' status. I was surprised this was necessary, since Ahmed had been in segregation most of the time I had known him.

'Why does this brother do this to me?' Bumgarner said, his head in his hands.

King suggested that five guards would make an FCE, a 'forced cell entry', to restrain Ahmed, cut off the brown suit and force him into an orange one. As I read this, I felt a brief pain in my chest. I could not believe they were speaking about Ahmed this way, talking about beating him up over something as trivial as a change in uniform.

'How's your relationship with The General?' Bumgarner asked King, looking for an alternative.

'Not bad,' King said.

'Well, do me a favour then. Go down there and talk to him, and tell him there's an easy way and a hard way,' said Bumgarner. 'It's his choice.' I guessed which choice Ahmed would make. He never took the easy way out.

When I read the Charlotte *Observer* report of this conversation, I immediately wrote to the government, threatening to sue them if they carried out this advertised beating of my mentally ill client. It was too late this time round, as the punishment would long since have been meted out, but perhaps the protest could save someone in the future.

As usual, the military tried to blame us, the lawyers, for the negative publicity they received when they let the North Carolina newspaper listen to their strategy meetings. 'Detainee lawyers seized on them and used them for a PR campaign in Europe to say their clients are being mistreated,' said Navy Lieutenant-Commander J. D. Gordon, referring to the news stories explaining why the Charlotte *Observer* reporters had to leave the base. 'Transparency's good, but you have to maintain situational awareness. Some people may not agree with how you do business, especially in Guantánamo. Guantánamo's a cause.'

It was only two weeks before he was scheduled to leave anyway, but Bumgarner was relieved of his position. Admiral Harry Harris had called for an inquiry 'to determine if classified and/or unclassified sensitive information about detention operations with respect to recent detainee suicides was disclosed to the public'. As usual, the information was only a threat to US national security if 'classified' meant 'embarrassing', but it looked like Bumgarner was going to be the one sacrificed this time.

I had asked for a meeting, but I had never been allowed to talk face to face with Colonel Bumgarner, a fact I regretted. There was too little trust in Guantánamo and if the suicides were the first major catastrophe on the base, it seemed very unlikely that they would be the last, unless everyone started treating each other like human beings. To date, based in part on Shaker's assessment that Bumgarner could be trusted, I still hoped that the colonel might be the one to recognise this. Now he was gone.

After he left, I learned more about him that made it seem unlikely that there had ever been much chance of a rapprochement. The week prior to his departure, as Bumgarner had talked to *The O'Reilly Factor*, Bill O'Reilly had played his normal role as cheerleader for the War on Terror. The two men discussed the escalating disturbances that had preceded the three deaths at the prison. Bumgarner rued the better treatment that some prisoners enjoyed in Camp Four, where the most compliant prisoners had been held, where there had been an incident the week before. The military version of the story had the prisoner laying a cunning trap to lure the soldiers in for a fight; from the prisoners' point of view, which I had already heard, it had been yet another incident where they had been provoked by guards showing disrespect for the Qur'an, a constant source of friction in the prison. Either way, the soldiers had come in with riot gear and rubber bullets to beat up the prisoners, who could never gather in groups of more than ten, because that was the maximum size of the cell block.

'Why I ever allowed that to happen, I don't know. But that's probably my biggest thing I . . .' Bumgarner began.

'You were being too nice?' O'Reilly suggested.

'I was being too nice,' repeated Bumgarner. He liked the sound of it, so he repeated himself. 'I was being too nice. But we responded the way I'd ask my guys to do. We had positioned everything. Nobody came out hurt. At the end of the day, everybody was fine. My guys are OK, detainees are OK. Just like a good old football game, it's about the extent of the injuries that came out of this escapade.'

'Were you surprised these guys tried to kill your guys?' O'Reilly spoke of the danger Bumgarner and his men had faced in almost reverential tones: after all, they had to go into a cell block in riot gear, firing rubber bullets and tear gas, against ten unarmed men.

'Absolutely not.'

'Why – you're nice to them! Why do they want to kill you?'

'These folks, they hate us. It's a strange thing . . .' Bumgarner began. 'It'd take me hours to try to explain this to you. They hate us, they hate Americans. I see it every day. I see a look in their eyes that I cannot explain to you. It is a crazy look when you're dealing with them.'

'All of them?'

'I'd say a large part of them. Depending on what's happening at the time. You can get – I do – I can get some guys who will sit and talk to me just like this, be a nice calm guy. And if you see him on the block with the other guys, and he gets spun up and they start spinning each other up, and they are . . . they get rather wild, rather radical.'

'They'd kill you in a heartbeat!' O'Reilly exclaimed excitedly.

'Sir, I characterise it to everybody that comes through here, make no mistake about it, they will cut your throat in a heartbeat. Make no mistake about it. We have information exactly right now . . . I haven't had . . . they had it going on this week that the deal was . . . they found a way to move two of my sinks, push button sinks,' Bumgarner began to explain, unsure of how far he should reveal potentially classified information. He cut to the conclusion. 'Well, we've taken out the springs now – they were going to use the springs to cut our throats.

We have information from various sources telling me that's what they ... my guards wear vests. And they said, well, their weak point now is the throat. So they're going for the throat, and we know it. And we'll be ready for it.'

Bumgarner seemed genuinely to believe that every prisoner had the same thing on his mind: how to kill Americans. Guantánamo Bay was not a prison but a battlefield. I had no doubt that Bumgarner spoke the mind of most soldiers, because this was the focus of all the training they received before reaching the base. Thus the cycle of mistrust became a self-fulfilling prophecy. The guards would edge nervously through each day, expecting an attack at any moment, reacting with excessive force to any perceived threat.

It was gripping stuff for the Fox TV audience, yet there was little evidence that it was true. The Pentagon routinely insisted that prisoners assaulted guards, sometimes throwing urine and faeces at them. Nevertheless Sean Baker, a member of the Kentucky National Guard, had suffered the most significant injury inflicted on a guard during the history of Guantánamo, and he wasn't injured by a homicidal Muslim but by his fellow soldiers. They had been rehearsing how they would deal with the prisoners. Baker was thirty-six, with a young-looking, soulful, slightly chubby face. He told his story to the CBS *Sixty Minutes* programme. He had joined the Guard in 1989, served in the Persian Gulf war, then quit. But it had only been a few hours after the September 11 attacks before he re-enlisted.

On 24 January 2003, not long after Baker was posted to Guantánamo, a sergeant called for a volunteer. Baker saw that no hand had gone up. 'Right here, Sarge,' he said, offering himself up again.

Second-Lieutenant Shaw Locke, in charge of an Emergency Reaction Force, told Baker what to do. 'We're going to put you in a cell and extract you,' he explained. 'Have the ERF team come in and extract you. And what I'd like you to do is go ahead and strip your uniform off and put on this orange suit.'

The jumpsuit was the same as those worn by the prisoners.

'I'd never questioned an order before. But ...' Baker recounted his story. 'At first I said, my only remark was, "Sir?" Just in the form of a question.'

'You'll be fine,' Locke assured him.

'Well, you know what's gonna happen when they come in there on me?'

'Trust me, Specialist Baker,' Locke said more emphatically. 'You will be fine.'

'Sir, you're going to tell that ERF team that I'm a US soldier?' Baker said.

'Yes, you'll be fine, Specialist Baker. Trust me.'

They agreed on a code word ('Red!') that would instantly stop the exercise if it got out of hand.

Locke wanted the training to seem real. Apparently he did not let the ERF team know that Baker was play-acting. In their subsequent statements each soldier swore he thought this was a real extraction.

As he was instructed, Baker refused the ERF team's orders and hid under the bunk. They entered the cell, beat him, choked him and slammed his head against the floor.

'Red!' Baker shouted.

The beating continued, particularly by the soldier on his back, a man called Scott Sinclair. 'That individual slammed my head against the floor and continued to choke me,' he said. 'Somehow I got enough air, I muttered out, "I'm a US soldier, I'm a US soldier."'

Even this – said with an American accent – failed to stop the attack, until one of the soldiers noticed something wrong. 'Whoa, whoa, whoa!' the man shouted.

Baker started having seizures that morning. He was taken to the naval hospital at Guantánamo.

'He'd had the crap beat out of him,' said Staff Sergeant Michael Riley, the platoon leader. 'He had a concussion. I mean, it was text-book – blank. You know, a dead stare, like he was seeing you, but really looking through you.'

Baker suffered brain damage. A military medical board determined that he suffered from mood and seizure disorders caused by a trau-matic brain injury he sustained while 'playing [the] role of detainee who [was] non-cooperative and was being extracted from detention cell in Guantánamo Bay, Cuba'.

'All I wanted to be is a soldier,' he said in the television interview. 'I feel like I've been betrayed by my own troops because ... what happened to me. I don't want this to happen to anyone else, what I'm living with daily.'

Baker was discharged from the military and is unemployed.

What would have happened if the subject had been a prisoner, instead of a soldier who ultimately shouted out with an American accent?

'I think they would have busted him up,' says Baker. 'I've seen detainees come outta there with blood on 'em – if there wasn't someone to say, "I'm a US soldier," if you were speaking Arabic or Pashto or Urdu or some other language in the camp, we may never know what would have happened to that individual.'

My clients had suffered injuries as part of the ERF routine – Omar Deghayes was blinded in one eye, Sami al-Laithi had his vertebrae fractured and there were daily beatings that occurred during the 'forcible cell extractions'. The prisoners can't take the military to court for their beatings because the McCain Amendment, designed to outlaw torture, also abolished the Guantánamo prisoner's right to bring a lawsuit against the United States. Sadly, neither can Specialist Baker, as soldiers are likewise forbidden from suing the military.

Colonel Bumgarner saw everything that happened on his watch through a particular lens. He saw all the prisoners as homicidal maniacs. Despite this, I had still believed that the colonel had acted in good faith when he sat down with Shaker and tried to resolve the hunger strike. But my faith was further shaken when Bumgarner revealed what he really thought about Shaker later in his interview with O'Reilly. The prisoners' identities remained classified, so Bumgarner never actually named Shaker, but it was easy enough to work out whom he meant.

'Is there a hierarchy in the prison?' O'Reilly had asked.

'Absolutely.' Bumgarner was emphatic.

'At the top, is –'

'At the very top there's a gentleman – I don't know if I'm allowed to tell you names – but he's clearly . . . we have a man at the top.'

'An al-Qaeda big shot.'

'Clearly al-Qaeda's big shot.'

'Saudi?'

'He is a Saudi,' Bumgarner continued. I was looking for a clue as to whom he meant. Shaker was Saudi, but surely Bumgarner could not believe that Shaker was the senior al-Qaeda prisoner on the base?

That would be even more improbable than elevating Ahmed Errachidi, the chef, to be The General. Shaker had lived in London for seven years minding his own business and raising his children; the idea that he was arm-in-arm with bin Laden was absurd.

'I've been able to cut the number one man out,' said the colonel. 'I keep him sort of in a . . . he stays where he's with other detainees, but not so that he could influence the larger population.'

So he did mean Shaker. Shaker was the only person who had been kept in total isolation for the year since the negotiations had collapsed. Because Shaker had worked so hard to help Bumgarner solve the hunger strike crisis, he had been tarred as 'leader of al-Qaeda'.

'And they fear him, the other detainees?'

'Oh, no, no. They respect him, tremendously,' said Bumgarner. 'The other brothers were in tears when they saw him —' If they were in tears, it was probably because they thought that a solution to their nightmare was at hand and Shaker was helping to engineer it.

'Right.'

'It was like they were bowing in reverence to him,' Bumgarner said.

'They've actually reconstituted their al-Qaeda cell in here?' O'Reilly asked, part aghast, part titillated.

'Oh, absolutely.'

According to Bumgarner, Guantánamo was full of al-Qaeda terrorists and here was Shaker at the top. And, Bumgarner said, the claim by lawyers that the prison was full of people swept up after September 11 in the white heat of overreaction was all nonsense. Nobody here was innocent.

'What about all these poor bakers and barbers whom they rounded up and threw in here for no reason?' asked O'Reilly, sneering at the camera.

'I'm looking for them, sir,' said Bumgarner with irony and a slight smile. 'I'm looking for them. They're out there somewhere, I reckon.'

'Because that's what the Human Rights Watch tells me,' said O'Reilly with another Elvis Presley sneer, ending the interview. 'Thanks, Colonel. We appreciate it.'

'Yes, sir.' Colonel Bumgarner nodded and disappeared off screen.

Shaker had trusted Bumgarner. He had worked hard, and put his reputation on the line, to try to resolve the hunger strike. And then he had been abandoned, left isolated in his cell for months, wondering why the colonel would not come back to see him. Yet the very fact that Shaker had been so persuasive had spelled his doom. Now, he was labelled a big shot in al-Qaeda, and the chance that he would get back to London to see his wife and four children any time soon was greatly diminished.

9

GULAG ARCHIPELAGO

Guantánamo Bay held the attention of the world in the War on Terror, but the US military always intended it to be a diversionary assault on the rule of law. People would ask me why our coalition of lawyers did not represent everyone in the prison. The first answer was that for over four years we did not even know who was there; second, the best intentioned do-gooder could not simply file a lawsuit just because we did not like what the Bush Administration was doing to these people's human rights – a lawyer had to have permission from the prisoner, or someone related to him.

For a long time the Pentagon took the position that it should not have to identify anyone in US custody, because this would provide information to the 'enemy' concerning who had been captured. Presumably it did not take long for the 'enemy' to figure this out and the Pentagon's position was undermined by the glee with which the Bush Administration would publicise the name of any significant member of al-Qaeda they seized.

Meanwhile the names of prisoners would leak out haphazardly. The US would generally inform the prisoner's home government that a particular person was in Guantánamo and the home government might inform the family, who might tell the local media. From shortly after Guantánamo's opening day, 21 January 2002, we tried to build a list of all the prisoners, compiled from media reports and assimilating the work of other organisations. By late 2004 the list had grown to 460 names. One aspect of the list remained consistent: it was always wildly inaccurate.

As much as any aspect of the Guantánamo process, the Pentagon's obdurate refusal to identify the prisoners seemed senseless and cruel. Stricken parents searched for their sons without knowing whether they were alive or dead, in Guantánamo or in some other prison. When I finally managed to get in touch with Yusuf el Gharani's family in Medina, they had not heard from him for three years. They thought that since Yusuf had made no contact their teenage son must have died; Yusuf had no idea whether his mother was still alive. Finally, on 15 May 2006, under court order in a Freedom of Information case, more than four years after the prison opened, the Pentagon released a list of the Guantánamo prisoners for the first time. There were 759 names, mostly with a date and place of birth.

After four years of intensive intelligence gathering, the list was still full of holes, even regarding the thirty-five people I was representing. Younis Chekkouri's name was implausibly mis-spelt. Hisham Sliti's nationality was wrong; the US military had not worked out the age of several prisoners. But for the first time we had an official list.

By the summer of 2006 we had only managed to get lawyers in to see about half of the prisoners then left in Guantánamo. We had plans to visit all the rest, but it would have costs hundreds of thousands of dollars, given the cost of translators. To visit 220 prisoners for a day each would run up half a million dollars in translator fees alone. The government would pay nothing.

Meanwhile, although we did not have the resources to provide adequate help even to those in Guantánamo, Reprieve and our allies at the Center for Constitutional Rights planned to move on to the next even more important stage of the investigation: the other secret prisons and the ghost prisoners held there.

We always knew that our initial objective – bringing the basic elements of the Constitution to Guantánamo Bay – was only going to be a beachhead in a far broader battle. As the numbers shrank in Guantánamo, the US military admitted to as many as 14,000 prisoners being held elsewhere. There were 500 in Bagram Air Force Base in Afghanistan, as many as 200 in Kandahar, over 12,000 in Iraq and others scattered worldwide in secret locations. The prisoners in Cuba made up only four per cent of the total.

These prisoners were ghosts held in secret prisons. In mid 2006 Reprieve was finally able to get a grant to commence work full time on a project that had been sputtering on my laptop for three years. We knew the locations of some prisons. We knew the names of many people who had gone missing. We knew that some of these people were still alive and presumably in US custody. But five years after the round-up had begun, we did not know the name of one person who could be linked definitively to a particular prison.

We had to track down all these missing people.

Khalid Sheikh Mohammed (KSM) was in his early forties. Pictures of him showed a man with a well-trimmed beard and thin receding hair. He sometimes wore glasses, slightly tinted, that broadened his long oval face. He was fluent in Arabic, English, Urdu and Baluchi.

His parents were from the Baluchistan province of Pakistan, an area that has long struggled for self-determination. He grew up in Kuwait and moved to the US in 1983, where he attended Chowan College, a small Baptist college in Murfreesboro in North Carolina, not too many miles east of Colonel Bumgarner's home town. He switched to North Carolina's Agricultural and Technical University, where he obtained a degree in mechanical engineering in 1986.

The next year he travelled to Peshawar in Pakistan and on to Afghanistan, to join the struggle against the Soviet Union in the waning days of the communist occupation. Notably, the thick dossier on KSM's activities in the next fifteen years came from proper intelligence work – there is no evidence that torture was used to compile the case against him in the years leading up to 2001. There is plenty of legitimate, unsoiled evidence that could form the basis of an honest prosecution of KSM in a legitimate US federal court, instead of a military tribunal.

When the Soviets left behind in Afghanistan a puppet communist regime, KSM remained to oppose it. In 1992, he went to Bosnia for a year to help the defence of Muslims being persecuted there, before moving his family to Qatar in 1993, where he was a project engineer for the Ministry of Electricity and Water. He was based there for the next three years, although he travelled widely to Sudan, Yemen, Malaysia, China and Brazil, building contacts with international Islamists.

In late 1994 he went to Malaysia, where he is alleged to have helped with the planning of Operation Bojinka, a Manila-based plot to destroy twelve commercial airliners flying routes between the United States and east and south-east Asia. He posed as a plywood exporter named Abdul Majid, and led an extravagant and thoroughly decadent lifestyle, hopping from go-go bars to karaoke clubs. One famous anecdote about his time in Malaysia describes him trying to impress one of his girlfriends, a dentist, by renting a helicopter to buzz the tower where she was working. He called her on a cell phone as he flew by, telling her to wave.

Operation Bojinka was discovered and foiled on 6 January 1995. In the meantime KSM had apparently developed a plot to assassinate President Bill Clinton during a trip to Manila in November 1994, as well as the Pope on his visit in 1995. Neither plot came to fruition.

With the evidence stacking up against him, the US asked the Qatari government to arrest KSM in 1996. One step ahead, he returned to Afghanistan, where he began to form a working relationship with Osama bin Laden, a little-known Islamist who had transplanted his own operations to Afghanistan after being evicted from the Sudan in the same year. Mohammed Atef, then bin Laden's chief of operations, arranged a meeting between bin Laden and KSM in Tora Bora some time in mid 1996. This was the first time they had met since the jihad against the Soviets in 1989. KSM apparently outlined a plan that would eventually become September 11.

Bin Laden urged KSM to become a full-fledged member of al-Qaeda, but KSM refused. KSM had grown to hate the US, motivated in part by his anger at American support for Israel. He wanted the fight taken to America, the country he blamed for causing all the misery in the Middle East, and he doubted bin Laden's commitment to this goal. Indeed, he only started working closely with a nascent al-Qaeda after the 1998 bombings of US embassies in Nairobi and Dar es Salaam. Only these actions convinced him of bin Laden's commitment to attacking the United States.

KSM accepted bin Laden's invitation to move to Kandahar. He became boastful of his role in al-Qaeda. He claimed that he was head of the media committee, responsible for producing propaganda videos of the attack on USS *Cole*. Given his extensive contacts around the world, KSM's job included extending the global reach of al-Qaeda. Meanwhile, he continued to mastermind the September 11 attacks. KSM, bin Laden and Mohammed Atef were the three people involved in the initial selection of targets.

Al-Jazeera journalist Yosri Fouda managed to interview KSM after the attacks.

'I am the head of the al-Qaeda military committee,' KSM boasted. When asked whether he played a role in September 11, he was proud: 'Yes, we did it.'

According to the allegations against him, his murderous acts did not stop with September 11. The French issued a warrant for his arrest in connection with the suicide bombing of the El Ghriba synagogue in the Tunisian resort island of Djerba in April 2002. German intelligence officers claimed they intercepted a call from the suicide bomber Nizar ben Mohammed Nawar to KSM three hours before the attack, with a final status update on the operation. KSM was also implicated in the Bali bombing, and the kidnap and murder of Daniel Pearl in Pakistan.

On the first anniversary of the World Trade Center attack, on 11 September 2002, the Pakistani Inter-Services Intelligence (ISI) claimed they had either killed or captured KSM during a raid in Karachi, at the same time as they seized another big name in al-Qaeda, Ramzi bin al-Hibh. This turned out to be false. Ultimately KSM was captured by the ISI on 1 March 2003 in a raid in Rawalpindi, Pakistan. He may have been captured as a result of a tip-off from two men interested in collecting the $25 million reward on his head. If so, they were disappointed. The US decided not to pay the fee and instead shipped both informants to Guantánamo Bay.

Pakistani officials said KSM was immediately transferred to US custody. Flight logs show a CIA plane leaving Washington Dulles Airport within forty-eight hours of his capture, flying to the area where he had been seized. From that time on KSM simply disappeared. In 2003 Binyam Mohamed was told by his Moroccan torturers that KSM was being held on a US base in Germany, which we later identified as probably being Coleman barracks in Mannheim. Later, on 12 October 2004, Human Rights Watch reported that eleven major al-Qaeda members, including KSM, had been held in a secret prison in Jordan, under the direction of the CIA.

Wherever he had been shuttled, it is unlikely that KSM had been having a happy time of it in US custody. In November 2005 the Bush Administration effectively conceded that KSM had been tortured in the course of the announcement that the US would not be prosecuting alleged dirty bomber Jose Padilla for the plot on New York. There were reports that water-boarding was just one of the methods of torture used on KSM – and that he was able to withstand two minutes under water, a feat formerly considered impossible. But such endurance would only have prolonged his suffering. His abusers had nothing but time.

The prisoners in Guantánamo were tagged the worst of the worst terrorists in the world, I have now personally met as many as fifty people who have been confined there, and talked to lawyers who have represented many more. I am confident that this label is wrong in the large majority of cases. Similar errors have probably been committed in other secret prisons.

Khalid Sheikh Mohammed is probably more than the unidimensional stick figure of evil portrayed by the Bush Administration. At the same time, he has boasted on television about his role in unconscionable offences. If he did commit the litany of crimes attributed to him, he has put himself well beyond the pale of free society, although that does not mean he should be beyond civilised justice. Most people would want him securely locked up; the Bush Administration would inevitably like him executed.

Since he is the highest level al-Qaeda prisoner in custody, the example of KSM fate has driven the Bush Administration's policy since his capture in March 2001. Without an honest ticking time bomb, KSM has been used as the bad case with which to make bad law.

On 6 September 2006, Bush strode up to the microphone to make an important announcement in the War on Terror. The summer had been desultory. Bush had been licking his wounds in the wake of the *Hamdan* decision: in late June 2006, the Supreme Court slapped Bush down again, declaring his military commissions illegal. The November congressional elections were looming, and with his approval ratings almost as low as Richard Nixon's during the Watergate scandal, Bush found that some Republican candidates were begging him to stay away from their constituencies. The Democrats were banging the anti-Iraq-war drum, ignoring the fact that most of them had originally voted in favour of attacking Saddam Hussein.

Bush had so few domestic friends that he had been reduced to making various placatory remarks to European leaders. Pressed by German Chancellor Angela Merkel, Bush promised that he, too, wanted to see the Guantánamo prison closed as soon as practicable.

Meanwhile I was prognosticating to anyone who would listen: Hamdan had been a godsend for Bush, I said, as it gave him a graceful way out. He could terminate his commissions and close the prison, ridding America of a particularly nasty running sore, and blame it all on 'those liberal Supreme Court justices'. Sure, Rumsfeld wouldn't like it, but Rumsfeld's star was waning. Most of the Guantánamo prisoners could be repatriated to their home countries, perhaps a small number would be put on trial in the US. The only uncertainty was what would happen to someone like KSM, currently held somewhere in his secret prison: would he simply disappear? Alternatively, there was plenty of legitimate evidence against him. Bush could bring him to the US and simply play his al-Jazeera interview. No jury in the country would take more than ten minutes finding him guilty, and they would almost certainly vote for the death penalty.

As so often proves the case, I was wrong. Bush looked in the mouth of his gift horse, and decided instead to launch another salvo of lawlessness. There were two issues on the table in his Cabinet – Guantánamo Bay, and the ghost prisoners held in secret prisons around the world. The State Department, speaking through Condoleezza Rice, generally preferred the option of closing Guantánamo, because they were constantly required to deal with foreign politicians patronising them about justice; they also wanted to bring the secret prisons into the light because international inquiries into the flight paths of CIA rendition planes were threatening daily embarrassment.

Vice President Cheney and then Secretary of Defense Rumsfeld wanted neither. So President Bush reached a solution that Karl Rove and the White House strategists thought would help shift the public eye away from Iraq. On 6 September 2006, President Bush dropped the latest of his PR bombshells in the War on Terror: he delivered a speech designed to change the agenda for the November elections, replacing the Iraq war with terrorism and homeland security.

'We're now approaching the five-year anniversary of the 9/11 attacks,' Bush said. 'And the families of those murdered that day have waited patiently for justice. Some of the families are with us today. They should have to wait no longer. So I'm announcing today that

Khalid Sheikh Mohammed, Abu Zubaydah, Ramzi bin al-Shibh, and eleven other terrorists in CIA custody have been transferred to the United States naval base at Guantánamo Bay. As soon as Congress acts to authorise the military commissions I have proposed, the men our intelligence officials believe orchestrated the deaths of nearly 3,000 Americans on September 11 2001 can face justice.'

There were cheers and applause from the carefully chosen crowd. He went on to announce that he was submitting a bill to Congress to re-establish the military commissions that had been struck down by the Supreme Court ten weeks earlier. He made it clear that passing this into law would be the most urgent priority of his government, apparently more important than the war in Iraq or, on the domestic front, the reconstruction of Katrina-torn New Orleans.

More applause.

The legislative compromise Bush had constructed was a power play, contrived to help Republicans at the November elections while mollifying the State Department. Bush dared the Democrats to advocate a more liberal law that might give rights to such a man as KSM, the architect of the World Trade Center attack, or even free him on some legal technicality. The timing of Bush's speech was carefully chosen: it was three days before September 11 2006. His message was that Republicans would be holding the line against evil, facing off against wishy-washy Democrats who simply wanted to understand how KSM's mother had abused him.

Whatever the politics of the plan, it was not a strategy for salvaging America's faltering international reputation. The prisoner transfer was an implicit repudiation of Bush's recent assurances that he would like to close down Guantánamo. The sore of Guantánamo would continue to fester.

Meanwhile, far away in some Peshawar hideaway, two days later bin Laden taunted the West by releasing his latest ninety-minute videotape to al-Jazeera. Like Bush's speech, it was timed to air immediately before the fifth anniversary of the September 11 attack. It included the martyrdom statements of various hijackers, taped before they left to fly planes into their various targets on that terrible day. It also contained footage of Ramzi bin al-Shibh discussing his part in the crime – ironically handing US prosecutors proof of guilt. Al-Shibh had arrived in Guantánamo a matter of days earlier.

I was perplexed. Bush could not be serious about this new military con-mission bill. Surely he could not expect it to pass muster before the Supreme Court, two or three years hence. Yet the bill became the focal point of all the Administration's efforts on Capitol Hill and the Democratic opposition was rarely even tepid. In the end, within six weeks the Senate passed the Military Commissions Act by a two-to-one margin.

The Act all but abolished the Guantánamo prisoners' right to habeas corpus, the challenge to the legality of their confinement. This rolled back our four years of the litigation to obtain legal visits for the prisoners – in many ways, we could soon be back where we had started, when we first went to court on 19 February 2002. Within two months of the passage of the new law, one of the more liberal judges in Washington had ruled that the prisoners could no longer bring their cases before him. The new law raised the spectre of the military trying to cut off legal visits to the prisoners altogether. Meanwhile, the part of the law that established new military commissions was in many respects a verbatim reincarnation of the earlier kangaroo court system. The 'jury' continued to be made up of military officers 'convened' (i.e. hand-picked) by the Secretary of Defense. A statement coerced out of the prisoner could still be used, so long as the hand-picked colonel in charge thought it might have some probative value. The accused could still be convicted based on evidence kept secret from him. The death penalty was still authorised for every crime – and if Bush had his way, KSM was surely going to meet his maker.

The case made by the Bush Administration for secret military trials still made little sense. The Administration argued that there was too much secret material in the War on Terror to allow for a normal trial, but this theory could not withstand the most superficial analysis. During the Cold War there were Soviet spies who worked long and hard to undermine the United States, sharing secrets about weapons that could bring about a nuclear holocaust. From the Rosenbergs on through the decades, such spies were regularly put on trial. There have long been procedures available to handle confidential evidence that is far more significant than anything KSM might have to say. The most damaging American secrets he knew would be the torture tactics of the US intelligence agencies; the Rosenbergs were intimately familiar with America's classified nuclear plans.

The second argument for eviscerating due process was that soldiers on the battlefield could not observe the niceties expected of a police investigation, like Miranda warnings, where the cops read the suspect his constitutional rights. This was a red herring: the Supreme Court had long since held that Miranda warnings do not have to be given when a suspect is seized abroad. Indeed, the Supreme Court recently sanctioned kidnapping a suspect in Mexico, at gunpoint and without a warrant, and bringing him back for trial in the United States.

The suggestion that the CIA must be free to coerce statements out of these terrorists required slightly more analysis. Here, the Administration said that force was necessary to secure life-saving intelligence, yet coerced confessions would be inadmissible in a normal court. Because this evidence would be excluded, the argument went, we would be unable to try KSM in a normal court, so we needed a different judicial process that would allow for 'flexibility' in the admission of evidence. 'Flexibility' was a euphemism for permitting the use of hearsay, coerced statements and secret evidence.

We have hundreds of years of experience and the very reason we have excluded such evidence from criminal trials is because it is unreliable. Yet this debate is a moot one. In order to convict KSM of the most reprehensible crime, there is no need to use statements coerced out of him; the prosecution need only play a videotape of his own volunteered statements. Likewise, bin Laden has provided videotaped evidence of Ramzi bin al-Shibh actually plotting the September 11 attack.

It is the nature of all criminal law, not just the cases of boastful terrorists, that a prosecutor selects charges that are most easily proved with admissible evidence. Ted Bundy is reputed to have committed more than thirty murders, but he was convicted for just one, for which he was executed in Florida in 1989. Harold Shipman killed at least 250 of his patients, perhaps as many as 400, but he was convicted on a sample of fifteen, and sentenced to life in prison in 2000. He committed suicide four years later.

Unless a prosecutor believes in reincarnation, there is little point in seeking more than one death sentence, or even more than one sentence of life imprisonment. This is particularly true in the US where, under normal federal law, the sentencing judge may take into account far-ranging information, going well beyond a single crime charged. To pretend that 200 years of criminal law must be jettisoned in the name of national security was simply another myth, propagated by Bush to justify another nightmare, the elimination of legal rules evolved over centuries to protect our most basic freedoms. Rather, this erosion of due process was really to prevent further details seeping out about America's role in torturing prisoners around the globe.

If the allegations against them prove correct, the American people have good reason to despise KSM, Abu Zubaydah and Ramzi bin al-Shibh. Until recently few Arabs had much reason to love them. However, a sham trial in Guantánamo Bay followed by executions carried out under the glare of the television cameras will elevate them to the status of martyrs. It seems clear to me that the American people will have far more reason to fear them dead than alive.

Nor is it necessary to create a law that puts only foreigners at the back of the due process bus – the harsh provisions of the Military Commissions Act explicitly do not apply to American citizens. Again the question is one of balance – what would America really gain by creating such discriminatory laws, versus the loss in respect for the United States and the rising temperature of hatred among those 'foreigners' (the ninety-six per cent of the world's population who are not American) deemed to be a class without legal rights?

There are very unsavoury reasons why certain people in the Bush Administration felt political pressure to neuter the right to a fair trial. Abu Zubaydah, a Saudi brought up in Palestine, was another of the men transferred to Guantánamo Bay. He was said to have inherited the mantle of al-Qaeda military operations chief when Mohammed Atef was killed by an American bomb in Afghanistan. More recent reports suggested that he was suffering from a serious mental illness, unsurprising given that he was badly wounded when captured and mistreated as he was shuttled around the world.

Abu Zubaydah had been in US custody even longer than KSM, and there may be even more embarrassing consequences to his appearance in a military commission. In his book *Why America Slept*, Gerald Posner describes how the US set up a fake Saudi detention centre in Afghanistan, with two agents posing as Saudi intelligence, to pretend that Abu Zubaydah had been flown to face the supposedly barbaric justice of Saudi Arabia. They expected Abu Zubaydah to tremble with fear when he discovered his 'rendition'.

However, when Abu Zubaydah was confronted by the false Saudis, 'his reaction was not fear', Posner writes, 'but utter relief'. He reeled off telephone numbers he had memorised for Prince Ahmed bin Salman bin Abdul Aziz, a nephew of King Fahd (and a racehorse owner whose horse War Emblem won the Kentucky Derby in 2002). To the amazement of the Americans, the numbers proved valid.

'He'll tell you what to do,' said Abu Zubaydah, who described the extensive assistance that Saudis had given to al-Qaeda. The final chapter of Posner's book suggests that the Saudis (inevitably tipped off by the Americans, and possibly working with them) found a solution to prevent the unwanted publicity that these revelations would have entailed. Prince Ahmed and two other Saudi royals named by Abu Zubaydah coincidentally died within days of each other, shortly after Abu Zubaydah's intelligence was passed along to the Saudi government. On 22 July 2002 Prince Ahmed died of a heart attack aged forty-three. The next day Prince Sultan bin Faisal bin Turki al-Saud was killed in what was called a high-speed car accident at the age of forty-one. The last of the three, Prince Fahd bin Turki bin Saud al-Kabir, expired one week later, officially dying 'of thirst' while travelling east of Riyadh.

Perhaps this was all coincidence. Perhaps the Saudis were cleaning up their own house without any input from the CIA. Or perhaps the United States was behind the assassinations. Seven months later, Posner writes, a fourth person named by Abu Zubaydah, Mushaf Ali Mir, a senior member of the Pakistani government, died in a plane crash in clear weather, along with his wife and some close confidants.

After five years of torture and assassinations a fair and open trial would be likely to result in indictments or impeachment of the officials responsible for these illegal acts. The Bush Administration, always more concerned with domestic publicity than long-term international goodwill and security, may find the temptation to suppress the truth too difficult to resist.

Once it began, where would the reign of the military con-mission end? For now, only foreigners can be sent before a military tribunal, but it has already been expanded to include non-citizens who live in the United States. Yet why limit the law to the current crop of people we fear, the shadowy world of al-Qaeda? All the same challenges to obtaining a conviction apply to members of the Mafia, or the Medellin cartel: close-knit conspiracies that resist police investigation and have a bad habit of eliminating informants. Loosening the rules of evidence would certainly make it easier to convict those charged with belonging to such groups, although there will be little confidence that we will convict the right people. Will the US kidnap foreign undesirables all around the world, prisoners in the war on crime or the war on drugs, and take them to various island gulags for con-missions of their own? Who says the Bush administration will stop at foreigners? Perhaps the law will ultimately be applied fairly to everyone, and undesirable Americans will lose their rights as well?

There was a second element of Bush's 6 September 2006 announce-ment that made me choke when I heard it. Perhaps to satisfy the State Department the Administration put out the idea that moving these fourteen big-name al-Qaeda prisoners to Guantánamo signalled that there are no more people in secret CIA prisons anywhere in the world. To spin the President's upcoming speech two men – furtively introduced as a 'Senior Administration Official' and a 'Senior Intel-ligence Official' – took to the microphones earlier on the morning of 6 September to prepare the soil.

'Can I just clarify . . .?' asked one journalist at the press conference. 'If you've drawn down your inventory of detainees to zero, first of all, let me just ask how recently it was that that number reached zero? And secondly, can you clarify . . . if you have put detainees in some other location, another country, some other venue, is that parsing, is that a way for you to split the details of the programme so that you can say you have zero? In other words, have you offloaded them to another location . . .?'

'No, no, no. We have been doing this – obviously, you asked the question – fourteen and . . . what happened to the rest,' the Senior Intelligence Official began, waffling vigorously but not very coher-ently. 'Clearly there has been movement within this programme for the life of the programme, so what we're seeing here today, what we're talking about here today is simply an extension of things that have been going on through the life of the programme. Not everyone who has entered this programme has stayed in this programme until just recently.'

'Let me answer your question,' interjected the Senior Administration Official, trying to bail his intelligence friend out of a tight corner. 'Tell me if this is right. What he's saying is there are no detainees in the CIA programme, held by the CIA, anywhere – in this country or overseas today.'

'Anywhere,' the Senior Intelligence Official underlined decisively.

'Let me say it again,' said the Senior Administration Official, wanting to ensure tomorrow's headlines. 'He is saying there are no – there are no detainees in CIA custody anywhere in the world. This is not a 'parsing trick' to say we're at zero because we've got them stashed someplace else. There's no funny accounting here.'

The idea that they had closed the secret prison programme was risible. Just twelve days previously the US government had published figures showing that there were almost 14,000 anonymous prisoners in Bagram Air Force Base and other detention centres, mostly in Afghanistan and Iraq. Now, twelve days later, all of fourteen had been moved. It was the tenth-of-one-per-cent solution.

The furtive officials had been careful to say only that the CIA was no longer holding prisoners, but implied that there were no ghost prisoners left at all. Yet there was no evidence that the CIA had been in charge of most of these prisons in the first place, so this merely meant that other US authorities or their allies played that role.

Could the Bush Administration really expect to get away with pretending that the secret prison programme was over, while continuing to hide prisoners from the world? If there is one lesson that President Nixon learned from Watergate, it is that the flotsam of criminal acts committed by people in power will ultimately wash ashore. Secret prisons are impractical, because in an open society they will never remain secret. Somebody, sometime, somewhere will inevitably tell.

Newsweek ran a story on the White House discussions held in the panic immediately post September 11: what should the United States do with the captives who would inevitably come into US hands? The magazine interviewed David Bowker, a lawyer who had worked in the State Department in these early days. He served on a working panel tasked with identifying the rights to which captured terror suspects were entitled while in US custody.

'White House hard-liners, led by Vice President Dick Cheney and his uncompromising lawyer, David Addington, made it clear that there was only one acceptable answer,' the magazine reported Bowker saying. 'One day, Bowker recalls, a colleague explained the goal: to "find the legal equivalent of outer space", a "lawless" universe. As Bowker understood it, the idea was to create a system where detainees would have no legal rights and US courts would have no power to intervene.'

Guantánamo Bay was boosted into orbit as the first legal black hole. The design followed a simple logic: since the 1890s the Supreme Court had made it clear that non-citizens enjoyed constitutional rights if they were on US soil. On the other hand two Supreme Court decisions in the wake of World War Two suggested that German or Japanese soldiers had no constitutional rights, so long as they were held abroad. No human rights treaty was relevant, since the US was not a party to any international convention that was enforceable in an international court.

So the White House came up with a recipe for dealing with 'terrorists': since there was a war going on, the prisoners could be held until the end of hostilities (in the case of the War on Terror, a date that may never arrive); since the prisoners had not complied with the rules of war (wearing uniforms and so on), they would be deemed 'illegal enemy combatants' and denied their Geneva Conventions rights. Then the White House simply had to find an offshore enclave that was not technically US soil and hold the prisoners incommunicado.

Guantánamo Bay clearly fitted the bill, as a tightly controlled naval base surrounded on three sides by the sea and on the fourth by a minefield. Yet, as the experiment unfolded, it became clear that there were flaws in the model. It was impossible to operate the base independently from the military. This was a significant disadvantage: the soldiers were transient and there was little chance that the sieve would hold its secrets for long. The base served the Bush Administration well for three years, past the re-election campaign in 2004, but it would be better to develop a prison that was run solely by long-term professional intelligence officers.

Guantánamo's profile was also partially public, and intentionally so. The presence of hundreds of alleged terrorists there served an important propaganda purpose, distracting attention from the failure to capture bin Laden and providing tangible evidence that the government was protecting America from dangerous maniacs. The planned show trials, like Binyam Mohamed's, were intended to provide evidence of extremism thwarted.

The logic of Guantánamo was hardly novel; indeed, history was being repeated. One afternoon I was walking into the Houses of Parliament by St Stephen's Gate for a meeting about the British prisoners in Guantánamo Bay. I noticed a marble statue of the Earl of Clarendon on the left, at the top of the stairs just before the central meeting hall. Quite why Clarendon had been honoured with a statue in the halls of democracy was unclear to me.

Edward Hyde, the first Earl of Clarendon, had been a favourite of King Charles II and had engineered the marriage of his daughter to Charles's son James. This meant that he would become the grandfather of two queens of England, but it did not prevent his fall from favour. He faced articles of impeachment in 1672. The charges against him included the allegation that he had been the architect of Britain's system of offshore island gulags around the country: 'That he hath advised and procured divers of his Majesty's Subjects to be imprisoned, against Law, in remote Islands, Garrisons, and other Places; thereby, to prevent them from the Benefit of the Law, and to introduce Precedents for imprisoning any other of his Majesty's Subjects in like Manner.'

The idea had been to lock people up on an island off the coast of Britain and deny them access to courts. Now facing an appearance in the dock himself, Clarendon chose not to wait until he was in jail and rely on the writ of habeas corpus to challenge the legality of his own detention: he fled the country before he could be convicted and spent the rest of his life in exile in France. The excesses alleged against Clarendon prompted the passage of the seminal Habeas Corpus Act of 1679.

The Bush Administration adopted the Earl of Clarendon's offshore plan, beginning with Guantánamo. But the experiment did not end there and it progressed with its own logic. US Air Force bases in Germany had a similar legal status to Guantánamo – technically not

US soil, but wholly under American control and large enough and secure enough to be free from prying eyes. At the same time as Chancellor Schroeder was trying to overcome his low poll ratings by loudly exploiting his anti-American sentiments, Germany was the European hub of rendition flights and was also playing its part in the secret prison programme. Binyam Mohamed was told by his Moroccan torturers that Khalid Sheikh Mohammed was being interrogated in Germany; Hassan bin Attash learned from his Jordanian abusers that his older brother Tawfig was there as well. Shaker Aamer described to me how Germany apparently allowed planes to land with prisoners en route to Guantánamo itself.

In the longer term, Germany would never prove a satisfactory alternative, since the local opposition to Bush's policies grew increasingly strong. An active German press would eventually expose what was going on.

The Bush Administration therefore refined its plan. The authoritarian nature of some US allies appealed to the architects on one level: there would be fewer legal or media eyes. The Middle East was home to plenty of despots who had their own motive to repress Islamic extremists. The Jordanians were a good example, loyal to the US, with the added advantage that they were competent interrogators. But Jordan also illustrated the limitations of the Middle Eastern proxy model: ninety-nine per cent of Arabs are sympathetic to the victims of American torture, as illustrated by the stories that have slipped through the net. For example, Hassan bin Attash had been rendered there for sixteen months of torture when he was still a teenager. A sympathetic guard smuggled out a letter to his family in Saudi Arabia. Later, the same guard went on haj and delivered additional messages between Hassan and his relatives in Mecca.

As Binyam Mohamed learned during eighteen months of torture, the Casablanca bombing prompted Morocco to invite the Americans to send prisoners to their secret prison at Tamara. President Hosni Mubarak's Egypt enjoyed a reputation as the country most likely to 'disappear' a prisoner. Even Syria was used for some renditions, on the old but ever-current maxim that the enemy of my enemy should be considered my friend.

However, the leakage of secrets in Arab countries was unacceptable to the United States. Early in the War on Terror some Far

Eastern allies – Thailand in particular – offered yet another possible solution. Taking prisoners there was attractive simply for its geographical distance and the locals were unlikely to be as sympathetic to the Arab prisoners who were being abused. But the Thais insisted on the removal of prisoners by 2004, jut as embarrassing rumours about cooperation with American illegalities began to seep out.

The next port of call, then, were the countries that were no longer authoritarian, but where the democratic tradition had a weaker hold and where a vigorous investigative press had yet to mature. Poland and Romania provided prisons – paradoxically, the cells were former Soviet jails of some sort – where some of the high-profile prisoners languished between 2003 and 2005. New Europe wanted to prove its use to America, but could not handle the heat when the news broke, so the US had to retreat from there also.

The world was shrinking under the influence of globalisation. The CIA and other intelligence agencies could run, but they just could not hide. There were rumours that two CIA centres were being built in Israel, one in Galilee, one in the Negev Desert. Israel had plenty of motive for hating KSM and his colleagues, and an equal motive to curry favour with its American financiers, but surely Israel would not be foolish enough to allow this kind of abuse to take place, long-term, on its territory? Only time and loose lips will tell.

There was, anyway, a far more sensible alternative consistent with the gradual distillation of the Bush Administration's logic: the Indian Ocean base at Diego Garcia. Bush could not use US territory for fear of US courts, so he would need a truly reliable ally to offer a quiet sanctuary for the next generation of secret prisons. Ultimately, and paradoxically, it would almost certainly be America's most democratic ally – Tony Blair's Britain – that would provide the latest incarnation of the Earl of Clarendon's island hell.

Blair had bought into the entire Bush campaign and had received the call for assistance – 'Yo, Blair!' Blair would not last for ever, but no New Labour successor would want to advertise that a shady deal had already been cut with the United States. Neither, if the Tories won an election, would the historically more conservative party rock such a sensitive boat.

Yet the prisoners could not be held physically on British territory, because it would be politically embarrassing and there might be unpleasantness to face in the European Court of Human Rights. The US might, rather, find inspiration from another archaic practice of penology: the hulk, or prison ship.

The Bush Administration had learned the dangers of using US naval vessels early in the War on Terror. Some prisoners, including the Australian David Hicks, had been flown out of Afghanistan to a US naval ship in the Indian Ocean prior to being taken to Guantánamo Bay. But naval vessels are legally US territory, so the ships would fall under the jurisdiction of the US courts and the prisoners would enjoy constitutional rights. The solution was to have a ship registered to a flag of convenience.

The prison ship would be manageably compact, so that the guards could all be intelligence officers. This would solve the problem of loose lips. The ship would be anchored slightly offshore of an island somewhere far from prying eyes. Using a ship would provide Blair with deniability – 'There are no prisoners being held on British sovereign territory,' the British government could bluster with technical accuracy. It would provide deniability to the US also. 'There are no secret prisons on US territory,' Bush could insist equally disarmingly.

The logic was obvious and so was the venue. Diego Garcia is the largest of fifty-two islands called the Chagos Archipelago, a roll of poker dice thrown across a patch of Indian Ocean, more than 1,000 miles from the southern point of India. The islanders were forcibly relocated in the years leading up to 1973, to provide a military facility for the British and Americans.

Diego Garcia has long been a British colony, but it has also been effectively taken over by the United States. The US borrowed the base as a massive staging post for anticipated conflicts in the Middle East. A number of ships had been permanently stationed there, so that mobile troops could be flown to vessels much closer to their ultimate destination.

As the Americans wondered what to do with their secret prisoners, Diego Garcia would have seemed an ideal solution. Whether the British and Americans actually conspired to use the base as a secret prison, time and investigation would ultimately tell. As ever, information began to leak out early on. One person speaks to another, and

247

the second talks publicly, perhaps without thinking of the consequences.

US Army General Barry McCaffrey was interviewed by Deborah
Norville for MSNBC Tonight on 6 May 2004 about the abuse of Iraqi
prisoners in Abu Ghraib. Although he was then retired, he still had
access to those deep inside the military. He had been the youngest
general in the US army, and his position had been running SOUTH-
COM, the command that now oversees the prison in Guantánamo Bay.
A question came up about the number of prisoners being held under
similar circumstances to Ahu Ghraib.

'We're probably holding around 3,000 people,' he said. 'You know,
Bagram Air Field, Diego Garcia, Guantánamo, sixteen camps throughout Iraq.'

General McCaffrey's comments helped to illustrate two important
facts: first, that the US was still taking prisoners in large numbers. In
the two years following May 2004, the admitted number of 'ghost
prisoners' would rise from 3,000 to 14,000, the official figure in the
congressional record, as of 25 August 2006. Second, as early as May
2004, there was a secret prison at Diego Garcia, and it had already
begun to leak information.

The latter fact did not undermine the plan to hold prisoners there,
as the location was too isolated for anyone to approach too close. Then,
on 11 May 2006, the British High Court ruled that the deportation of
the Chagos Islanders had been illegal. 'The suggestion that a minister
can ... exile a whole population from a British Overseas Territory and
claim he is doing so for the "peace, order and good government" of
the Territory is repugnant,' wrote the court in a withering criticism
of the government's removal of the people from their ancestral homes.

The ruling was clear: the islanders would have the right to return
home. The Americans seemed more interested in the outcome than
the British. They were having none of this pandering to a bunch of
islanders. According to a State Department official, Lincoln Bloomfield
Jr, to allow civilians on to the archipelago could potentially lead to
'terrorists infiltrating the islands'. Perhaps the Bush Administration
wanted only a particular group of terrorists to be sneaking into Diego
Garcia – those being rendered there illegally to a secret prison hulk.

Certainly, Guantánamo is no longer the place to do secret interrogations. Meanwhile, the problem of prisoners in the War on Terror

is not going to go away: there are thousands being held now and there will be thousands more in the future. If America continues along the Bush path, these prisoners will have to be taken somewhere.

This has become our greatest challenge – locating the prisoners in all the other secret prisons around the world and reuniting them with the rule of law.

While fourteen big-name al-Qaeda operatives appeared in Guantánamo on 6 September 2006, many other prisoners had been shuffled on elsewhere, suffering the various fates that await the carcass of a prisoner whose intelligence value has expired. Some of the prisoners and the disappeared may be small fry, but others are as significant as the fourteen. Top of that list is Ibn Sheikh al-Libi, a Libyan who was captured in November 2001, the first big name of al-Qaeda who found himself in US custody. He was initially held by the FBI at the airport in Kandahar, then aboard the USS *Bataan*, an amphibious assault ship in the Arabian Sea, before vanishing to other secret locations. Jack Cloonan, an officer who had worked for the agency since 1972, claimed that the FBI was developing a good relationship with – and good intelligence from – al-Libi.

Talking to Jason Vest of the *American Prospect* magazine, Cloonan described the patient and effective approach that he had outlined to his agents for al-Libi's interrogation. 'I told them, "When you get access, don't say anything at first. Sit. Say hello after a while. Offer him tea, dates, figs. Point out where Mecca is. Ask him if he wants to pray. And sit. And when he starts to look a little inquisitive, tell him who you are, and that he has rights and privileges, and that you're going to give him his rights. Just like any other interview." So they do all this. And they start building rapport. And he starts talking. . . . They're getting good stuff, and everyone's getting the raw 302s [interview summaries] – the agency, the military, the director. But for some reason, the CIA chief of station in Kabul is taking issue with our approach. . . . A series of conference calls ensued among military, CIA, and FBI officials; in the end . . . the CIA's prerogative carried the day.'

At this point a Toyota Tundra pulled up at the detention centre where FBI agents were conducting the interrogations. There was a box in the back. The CIA agents started shackling him up and al-Libi spoke to the FBI for the last time. 'I know this isn't your fault,' he said, just before they taped up his mouth.

A CIA agent leant close into al-Libi's gagged face. 'You're going to Cairo, you know. Before you get there I'm going to find your mother and I'm going to fuck her!' he screamed, before stuffing al-Libi into the box to begin his trip. The CIA apparently thought that by rendering him to Egypt they could expedite the 'mining' of his information.

While it will be a long time before the whole story floats to the surface, we already know enough about al-Libi to prove the folly of the rendition programme. When he was in Egypt, al-Libi told his torturers what the US wanted to hear: that al-Qaeda was in league with Saddam Hussein in developing weapons of mass destruction.

This intelligence found its way into Bush's public argument in support of the Iraq invasion. On 7 October 2002 Bush gave a speech in Cincinnati in which he emphasised Saddam's ties to al-Qaeda. 'We've learned that Iraq has trained al-Qaeda members in bomb-making and poisons and deadly gases,' he said, relying directly on evidence tortured out of al-Libi.

The normally cautious Colin Powell, then Secretary of State, was encouraged to rely on the same intelligence in his address to the UN Security Council in February 2003, arguing the case for pre-emptive war. Supposedly, Saddam had offered to train al-Qaeda operatives in chemical and biological weapons.

Even when President Bush was reciting them, the CIA doubted the reliability of al-Libi's information. By January 2004 al-Libi had recanted, saying he had made the statements to satisfy his Egyptian torturers. After the loss of more than three thousand American lives and several hundred thousand Iraqis, and counting, we all know the price paid for false intelligence.

'He's an entirely unreliable individual upon whom the White House was placing substantial intelligence trust,' Democratic Senator Jay Rockefeller said of al-Libi. 'And that is a classic example of a lack of accountability to the American people.'

Unfortunately, Senator Rockefeller was speaking in November 2005, long after the damage was done.

By 2006 al-Libi had been milked of all his intelligence, true or false, and was another empty carton requiring disposal. But he was not one of the fourteen men who surfaced in Guantánamo Bay. Where was he and what had become of him? Was he bound for his home in Libya, where Colonel Gaddafi had recently become a dependable ally in the War on Terror? If so, he might want to consider a painless way of committing suicide.

10

REPATRIATION

Many people find themselves unable to work up much sympathy for someone like Sheikh bin al-Libi, even if he has been repatriated to Libya to face persecution, but the rules regarding refugees were not written just for him – they apply to people who used to be our heroes, those willing to languish in prison cells for their beliefs. A refugee might have challenged totalitarianism in the Soviet Union, an authoritarian regime in South America, or a tyrant in Libya.

Today, some politicians spit out the phrase 'asylum seeker' as if it were sour milk. There have been many casualties in the War on Terror, and among the most tragic has been the Refugee Convention, which lies seriously injured, close to expiring.

The dynamics of the politics of hatred are simple: it is much easier for a politician to convince the electorate to hate a particular group of people and blame them for society's ills, than it is to resolve the complex issues that are really the cause of the problems. An increasing number of politicians employ this strategy. In America, for example, the death penalty was perhaps the most politicised issue of the Eighties. The politician would point to a society racked by crime and claim that the solution was to purge the tiny group of people on Death Row. This became the holy grail of each election. Inordinate energy and expense were devoted to claims and counter-claims about the efficacy of the death penalty, and elections would be won by those who promised the harshest punishment. The distillation of this hatred came at the end of the process, the execution. I was driving on a miserable mission to attend Mississippi's gassing of Edward Earl Johnson in 1987 when I turned on the radio. One station was conducting a call-in programme, asking for votes on whether and how Edward should die. Mississippians felt the need to phone in and express their opinion: the gas chamber was too kind and we should do to Edward what he had allegedly done to the victim. Of course, the callers had not taken the time to find out who Edward was, or even learn that he was probably innocent.

Politicians around the world employ the same ugly principles, not just the Americans. The US would like to have Yemen as an ally in the War on Terror, but that does not suit the interests of Yemeni President Saleh, whose people have a current per capita income of just US$300, one per cent that of America or Europe. Saleh has two options when he considers the future of his country: he can tell everyone to be patient, to work hard, and in a couple of generations perhaps they will be able to afford one of the Big Macs that are being advertised on their television screens. Or he can tell his people to hate the Americans: who else could be to blame for Yemen's woes, if not the bloodsucking capitalists who are daily draining the oil from the Arabian peninsula? Because he is a politician and lives in the short term, he is unlikely to opt for patience.

Some of the variations on the politics of hatred astound me, as I cannot believe they work. In 2001 the Conservative party claimed on its website that Britain was Number One in the Premier League of crime. How can anyone say that with a straight face? When I lived in New Orleans I got held up several times at gunpoint and the US has a crime rate that clearly puts it in a different division. Paradoxically, then, once politicians decide to focus on the blame game, they try to convince us that we live in a society that is much worse than in reality.

The most bizarre manifestation of the disease involves asylum seekers. Persuading voters to fear economic migrants is one thing – the spectre of a tide of people competing for scarce jobs, while often hugely overstated, is at least plausible. But how can governments have the gall to single out as a threat to the nation asylum seekers, the tiny fraction of people fleeing from one country to another to avoid persecution?

In recent times this attitude seems to have taken hold first in Australia, where pictures of boat people flooded the news. Many of those being excluded by Prime Minister John Howard were fleeing Afghanistan at precisely the moment that Australian soldiers were helping to expel the intolerant Taliban regime.

More recently, Tony Blair has turned the spotlight on those seeking asylum in Britain, calling on the tabloids to man the barricades. Yet the Home Office reports that there were just 25,710 asylum applications in 2005, and only 17 per cent of cases considered that year were granted. This means that roughly 4,370 would prevail. These represent just fewer than one per cent of the 565,000 people who migrated to Britain, or one political refugee per 13,000 citizens. The chance that the average British person would ever encounter a 2005 asylum seeker – let alone lose a job to one – was infinitesimal.

The cynical attitude of the British government to the plight of such people is pitiful and the ramifications of these policies reached deep into Guantánamo Bay, where British refugees waited in vain for assistance.

'We are dying a slow death in here,' said Omar Deghayes, as we discussed his situation in Guantánamo in August 2005. Omar's father had died a slow death in Tripoli twenty-five years before, tortured by Gaddafi, and Omar's entire family had eventually escaped to Brighton, where they were recognised as refugees. 'And you have to remember that we have not been charged with any crime. I do not understand what America is doing.'

Omar was having a hard time understanding what he was meant to have done wrong, as he languished in Guantánamo Bay for a fifth year. The US military had never formally charged him with a crime, but they did accuse him of being an 'enemy combatant'. 'The detainee is suspected of appearing in a confiscated Islamic extremist military training video showing atrocities in Chechnya,' the allegations read.

Once a year the military would put in writing some justifications for each prisoner's continued detention. The allegations against Omar in 2005 varied slightly from the year before. It was a minor victory. Now, Omar was only 'suspected' of fighting in Chechnya; previously the assertion had been bolder, that Omar Deghayes had definitely been brandishing a Kalashnikov on the Chechen rebel videotape.

Omar insisted that he had never been near Chechnya and was mystified by the whole situation. For more than three years the US military had refused to let him see this video. Even after I took on his case, I was not able to get a copy.

Where the legal system failed, I asked some journalists at the BBC to see if they could do any better. Peter Marshall, reporting for

Newsnight, managed somehow to put his hands on a copy and called to ask Taher Deghayes to come to the studio to identify his brother Omar on the video. I rode over with Taher in a taxi to White City.

'I don't *think* he ever went to Chechnya,' Taher said. From the heavy emphasis on the word, it was clear that doubts were taking hold now that we were headed to see the actual evidence. Taher was family and his worries were a testament to the prejudicial power of an accusation.

When Peter plugged in the videotape, I was on tenterhooks myself, caught up in the moment. Almost immediately a bearded radical appeared, waving an automatic weapon. The image was subtitled 'MR DEGHAYES' in capital letters, in case anyone might miss it.

Taher's relieved laugh was immediate. The man on the television looked like a young Fidel Castro, but aside from the beard there was no resemblance to Omar.

'How can you be sure it's not him?' Peter demanded.

'Of course I can be sure!' Taher has a very clipped, proper accent. 'Omar is my brother. And that's not my brother.'

We rewound the tape and it was obvious that all the subtitles were done in the same style, including the Spanish introduction. Copies of the tape had been seized by the Spanish authorities in various separate searches of the houses of Muslim suspects some years before. Apparently the Spanish had shown it to an unknown informant who had somehow identified one person on the tape as Omar Deghayes. The Spanish had then passed the tape along to the US authorities with the added captions, and the US used it as the basis for seizing Omar in Pakistan. Despite Omar's insistence that he had never been to Chechnya, he had been held for three years before anyone who actually knew him was allowed to review a copy.

Sometimes I feel that the job requires us to prove to non-believers that the sun rises in the east each morning. Some years ago a colleague did a massive study to prove that racism infects the application of the death penalty in America, as if there could be any doubt. Now we had to prove something that was obvious to anyone who knew Omar: that the man in the video was not him. We consulted an independent identification expert, Dr Timothy Valentine. He compared the images on the videotape with known pictures of Omar.

'I conclude', he wrote in his report, 'that comparison of four photographs of Omar Deghayes with the facial image from the video supplied provides no support for the contention that the video is of the same person as the passport photographs.'

The conclusion was hardly controversial. When Omar was a young child he had got too close when Taher and a friend had been fighting with wooden swords and one of them accidentally caught Omar's eye. In every picture since the age of four Omar's injury has been obvious, yet there was no mark over the right eye of the person in the video.

That night Peter Marshall put out his *Newsnight* report, and the confidence of the most hardened prosecutor should have dissolved. A British terrorism expert was watching and he contacted the programme to say that the person waving the gun was certainly not Omar, but was a man called Abu Walid – unsurprisingly, a well-known Chechen rebel. Abu Walid had been killed some time before, in April 2004.

I immediately sent all this evidence to the US military authorities and asked that Omar be set free. Yet a year later, all this had achieved was a slight rewording of the allegations against Omar. Now he was only 'suspected' of being in the Chechen tape. That remained sufficient reason to hold him indefinitely.

Even public justice can end up being a miscarriage of justice; secret justice is no justice at all. The US military preferred to continue to believe that Omar was on the tape, rather than admitting that he had been held in error for three years.

Ironically, Omar stood as a human barrier to the closure of Guantánamo Bay, because he was a political refugee from Libya, and the only people with power who could stand up for his rights – the British government – showed no interest in helping him.

Like father, like son. Omar's father, Amer, had faced persecution in Libya a quarter of a century earlier. Amer was a prominent lawyer in Tripoli who pioneered the Libyan trade union movement. When Gaddafi came to power in 1969, the year Omar was born, he offered Amer the post of Foreign Minister. Amer already knew that the regime was oppressive, for all its socialist pretensions. Amer was a man of integrity, an idealist who believed in justice, so he refused to be a part of the machine. Because of this, Amer was consistently harassed and threatened.

One Sunday in February 1980, Amer was conducting the family's weekly poetry reading when Gaddafi's men came for him. Amnesty International tried to intervene on his behalf, but it was too late. The ten-year-old Omar and his mother Zohra went to the morgue to identify the body. Tongues whispered that Amer had been tortured before he was killed.

Viewed as counter-revolutionaries, the Deghayes family were a target for persecution. Taking an exam a year after his father's death, Omar was required to write an essay on the glories of the wonderful Libyan leader. Omar had inherited his father's obstinacy, so he wrote about the Great Criminal Gaddafi. Only a sympathetic schoolteacher who brought his essay to his home and talked to Zohra prevented him from suffering the same fate as his father.

The family had to escape if they were to survive. Each year, Omar had visited Switzerland for treatment to save the sight in his right eye, after the swordfighting accident. This was the excuse for him to leave the country, but for the first six years after his father's death at least one member of the family always had to remain behind as a hostage to the regime. Finally Zohra worked out how they could all be abroad simultaneously, in two groups. Once free, they were never going back.

Naturally they went to the UK, where they had visited Brighton since 1973 and had friends. The entire family was given refugee status in 1987, recognised by the UK and the United Nations High Commission for Refugees (UNHCR). Even in the UK the family continued to receive threats from Libya.

Living in Brighton, Omar and his brother Monder played football on Sundays for their local team. Omar was an avid reader and watched *Newsnight* on the BBC. As he came to grips with his religious faith, he volunteered for Sussex Prison Services, where the authorities asked him to give religious assistance to Muslim prisoners. Once he persuaded three Muslim asylum seekers to stop their hunger strike.

Omar had seen his father's mutilated body. That vision continually reminded him that the Libyan people deserved justice. While the rest of his family took out British citizenship, for a long time he did not. He was committed to challenging the Libyan despot. He was the archetypical political refugee, willing to risk persecution for his ideals.

But now Omar was in Guantánamo. He was certainly not a Chechen rebel, and he denied being a member of any extremist group. He had visited Afghanistan briefly. He had been brought up in England, but he had wanted to see the Taliban at first hand, as he was unwilling to accept, unquestioning, the condemnation of the regime by the Western media. On his way home through Pakistan, he had been seized and sold to the US. There was no doubt what Omar's fate would be if he returned to Libya.

On 9 September 2004, in the late afternoon, a guard told Omar that he had a 'reservation' to meet with some people in another Guantánamo camp. He was taken there in shackles, with his head covered, and left for several hours in an extremely cold room with the air conditioning turned up full. He was trembling from the freezing cold.

Around midnight four Libyans entered the room, along with three Americans in civilian clothes. The first Libyan was in his forties, overweight, with a dark complexion. Omar guessed that he was from Libyan intelligence or interior security. The second Libyan was also in his forties, his face perpetually angry and hostile. He gave the impression that he was from Libyan exterior intelligence. The third was slightly overweight, with curly hair and a small Charlie Chaplin moustache. Omar was not sure of this man's role, but thought that he might have been brought along to provide information, as he said he had visited Afghanistan years before. The final one seemed to be the leader. He impressed Omar as being from the Sirtani tribe, which is Gaddafi's.

Omar was still shaking from the cold and was horrified to find himself in a room with these people. Although the US knew Gaddafi's oppressive history, they had allowed these people to come to Cuba and were now prepared to cooperate with the Libyans against him. He worked out that American intelligence had filled them in with some facts about his opposition to Gaddafi. What he did not know, until I told him much later, was that the Libyans had been given a ride from Tripoli to Guantánamo in a CIA plane.

Over the previous four years Omar's US interrogators had frequently threatened to hand him over to the Libyans and now they seemed about to do it. Omar decided to be as polite as he possibly could, because he did not want to antagonise his visitors. Despite his best efforts the Libyans were aggressive from the start.

One of the men began to talk about Amer Deghayes. 'He was nothing,' the man sneered. Omar coldly replied that they had better not say anything more in denigration of his father.

They showed Omar pictures of two people who had been forced to return to Libya by the countries where they had sought asylum. The men were Sami Abu Munder and Abdullah Sadiq, they said, people whose names Omar should know. Omar knew neither, although he had heard of Abu Munder, a well-known writer who had penned many pieces in opposition to Gaddafi's dictatorship. Abu Munder had lived in China for over a year, but under pressure he had been turned over to the United States and flown to a secret prison for several months' interrogation. Eventually he had been rendered to Libya on a CIA plane similar to the one that brought the Libyans to Guantánamo.

'Sami Abu Munder said that you are a close friend of his,' the third Libyan remarked. 'You and him joked about a lot when you were both living in London.' It was false, but Omar was not surprised that the man had cracked, given what he must have been through.

The pictures showed that Abu Munder and Sadiq had been badly abused. The second Libyan sitting now in the room with Omar appeared in some of the pictures, smiling happily at the camera. The man pointed himself out. 'Do not say these are faked pictures,' he said cheerfully. 'They are real and the world today is very small. Nobody can hide from us.'

'You are a member of LIG,' one of the Libyans said, accusing Omar of working with the Libyan Islamic Group, a group of expatriates who opposed the regime. They sneered at his denials. Another dissident called Habib had been rendered with his family from Indonesia to Libya. Under torture, Habib had implicated Omar and hundreds of others as opponents of the Gaddafi dictatorship. Omar knew of many examples where prisoners in Guantánamo were being held based on evidence coerced out of them by the Americans. In Omar's case, it seemed that the Americans were going to return him to Libya based on false information tortured by the Libyans out of people whom he did not even know.

Omar knew that these kinds of accusations meant death in Libya, with no opportunity for any kind of a fair trial. Indeed, the Libyans were explicit.

'You have no problems with the US,' said one with a dramatic pause. 'Your problems are with us.' That night they threatened and interrogated him for roughly three hours before they left.

Omar was taken, shackled, back to his cell to mull over his plight. Two days later he was forced to meet with the Libyans again for two more hours.

'It is clear as the sun that you, Omar Amer Deghayes, are one of the opposition,' the second Libyan told him. 'You will be brought to judgement in Libya. God knows who is the misguided one and who is on the correct path, and when we bring you to Libya I will personally teach you the meaning of this.'

The meaning of this was clear as the sun to Omar. 'Opposition in Libya means hanging in the streets. One of Gaddafi's slogans says this,' he explained, as we discussed it later.

The Libyan became more direct with his threats. 'In here I cannot do anything, but if I meet you later I will kill you, if you don't kill me.' The man then left.

Later Omar talked to some of the other Libyan prisoners, each of whom had received a personal visit. Some of them had spoken openly of their opposition to Gaddafi. They had also received direct threats of physical harm from the Libyan delegation.

What were the Americans doing cavorting with Gaddafi, a tyrant with a long and consistent history of atrocities? Gaddafi had been friends with almost any terror group in the world, including the IRA. His pursuit of the opponents of his regime has been obsessive and he has sent his agents chasing them around the globe, including London. Britain broke off diplomatic relations with Libya in 1984 after WPC Yvonne Fletcher was shot in St James's Square, as Libyan operatives fired at demonstrating dissidents. The Libyans accepted 'general responsibility' for this murder fifteen years later. Meanwhile relations had deteriorated further following the seizure of the *Eksund* in 1987, a ship loaded with Libyan arms and explosives destined for the IRA.

In 1986 President Reagan famously referred to Gaddafi as a 'mad dog'. Despite plenty of examples that Reagan was right, there were powerful US interests in favour of painting out the leopard's spots. In the new world order, after September 11 the Bush Administration designated the main opposition group to Gaddafi, the LIG, a 'terrorist organisation'. In March 2005 a United States official announced plans to drop Libya from its list of sponsors of terrorism. Reuters noted that 'troubling questions remain[ed]' with respect to a recently reported Libyan plot to kill Saudi Crown Prince Abdullah, but any such qualms were soon cast aside.

In November 2005 the CIA's deputy director, Vice-Admiral Albert M. Calland III, visited Tripoli for secret meetings to expand Libya's role in fighting terrorism. Calland met with Colonel Gaddafi and his intelligence aide Abdullah Sanusi. To place Sanusi in historical perspective, he was not just Gaddafi's brother-in-law; he was wanted in France, too, for the bombing of a civilian jetliner over Africa in 1989 that killed 170 people. He was convicted *in absentia* and barred from travelling to many European countries and the United States. Sanusi was also accused of killing hundreds of detainees at the Abu Salim prison.

'Sources familiar with the talks between Libyan officials and Calland described them as positive and fruitful,' wrote the *New York Times*, summarising the meeting. In 2006 Washington officially restored diplomatic ties with Tripoli.

Meanwhile the British had been rushing even faster into Gaddafi's welcoming arms. With more than 190 countries to choose from, Prime Minister Tony Blair decided to go on an official visit to Libya in 2004. Why would the man who had pressed Britain to accept the European Human Rights Convention work hand in hand with one of the world's premier dictators?

The answer was simple: in the immediate wake of the Iraq war, Gaddafi declared that he was 'renouncing' his weapons of mass destruction. For Bush and Blair this was welcome evidence that the war had a deterrent effect, moving a rogue nation into line. Neither leader honestly questioned whether Gaddafi had WMD, or why renouncing WMD might be construed as evidence that Gaddafi had given up other unsavoury practices such as torture and persecution. They tripped over each other to welcome him into the coalition fighting terrorism. In doing so they betrayed those who were fighting for justice.

For many years Britain provided sanctuary to those who would oppose Gaddafi. However, in the wake of the 7 July bombings, the British signed an agreement with Colonel Gaddafi to deport various dissidents to Libya.

On 24 May 2006 500 police officers were reported to have carried out raids targeting Libyans in Britain suspected of helping to plot and finance terrorist attacks in Libya.

'We are not talking about a direct threat to the UK,' said Michael Todd, Chief Constable of Greater Manchester Police, explaining the focus of the raids. 'We are talking about the facilitation of terrorism overseas.' In other words the British police were cracking down on people who opposed Gaddafi, allying the Manchester police with one of the most despicable governments in the world today.

Amnesty International continued to recognise Omar as a victim of the Guantánamo experiment, issuing bulletins on his case. Hundreds of concerned citizens wrote to their Member of Parliament, to President Bush and to Omar in his prison cell, expressing concern about his plight. The Save Omar campaign marched on Downing Street. The *Brighton Argus* tirelessly told the stories of his suffering in Guantánamo Bay.

Even the Law Society intervened on his behalf, since Omar had been a student member.

The problem is that Omar Deghayes is a member of the group New Labour has taught us to resent – asylum seekers. Omar wants to bring his politically inconvenient opposition to Gaddafi to Britain and this can no longer be allowed. If the government continues to recognise Omar as a refugee, it would necessarily mean acknowledging that Omar has a 'well-founded fear of persecution' at the hands of the mad dog of Tripoli. This cannot be done without offending a new ally and undercutting the claim that the Iraq war – that albatross round the Labour government's neck – achieved a victory for democracy.

During his years in US custody Omar has been visited by British officials on at least seven occasions – in Pakistan (around the time he was sold to the Americans), Afghanistan (where he was taken by the US) and eventually in Guantánamo Bay. The first British visit was by a man who gave the name 'Andrew'.

'If you help me and the Americans, soon you will be back home in the UK,' promised this Andrew.

Omar cooperated fully. He was taken to Guantánamo Bay.

Omar denied fighting in Chechnya. There was a time when the British authorities might have conducted an independent investigation – perhaps they could have compared the man on the video with the man sitting in front of them. But instead the British intelligence agents accused him of lying about it.

Instead of lending Omar assistance in his hour of need, then Foreign Secretary Jack Straw took the position that British refugees in Guantánamo Bay must apply to their country of origin for diplomatic support. In other words Omar should get help from Gaddafi. The visit of the four Libyans to Guantánamo in September 2004 proved the type of assistance he could expect.

On 10 March 2005 the Brighton City Council voted overwhelmingly to welcome Omar back to his home town. If only all politics truly were local. In London the British government steadfastly refused to take any step to help him.

Omar was only one of the victims when the British and American governments abandoned the principles of the Refugee Convention.

Until President Bush transferred the fourteen big-name members of al-Qaeda to Guantánamo Bay in September 2006, there were few genuine terrorists there, but there were plenty of people who had been in Pakistan or Afghanistan for various reasons, sometimes finding them convenient to escape an oppressive government. Even among my small group of clients there were several. Sami al-Laithi, an Egyptian, had been one of them, living first in Pakistan, then Afghanistan, teaching English and playing football, preaching democracy and trying to avoid the long arm of President Mubarak. At the best estimate, our Guantánamo legal team thought there were probably as many as a hundred people among the prisoners who needed to claim asylum. Who knew how many political refugees there were in the other secret prisons?

What would the US do with them? From President Bush downwards, the Administration had already labelled the prisoners as 'bad men', the 'worst of the worst' terrorists; how could they now expect other countries, with their own domestic political agendas, to accept these men as refugees?

The harsh conditions at Guantánamo did help partially to resolve this dilemma: many prisoners, like Sami al-Laithi, who feared persecution by their own governments, now preferred to return home and face the music rather than stay in Guantánamo.

However, there were plenty of people in Omar's position who knew that repatriation meant certain death. No matter how bad life had been in Guantánamo, these men were not inclined to believe that the Iraq war had turned tyrants into democrats.

For instance, there were twenty-three Uighurs held in Guantánamo Bay, five of whom were found not to be enemy combatants in their CSRT hearings. There was no justification for holding them. When I first heard the term I had no idea where the Uighurs were from. I soon learned that none of them was an enemy of the US, as they had already signed up as enemies of China, the nation that had annexed their homeland, Turkestan, in 1949 and had repressed its inhabitants ever since.

The Chinese-American lobby was very vocal and pressured the Bush Administration to promise that the Uighur freedom fighters would not be returned to China. Where, then, should they be sent? The US State Department struggled to find an asylum state. The Europeans were not going to bail Bush out. The Turks, often friends to the ethnically related people fleeing Turkestan, also refused.

Months went by and the Uighurs' lawyer waged a constant campaign in the courts. He was P. Sabin Willett, who came to the battle with the backing of one of the largest law firms in the country, Bingham, McCutcheon. Sabin forced the authorities to move some of the Uighurs to Camp Iguana, once the block for the juveniles, where conditions were better. He persuaded the courts to allow regular telephone calls to these prisoners. He raised his clients' right to maintain a prison garden, as mandated by the Geneva Conventions. Denied spades and seeds, the prisoners in Camp Iguana were reduced to digging with a spork (the plastic mutation of a fork and spoon). They patiently scraped a small square of soil and irrigated it with the yellow Guantánamo water, softening the earth. They scraped and irrigated; scraped and irrigated. Finally they sowed seeds hoarded from the fruit and vegetables they were fed. The watermelon died; a two-inch lemon tree clung to life.

Eventually the military wilted. The US authorities found the only country in the world that would offer asylum and five innocent Uighurs were shipped off to Albania. After suffering for decades under the bizarre Enver Hoxha and his Maoist regime, and after finally throwing off the yoke, Albania was willing to stand up to complaints from China, which demanded the return of these 'terrorists'. While they exchanged Camp Iguana for an Albanian refugee camp and life was still miserable for the men, it was a step up from Guantánamo and Sabin continued to look for a better alternative.

The Uighurs' story underscored the problem that the Bush Administration had created for itself in Guantánamo Bay. Scores of refugees remained in the prison, and there were others in even shadier detention centres around the world. Now that these prisoners had all been tarred as terrorists, it would prove very difficult to find asylum countries for many. The US would be tempted to succumb and force many of these prisoners to return home no matter what the consequences.

11

DEFENDING FREEDOM

On 12 September 2001 the United States awoke to find a reservoir of international goodwill. Former enemies competed in their condolences. Political criticisms and jealousies were swept to one side and, with hardly a dissenting voice, the world demanded that those who had planned the horror at the World Trade Center be brought to justice. Nothing, everyone agreed, could have justified this crime against thousands of innocent people.

On 12 September 2001 President George W. Bush stepped up to the microphone, poised to shed his bumbling image. World leaders recognised that the United States was the victim and offered the victim the opportunity to lead. Bush was given the chance to become a statesman.

On 12 September 2001 the name of al-Qaeda had barely penetrated the consciousness of even the well informed. The gang had carried off one of the most shocking crimes in history, but it was a tiny group of zealots with no realistic chance of denting the awesome power of the United States: the complete ranks of this enemy could be printed on a couple of pages of paper.

Disgusting though the crime was, there was no doubt that America would survive it. Now was the time for the US to run with the tide of global sympathy to press forward its agenda of democracy and freedom.

Just five years later, the United States was regarded in the international community with disappointment, anger and even revulsion. More people had a negative opinion of the US than at any other time in the nation's history. Al-Qaeda had failed to make a single additional attack on US soil, yet it had achieved a notoriety and an ability to inspire fear massively out of proportion to its size. Instead of sitting impotent in prison or a Peshawar cave, bin Laden attracted thousands to his banner of hate.

Far from growing into a statesman, President Bush was internationally despised and reviled. Abroad, his credibility was lower than Richard Nixon's; sadly, if a prisoner in Guantánamo Bay alleged abuse, the overwhelming majority of the world's population was likely to believe the prisoner over any denial by the President, and with good cause.

Outside the supposedly secure homeland an American passport had become a dangerous commodity. There was talk of Armageddon in the Middle East. In just five years the world had become a dramatically more perilous place.

How could it all have gone so terribly wrong?

With the benefit of years' hindsight, condemning liberals have leapt to the podium to denounce their neocon enemies. After the looming Soviet bear lost its claws, the US had drifted, somehow less certain of itself as the hyperpower in a unipolar world. Bush had been wafting along – would he be a compassionate conservative or a conservative zealot? But from September 11 on his world became black and white – or bearded versus clean-shaven.

The liberals suggest that the Bush Administration bought the idea of Guantánamo Bay at a fire sale and rushed it into production without a second thought. The experiment was so ad hoc that the base commander was given only ninety-six hours to prepare Guantánamo for the arrival of the first prisoners in January 2002. The architects of the plan, we are told, soon saw that Guantánamo would yield little intelligence of any consequence – it was all a cynical effort to demonstrate to the American people that something was being done to combat terrorism. The Bush Administration could not capture bin Laden or Mullah Omar, so they incarcerated 773 prisoners in Guantánamo to pretend that the war was somehow being won.

Life would be much simpler if the liberals were right and the neocons concocted this as a conspiracy to distract the electorate. Yet it just is not the case. From the perspective of the Bush Administration the Guantánamo experiment was thoroughly successful for a long time. It drew negligible dissent within the US well into 2006. As late as 27 June of that year, when some of our clients had been held for four and a half years without charges, a *Washington Post* poll showed that fifty-seven per cent of Americans supported the use of Guantánamo to hold 'suspected terrorists', with only thirty-seven per cent opposed. Even more – sixty-seven per cent – believed that the government was protecting the rights of the prisoners. A smaller majority, fifty-one per cent, felt that the base had made America more secure; the rest did not necessarily condemn it, they merely doubted that it contributed much to security. Even as late as October 2006, the Military Commissions Act, Bush's proposal to create new kangaroo courts for the prisoners, passed Congress with little debate and by an overwhelming margin.

American politicians have always been more realistic than their European counterparts. They know who elects them: foreigners have no vote at all and not many of the American votes really matter. In order to win, the President needs only a slim majority of those citizens who bother to go to the polls. Among the right-wing voters upon whom Bush relied, support for Guantánamo remained strong.

Meanwhile there was a thin sliver of the US population where Guantánamo continued to find almost unanimous support well into 2006: the Bush Cabinet. Bush's three most influential advisors, Vice President Dick Cheney, Secretary of Defense Donald Rumsfeld and Rumsfeld's former deputy Paul Wolfowitz, did not champion Guantánamo Bay out of cynicism. The truth was much more dangerous: they were unshakeable in their belief that Guantánamo and the archipelago of secret prisons served a crucial purpose.

There were various predictable reasons why Cheney–Rumsfeld–Wolfowitz would cling to this view. First, their perspective was shaped during the Cold War, and they harboured a knowing certainty that the world outside the US was nasty and brutish. They saw everything through this prism. The trio had long since developed a plan to protect American interests against these threats – a plan that began and essentially ended with the role of the US military and other security services.

History teaches us, they said, that only the threat of force under President Reagan toppled the Soviet Union – the US had more bombs and more money, so it was a battle that the 'Evil Empire' could not win. Today's terrorists are hell-bent on violence and destruction, and it is naïve to think that anything other than force will protect the United States. The US military and the newly created Department of Homeland Security would be the bulwarks against this peril.

The neocon three would pay lip service to the possibility that the military might make mistakes, but they would belittle the chance of errors on a large scale. After all, these prisoners were Arabs, seized by the US military close to the Afghan battlefield, far away from their Middle Eastern homes. They could have no innocent reason for being there.

For someone in the office of vice president or secretary of defense there would be an additional factor that would prevent them from recognising the innocence of prisoners in Guantánamo. Most of us, when we latch on to an improbable belief, are surrounded by reminders that we might be mistaken. For a politician in the stratosphere of government there is rarely anyone available to deliver the long brown envelope of home truths on a regular basis. His acolytes are likely to be sycophantic, and his tour of the Guantánamo prison will be sterilised. It was therefore virtually inevitable that Cheney–Rumsfeld–Wolfowitz would remain convinced that the chance of a mistake in Guantánamo was infinitesimal.

Thus the trio would see little practical need for checks against the power of the military as jailers. Meanwhile step two of their plan involved ensuring military effectiveness against the enemy. It is vital, they would say, to avoid bureaucracy and ensure that a mean, lean fighting machine can sweep into action with maximum efficiency. The Constitution gives the President the power to conduct war rather than Congress for this very reason: it would be impossible to wage an effective military campaign if the Democrats and Republicans had to debate every deployment. Thus the trio's philosophy would seek to enhance the power of the President over the Congress at every stage.

As for the other branch of government – the judiciary – it has nothing to contribute to the War on Terror. The long-established Cheney–Rumsfeld–Wolfowitz mantra is repeated over and over: surely enemies on the battlefield cannot have legal rights? How do you expect our brave boys to call timeout during a firefight to summon the judges and lawyers?

Indeed, the trio firmly believed that foreign citizens held on 'foreign' soil in Cuba have no enforceable legal rights anyway, so there was no need for lawyers. It bears repeating that in the United States the notion of human rights is philosophical and the source of legal rights – the Constitution – is a pact between US citizens and their government, without reference to anyone who does not carry an American passport. There was no need for Cheney–Rumsfeld–Wolfowitz to justify why foreigners have no legal rights – they just don't.

The struggle to keep lawyers and judges out of Guantánamo Bay also grows out of an antipathy towards the judicial process. Cheney–Rumsfeld–Wolfowitz would regard the injection of lawyers into every aspect of life as symptomatic of the American malaise, where men of action – not just on the battlefield but also in the boardroom – are hampered from getting on with the job. Thus Guantánamo is not an isolated skirmish where a strategic retreat is acceptable, but a symbol of a far broader struggle for the lifeblood of the American Way.

Contrary to the expectations of the liberal cynics, Cheney–Rumsfeld–Wolfowitz were not going to back away from Guantánamo because they knew they had done wrong. They did not believe this for one moment. They were fighting a fierce rearguard action against forces who, they believed, were chipping away at the foundations of America.

Of course, it would be wrong to view the Bush Administration's approach as wholly monolithic. There are two poles of the Cabinet. To some extent every government operates a series of push-me, pull-you policies, the inevitable compromise between one democratic interest and another. Nonetheless, from an international perspective the Bush administration is an anomaly: the two poles are not liberal and conservative, but rather the far right and the extreme right.

The extreme right, represented by Cheney–Rumsfeld–Wolfowitz, has goals that are clear and remain consistent. For them Guantánamo Bay has been an opportunity to implement their ideology, allowing the military to defend freedom in whatever manner the military might see fit. While Condoleezza Rice is less comfortable when it comes to sacrificing core American values – such as the Constitution – she shares much of the trio's Hobbesian view of the world. Inevitably, someone in the position of Secretary of State tends to take a more nuanced position, because she is forced into a daily communion with the diverse views of foreign governments, instead of the more homogeneous environment of domestic politics or the US military.

Yet Rice was more conservative than her predecessor, Colin Powell. On 13 September 2006 he sent an open letter to Senator John McCain, the Republican who was leading the fight for a ban on torture, urging that the Military Commissions Act be rejected.

'The world is beginning to doubt the moral basis of our fight against terrorism,' Powell wrote, opposing the White House effort to undercut various legal rights.

But Powell had resigned after the 2004 election, and the Bush Cabinet had consolidated its move to the right, away from Powell's moderate influence. Now, Bush dismissed this criticism out of hand saying simply that his former Secretary of State did not understand what was at stake.

Guantánamo was introduced to the world, almost fully formed, in January 2002. There may be plenty of naysayers now, but international criticism of Guantánamo was slow in coming. The balance of world opinion shifted gradually, gathering little momentum until the spring of 2004, when the photographs of Abu Ghraib added credibility to the abuse allegations that lawyers were making about their clients in Guantánamo.

The international disdain did not come from the creation of the prison itself, but from the manifestly hypocritical rules that governed its operation. There has always been torture, but the Bush Administration added a new twist – torture committed by those who were loudly condemning it at the same time. The prison base evolved into an icon of US hypocrisy, established in the name of democracy and the rule of law to preserve 'our values' against the onslaught of Islamic fundamentalism.

Internationally, Guantánamo began to drain a large quantity of the September 2001 reservoir of goodwill. For a long time, with polls running high at home, the Bush Administration shrugged at international opinion. The US is the leading proponent of domestic democracy in the world, yet American antipathy towards international democracy is pathological. Democracy requires a reasonably balanced system of voting, yet when all 192 members of the UN have exercised their right to vote, the US insists that five members of the Security

Council should have a permanent power of veto (with an equal lack of justification, the British and the French assert the same right). In a democracy no citizen can refuse to pay taxes because he disagrees with a particular government policy, yet the US has withheld its payments so long as the UN provides support for abortion. A citizen in a democracy can hardly refuse to submit to the government's criminal laws, yet the US declines to recognise the International Criminal Court for fear an American might actually get charged and convicted for a war crime. The US has still to sign up to its first human rights document that is enforceable in an international court. And so the litany of hypocrisy goes on, all cheered by a domestic audience that perceives no irony.

Meanwhile, the Bush War on Terror failed in its most obvious task: the most powerful nation on earth could not capture one man, Osama bin Laden. At the same time, Bush's tactics created a world full of new dangers for those holding American and British passports. Yet the politicians had established their policy, and now clung to it with uncompromising rhetoric.

'The new anxiety is the global struggle against terrorism without mercy or limit,' Tony Blair exhorted the Labour Party Conference at his swansong speech in September 2006. 'This is a struggle that will last a generation and more. But this I believe passionately: we will not win until we shake ourselves of the wretched capitulation to the propaganda of the enemy, that somehow we are the ones responsible . . .'

There are various responses to Blair's position and the first came from the British judges . Al-Qaeda was hardly 'without limit' in 2001 — the original al-Qaeda lunatic fringe consisted of bin Laden and a very small band of associates. As Blair used their crimes as an excuse to dismantle legal rights, the judiciary fought back.

The law lords declared illegal the Belmarsh experiment where the Blair government locked up various perceived extremists without trial. 'This is a nation which has been tested in adversity, which has survived physical destruction and catastrophic loss of life,' wrote Lord Bingham. 'I do not underestimate the ability of fanatical groups of terrorists to kill and destroy, but they do not threaten the life of the nation. Whether we would survive Hitler hung in the balance, but there is no doubt that we shall survive al-Qaeda.'

Bingham went on to a broader question: what is it about the British nation that we should be trying to protect?

'What is meant by "threatening the life of the nation"?' he asked. 'The Armada threatened to destroy the life of the nation, not by loss of life in battle, but by subjecting English institutions to the rule of Spain and the Inquisition. The same was true of the threat posed to the United Kingdom by Nazi Germany in the Second World War. This country, more than any other in the world, has an unbroken history of living for centuries under institutions and in accordance with values which show a recognisable continuity.' Ultimately, consistent application of the rule of law has been the basic right of anyone living in Britain.

On a second point, Blair was protesting too much when he denied that 'we are the ones responsible' for the escalation of hatred. No matter what the policies of the West may have been, of course there was no excuse for the wanton slaughter of 3,000 New Yorkers. To be sure, Blair did not create the original al-Qaeda gang, who had their own mixed bag of complaints that Britain neither provided nor could negate. But the subsequent actions of Bush and Blair have provoked much of the hostility that now exists.

Bush has been the greatest recruiting sergeant that al-Qaeda could have imagined, and the new 'home-grown British terrorists' are the direct and bitter fruit of Blair's policies. Blair's actions did not simply light the fuse on a pre-existing extremist. The four British men who blew up themselves and their victims on 7 July 2005 had not been contemplating murderous attacks since childbirth, waiting for a convenient pretext to vent their latent homicidal tendencies. They were goaded to commit a terrible, criminal act by the policies that Bush and Blair adopted. Egged on by its own populist oratory, the British government, which was morally obliged to provide the safest possible society for all, instead provoked discord and violence. To pretend otherwise is to adopt the fantasy that foreign policy – be it Guantánamo or Iraq – can exist in a vacuum.

Bush and Blair have contrived to make the lives of every person on this planet vastly less secure.

*

It isn't just me saying this. Consider the 2006 National Intelligence Estimate, a report compiled by all the US agencies and approved by John D. Negroponte, director of national intelligence. Although such a document is heavily political, it could not avoid the inevitable: 'An opening section of the report, "Indicators of the Spread of the Global Jihadist Movement", cites the Iraq war as a reason for the diffusion of jihad ideology,' the *New York Times* reported. '"The Iraq war has made the overall terrorism problem worse," said one American intelligence official.'

Of course this is true. Bush resisted publication of the full report, for fear of other truths that might make the front pages. What might the National Intelligence Estimate have made of the Guantánamo prison experiment? Any assessment would balance the two sides: the military's assertion that Guantánamo Bay is playing a crucial role in the War on Terror, and the critics' belief that Guantánamo has been a moral and practical disaster.

On the military side of the scale, the justification for holding the prisoners was to extract intelligence and to prevent them from committing crimes in the future. Successive generals and admirals running the base have boasted about the 'very significant intelligence' that has been obtained from the prisoners; I have seen some of it and, while I cannot reveal what I have seen, I have yet to see intelligence that is of any real value in protecting the US or the UK. The unclassified evidence that I am permitted to discuss illustrates the problem: Omar Deghayes was not a Chechen rebel – he has never been to Chechnya, and he is not the man brandishing the Kalashnikov in the US military video. British prisoners Shafiq Rasul, Asif Iqbal and Rhuhel Ahmed were not the three shady figures beside bin Laden in another videotape – at the time it was made in 2000, they were in Birmingham. Yusuf el Gharani was not a twenty-year-old member of the London al-Qaeda cell in 1998 – he was eleven, and had never left Saudi Arabia. Ahmed Errachidi was not The General of al-Qaeda in Afghanistan in July 2001 – he was a chef at the Westbury Hotel in London. These are just examples from my own small group of clients. Other prisoners probably have even more compelling stories, but many have no lawyer to tell.

To be sure, there must be some intelligence of value that has come from the base, but – as former CIA Agent Mike Baker told me – it is probably impossible to sort the wheat from the chaff, because so much coercion has been used. Foolish decisions made based on false intelligence can cause immense harm, as when Bush marched to war in Iraq relying on the coerced confession from Sheikh al-Libi, that purported to link Saddam Hussein and al-Qaeda. Certainly, there is no evidence that the prisoners, locked up for five years, have any current knowledge of crimes planned for the future, so that whatever value Guantánamo might once have had has surely dissolved by now. As 'Big Bill' Cowan said, if there is any excuse for torture, it has evaporated 24 hours after the prisoner's capture.

The military does have one argument that it makes without fear of contradiction: while they are being held in Guantánamo, none of the prisoners will launch a violent attack on the US mainland. Yet, in all probability, the majority of prisoners had never planned any such action. While I have heard none of my clients advocate violence, now their disaffection with the US is complete.

Ultimately, the purported 'benefits' of Guantánamo cannot easily be measured because the US military insists on secrecy, but it is still possible to assess whether experiment with a lawless prison has been a success. The 'cost' of Guantánamo to the US is readily quantifiable: how much free and, from bin Laden's perspective, 'positive' media coverage has al-Qaeda received as a result of the endless stories about injustice at the prison? This can be identified from the hundreds of thousands of articles that have been published worldwide condemning the hypocrisy of holding the prisoners without trial. It is also measurable from opinion polls: by the summer of 2006 the proportion of Europeans who felt that the United States was a leader in human rights had halved since 2001. In Muslim countries where many people had formerly admired the United States, the situation had become even worse – a poll covering Egypt, Pakistan, Jordan and Turkey found that more than two-thirds in each country now had a negative view of America.

'It's an international public relations disaster,' said an anonymous 'Senior Defense Intelligence Agency Official' in early 2004, quoted by journalist David Rose in his book *Guantánamo*. 'For every detainee, I'd guess you create another ten terrorists or supporters of terrorism.' When I discussed this with David two years later, we agreed that the intelligence officer would now have revised his estimate from ten to a hundred new heads to the al-Quaeda hydra for each prisoner held.

So why did both the British and the American governments latch on to the idea that by dissolving human rights we could better protect a society that has been built to preserve the rule of law?

There is a bizarre and fascinating paradox in many actions of government: politicians seem to believe that we can best approach our ideal world by marching firmly in the opposite direction. You don't need to be an idealist to find this attitude perplexing.

While the finer points have been debated for centuries, most people agree in general terms on the elements of Utopia. An ideal society would reflect equality between citizens, no war, no violence, justice for resolving disputes and so forth. Admittedly, Utopia is by definition not our reality, but it is the Pole Star that leads us towards the future. Reasonable people may differ on the best path towards that goal, but there are some routes that are so obviously wrong that we can reject them out of hand.

Our current politicians try to convince us that we should impose democracy at the end of a gun barrel, a solution that has little logical appeal, and that proved wrong in Vietnam and wrong in Iraq. In a stampede of tabloid hysteria, the government dissolves elements of the rule of law that have been carefully constructed over generations. So men with beards in our country should not have legal rights because they may be dangerous, as if the serial killers who still have these rights are not.

Both America and Britain have been admired around the world for their evolving standards of decency and freedom. The idea that we can move an incremental step closer to ideal justice by abolishing various elements of due process – whether in Guantánamo or Belmarsh – is a very difficult proposition to defend, yet in the wake of September 11 it was adopted as government policy in both countries.

Indeed, Belmarsh prison in London is as good an example of this as Guantánamo. In the wake of September 11 it was used to detain a dozen prisoners without trial until the House of Lords struck it down. When this detention ledger is totted up, what did it achieve?

The Belmarsh policy focused on a small number of individuals who might one day commit some unspecified offence, while alienating and angering thousands of others – many Muslims included – who saw the policy as unfair. It was not just wrong, it was ill-advised.

There are many other examples of policies where our politicians lead us directly away from our ideals. Take the endless propping up of repressive governments. American support for one repressive dictator (Iran's Shah) ended in tears with the 1979 revolution, leaving an implacable enemy of the US in power. The US chequebook then bounded across the Iraqi border to support another dictator (Saddam Hussein), who launched a bloody war against Iran that created a generation of victims. When Hussein slipped his collar to invade Kuwait, the US transferred its allegiance to another regional mastodon, Saudi Arabia. Now, in addition, Bush and Blair support dictators against 'terrorists' across the globe, from Libya to Pakistan. This immoral support for immoral governments spins an inevitable cycle where the new regime that ultimately turfs the dictator out of office knows America (and now Britain) only as its enemy.

I once had the opportunity to ask Robin Cook about the phrase most often ascribed to him as Foreign Secretary.

'I never used the phrase "an ethical foreign policy",' he replied, rather testily.

I was not sure why he denied it so emphatically. It is an aspiration that should guide any sensible government.

Both the Bush Administration and the British government have gone horribly astray since September 11 2001. Why is this? How can so many intelligent people have got it so terribly wrong?

Part of the explanation is that they have been seeking to answer the wrong question. It is therefore unsurprising that they get the wrong answer.

After September 11 it was perhaps predictable that the Bush Administration concentrated on identifying the best way to prevent a recurrence of a similar specific event, sidelining many other concerns. Bush adopted harsher laws like the Military Commissions Act, retrenched civil liberties, and incarcerated plausible suspects without trial. In adopting this course of action, the focus of the Bush Administration remained fixed on how to stop an individual crime that might happen in the future.

The lesson of Guantánamo, and its parallel at Belmarsh, is clear: in seeking to prevent a particular suspected terrorist from committing a hypothetical crime, Bush and Blair jettisoned the values they were trying to protect. By doing so, they radicalised thousands, if not millions.

Bush and Blair seem to share a profound misunderstanding of a government's obligations towards its citizens. The government must accept responsibility for the overarching safety and well-being of society, rather than just the prevention of particular criminal acts. If we look to the well-being of society as a whole, the answers become both very different and, for the most part, much more obvious. For Britain, the main question posed by the government should not be how to minimise the chance that one particular event (a plane flying into a building, or a bomb in the Underground) will take place some time in the future carried out by a particular person who we can detain or deter. Rather, the driving question becomes a broader one: how do we minimise the number of people who will be victims of violence, while at the same time adhering to our moral values? Ensuring that we make no more enemies becomes more important than eliminating enemies who already exist.

The answer to the questions facing us are often much simpler than the politicians would have us believe. By far the most efficient counter-terrorism weapon in our arsenal is the effective enforcement of human rights.

The first rule in my counter-terrorism handbook is that if you behave with decency, upholding your own standards, there will be fewer people who want to kill you. In the summer of 2001, there were extremists of all types who were preaching bizarre opinions, yet few people listened to them, and the UK was deemed secure. It is not difficult to figure out why, five years later, people staggered out of London Underground stations with glass embedded in their faces. We ceded our claim to the moral high ground and strengthened the position of certain extremists who were offering a stark alternative. The extremists' message of hate has been peddled for centuries.

Years ago, I bought a copy of *Mein Kampf* because I wanted to compare it to what the prosecutors were telling jurors in their efforts to execute my clients in the Deep South. I sidled around bookshops, coyly approaching the sales personnel.

'Do you have a copy of *My Struggle* by A. Hitler?' I asked, hoping somehow to disguise the name with an initial. They would frown at me, and suggest that I try the local Ku Klux Klan bookshop. I finally found a copy.

Early on, Hitler's career ran parallel to that of Oswald Mosley in Britain. Mosley wrote a book as well, called *My Life*. His book immediately disappeared into the rubbish bin of literary history because he never became more than a fringe figure. The British people had an acceptable choice between parties that offered some hope for the future. The Germans felt they did not. In the Treaty of Versailles, the Allies kicked a dog when it was already down. Versailles was understandable, given the millions of dead strewn all over Flanders, but nevertheless a disaster. The German people became desperate, and saw no viable alternative to Hitler and his nationalist populism. Millions more became his victims.

Osama bin Laden was an extremist long before September 11. His fifteen minutes of infamy could have been rapidly swallowed up in international condemnation. Instead, President Bush chose a series of policies that undercut his own moral platform. In 2004 bin Laden would have supported George Bush for re-election against the moderate Democrat John Kerry because he knew which candidate would best attract Muslims to the banner of al-Qaeda.

These are hardly novel insights: the IRA credited the harsh policies of the British government, such as internment, with recruiting more volunteers than the group could hope to attract on its own. Guantánamo Bay has played the same role for bin Laden. Abu Ghraib is another example. Whatever dubious intelligence may have been obtained by abusing prisoners, those photographs were responsible for attracting hundreds of horrified Muslims to fight alongside insurgents in Iraq, each intent on driving the American infidels from the Middle East.

The second rule of counter-terrorism is that if you behave decently, you will get better intelligence from your subjects than if you torture people. There are two elements to this: more people will want to help you, and you are more likely to obtain the truth – and know that it is the truth – when you are asking questions.

Whether I was talking to Mike Baker of the CIA, or to prisoners who have faced torture, it was clear that someone was much more likely to tell the truth if he was treated with respect rather than abuse. The majority of prisoners I have met in Guantánamo initially had no reason to dislike America and were willing to talk honestly. When they were abused, they were willing to say anything and only wanted to repeat what their abusers wished to hear. The resulting intelligence was worthless, as the interrogator could not know what was true and what was false.

The third rule of counter-terrorism is that decency is not the equivalent of appeasement. It is the opposite. We do not have to sympathise with bin Laden to advocate an end to Belmarsh, Guantánamo and the secret prisons.

Likewise, countries that refused to join the Iraq invasion were not appeasing Saddam Hussein – they were respecting the overwhelming will of the international community. We do not have to be pacifists to say that the US military should stop bombing innocent civilians in Iraq and Afghanistan.

It is not a matter of 'coddling terrorists' – it is simply a matter of living up to our ideals. Ultimately, it is also common sense.

The fourth rule of counter-terrorism is that we should not ditch our values at the first sign of trouble. Such a reaction is no more justified today than it was when our society was threatened by other enemies – whether they were the Nazis with their gas chambers, the Japanese with their kamikaze bombers, or the Soviets with their nuclear missiles. Each time we have retreated from the rule of law in response to such threats, history has taught us that we acted in haste and we now regret at leisure.

If a prisoner is suspected of a crime, a fair trial has been the preferred mechanism for passing judgement for hundreds of years in both Britain and the United States. The trial system may be imperfect, but it remains the best way to go about the task – and it is generally effective. There is no need to resort to torture evidence, or military commissions, to obtain convictions.

There is nothing intrinsically ironic about the Guantánamo military motto 'Honor Bound to Defend Freedom'. Our leaders made it so, not the soldiers who must recite it daily. We are all bound to defend the rights and freedoms of those who are the most despised. Some will think me delusional but it is what I hope I am doing when I struggle halfway across the world to meet with the 'bad men' whom I represent. Dostoyevsky said that a society should be judged by the way it treats those accused of the worst crimes. Bush and Blair have earned our society harsh condemnation on this score, but there is still a chance to temper the verdict.

APPENDIX A

TIME LINE OF RELEVANT EVENTS

30 April 1494   Guantánamo Bay 'discovered' by Christopher Columbus on his second voyage of exploration to the New World.

1898   Spanish-American War begins, purportedly in response to Spanish mistreatment of Cubans. Americans land troops at Guantánamo Bay.

1903   Original lease agreement between the US and the newly independent Cuban government grants the Guantánamo Bay base to the US as a naval and coaling station.

1934   Lease renewed, without any termination date.

1953–9   Cuban Revolution led by Fidel Castro. His advance on Havana begins from 40 miles west of the base.

10 March 1957   Osama bin Laden born in Saudi Arabia.

4 January 1961   US severs diplomatic relations with 'communist' Cuba.

17 April 1961   Bay of Pigs invasion by exiled Cubans, sponsored by the CIA, takes place several hundred miles to the north-west of the base.

Late 1961   Castro tries to stem the flow of refugees seeking asylum by building the 'Cactus Curtain' along eight miles of the north-eastern border of the Guantánamo base.

October 1962   Cuban Missile Crisis. Seventy-five thousand landmines subsequently placed along the border of the base.

1979   Bin Laden goes to Afghanistan to fight jihad against the Russian invaders. At the time, the mujahideen receive significant support from the CIA. Bin Laden later goes to the Sudan.

May 1996   Under pressure from the US and other countries, the Sudan orders bin Laden to leave the country. He goes to Afghanistan.

26 February 1993   First attempted bombing of the World Trade Center. Several people are later convicted after a lengthy trial in US federal court in New York.

20 November 2000   US presidential election.

9 December 2000   US Supreme Court stops recount and effectively declares the election for George W. Bush in *Bush v. Gore*.

20 January 2001   President Bush inaugurated.

16 August 2001   Zaccarias Moussoui arrested on immigration charges in Minnesota, 26 days before 9/11. The significance of his flight training is not recognised. Long after the fact, he will be charged as the twentieth hijacker in the 9/11 attacks, convicted and sentenced in US federal court to life imprisonment.

11 September 2001   Little-known terrorist group called al-Qaeda attacks the United States.

16 September 2001   Bin Laden releases a videotape denying responsibility for the September 11 attack: 'I stress that I have not carried out this act, which appears to have been carried out by individuals with their own motivation.'

7 October 2001   Afghanistan War (dubbed 'Operation Enduring Freedom') begins with coalition bombing of Afghanistan.

11 November 2001   Sheikh al-Libi, associate of bin Laden and head of the Khaldan al-Qaeda training camp in Afghanistan, captured by Pakistani security forces after fleeing the fighting in the Tora Bora mountains of Afghanistan.

12 November 2001   The Taliban retreats from Kabul.

15 December 2001   Sami al-Haj, al-Jazeera cameraman, is detained by the Pakistani authorities when returning to Afghanistan with his crew.

17 December 2001   Tora Bora defensive positions overrun.

22 December 2001   Richard Reid (the British man dubbed the 'Shoe Bomber') arrested for trying to blow up American Airlines Flight 63 from Paris to Miami. He is later convicted and sentenced in a US federal court to life imprisonment.

27 December 2001   Bin Laden issues his second videotaped statement, stopping short of claiming responsibility for September 11, but asserting: 'Terrorism against America deserves to be praised because it was a reponse to injustice, aimed at forcing America to stop its support for Israel, which kills our people.'

7 January 2002   Sami al-Haj turned over to US authorities.

8 January 2002   Sheikh al-Libi is reportedly held on the USS *Bataan* in the Indian Ocean. Later in January he is among the 150 prisoners secretly handed over to Egyptian authorities for interrogation. Under torture, he 'admits' that al-Qaeda was working with Saddam Hussein on weapons of mass destruction.

11 January 2002   Announcement that prisoners from Afghanistan will be taken for detention in Guantánamo Bay.

21 January 2002   First flight brings prisoners from Afghanistan to Guantánamo Bay. They are held in open cages in an area called Camp X-Ray (which is closed at the end of April 2002).

February 2002   For the first time, in classified documents, the CIA expresses doubt about al-Libi's confession to the link between al-Qaeda and Saddam Hussein.

19 February 2002   Litigation brought by the Center for Constitutional Rights (CCR), Prof. Joe Margulies, and Clive Stafford Smith in federal court in Washington, DC on behalf of two British prisoners in Guantánamo Bay (Shafiq Rasul and Asif Iqbal) in a case styled *Rasul v. Bush*.

27 February 2002   US military begins building Camp Delta at Guantánamo Bay. It opens in April 2002.

28 March 2002   Abu Zubaydah, thought to have served as bin Laden's field commander, is captured in Pakistan.

10 April 2002   Binyam Mohamed, a British resident from Kensington, is detained at the airport by Pakistani authorities.

29 April 2002   Camp X-Ray closed at Guantánamo Bay.

21 July 2002   Binyam Mohamed is rendered by CIA plane to Morocco, where he faces 18 months of torture.

10 September 2002   Ramzi bin al-Shibh, a senior al-Qaeda member who allegedly helped plan 9/11 from Hamburg, Germany, is captured in Pakistan.

7 October 2002   President Bush gives a speech in Cincinnati in support of war plans for Iraq where he relies on evidence tortured out of al-Libi in Egypt, and strongly emphasises Saddam Hussein's ties to al-Qaeda: 'We've learned that Iraq has trained al-Qaeda members in bomb-making and poisons and deadly gases.'

November 2002   Chaplain James Yee begins his assignment as Muslim imam for the prisoners in Guantánamo Bay.

8 November 2002   Abd al-Rahim al-Nashri, alleged to be al-Qaeda operational chief in the Persian Gulf region, is captured.

February 2003   After torture in Egypt, al-Libi is returned to US custody, and is held for some months in secret in Guantánamo Bay, along with other high-level al-Qaeda prisoners.

6 February 2003   US Secretary of State Colin Powell addresses the UN urging preemptive war with Iraq, relying on evidence tortured out of al-Libi in Egypt linking al-Qaeda and Saddam Hussein.

1 March 2003   Khalid Sheikh Mohammed (KSM), allegedly the third-ranking member of al-Qaeda, is captured by Pakistani intelligence in Rawalpindi.

23 March 2003   Invasion of Iraq ('Operation Iraqi Freedom').

2 May 2003   President Bush announces 'Mission Accomplished' on board USS *Lincoln*.

July 2003   President Bush names the first six prisoners who will face military commissions in Guantánamo Bay, including two British men (Feroz Abbasi and Moazzam Begg) and one Australian (David Hicks). For the first time there is widespread criticism of the prison in the British press.

17 July 2003 At a press conference with Prime Minister Tony Blair, President Bush discusses the 'War on Terror' and then responds to a question about the prisoners in Guantánamo: 'The only thing I know for certain is that these are bad people . . .'

10 September 2003 Chaplain Yee, the Guantánamo imam, is arrested on charges that he is a spy for Syria. His wife searches for him as he spends 76 days incommunicado. Ultimately, the espionage charges are dropped and he is accused of adultery and downloading pornography on a government computer.

26 November 2003 British Lord Justice Steyn brands the proposed military commission tribunals 'kangaroo courts'.

January 2004 Al-Libi recants all allegations that al-Qaeda had links with Saddam Hussein.

21 January 2004 Binyam Mohamed, after 18 months of torture in Morocco, is rendered to the Dark Prison in Kabul.

29 January 2004 Pentagon spokesperson, Lieutenant Commander Barbara Burfeind, states to BBC journalist Jon Monel on Radio 4 that with the release of three Afghans aged between 11 and 15, no juveniles remain in US custody in Guantánamo. A Reprieve report later demonstrates that as many as sixty-four juveniles have been held at the base, and as many as nineteen remain incarcerated in 2005.

8 February 2004 President Bush pronounces himself a 'War President'.

March 2004 Five British nationals (Asif Iqbal, Shafiq Rasul, Rhuhel Ahmed, Tarek Dergoul, Jamal Udeen) are released from Guantánamo Bay, leaving four British nationals and ten British residents behind.

May 2004 The first permanent, maximum security facility (Camp V) is completed at Guantánamo Bay, housing up to 100 prisoners. Kellogg, Brown & Root (KBR), a subsidiary of Halliburton formerly run by Vice President Dick Cheney, is the main contractor. The cost was $31 million.

9 May 2004 The *Washington Post* publicises classified documents that show Pentagon approval of sleep deprivation, exposure to heat and cold, bright lights, and loud music during interrogations at Guantánamo.

June 2004 In a confidential report leaked to the *New York Times*, Red Cross inspectors accuse the US military of using 'humiliating acts, solitary confinement, temperature extremes, use of forced positions' against prisoners, concluding that 'the construction of such a system, whose stated purpose is the production of intelligence, cannot be considered other than an intentional system of cruel, unusual and degrading treatment and a form of torture'.

15 June 2004 Brigadier General Janis Karpinski, commander at the Abu Ghraib prison in Iraq, says she was told by General Miller (former commander at Guantánamo) to treat detainees like dogs 'as it is done in Guantánamo'.

28 June 2004 US Supreme Court rules in *Rasul v. Bush* that prisoners in Guantánamo Bay have the basic legal right to challenge their detention by the ancient writ of habeas corpus in US federal civilian courts.

July 2004 Al-Libi, Abu Zubaydah and other high-ranking al-Qaeda members who have apparently been held in a secret part of Guantánamo Bay are moved now that the rule of law has reached it. They are moved to a secret prison in Eastern Europe. Al-Libi is later reportedly moved to a secret prison somewhere in North Africa.

29 July 2004 FBI report (revealed later in the *New York Times*) specifically describes and criticises the abuse of prisoners for the first time: 'I entered interview rooms to find a detainee chained hand and foot in a fetal position to the floor, with no chair, food or water. Most times they had urinated or defecated on themselves and had been left there for 18, 24 hours or more.'

August 2004 Gita Gutierrez of the Center for Constitutional Rights becomes the first lawyer to visit the base. Under compulsion by the Supreme Court, the military creates the Combatant Status Review Tribunals (CSRT) system for assessing whether a prisoner is an 'enemy combatant'. The system is heavily criticised for using secret evidence, relying on evidence extracted by torture, and excluding lawyers.

24 August 2004 After two and a half years at the prison, Salim Hamdan, a Yemeni prisoner at Guantánamo Bay who allegedly once drove for bin Laden, becomes the first person to have a hearing in a military commission. This process is later stopped by the courts, and ultimately declared unconstitutional by the Supreme Court.

22 September 2004 Rendition of prisoners to Guantánamo from Afghanistan suspended for two years after the last plane brings Binyam Mohamed and nine others to the prison.

30 October 2004 In a videotape timed to coincide with the US presidential elections, bin Laden publicly acknowledges al-Qaeda's involvement in the attacks on the US for the first time. He says that the attacks were carried out because 'we are free and do not accept injustice. We want to restore freedom to our nation.'

2 November 2004 George W. Bush wins re-election against Senator John Kerry.

18 November 2004 After 15 months' delay (in a process that is meant to take three weeks), and after 'losing' the application twice, the military finally provides Clive Stafford Smith with a security clearance and allows him to visit British citizens Moazzam Begg and Richard Belmar. After that time, Stafford Smith visited prisoners for roughly ten days every six weeks, sixteen visits in all by the end of 2006.

14 December 2004 The first Annual Review Board (ARB) is held to determine whether those prisoners deemed to be enemy combatants are a 'continuing threat' to the US. The ARBs provide even fewer rights than the military commissions or CSRTs and are strongly criticised.

25 January 2005 The four remaining British citizens (Feroz Abbasi, Moazzam Begg, Richard Belmar and Martin Mubanga) are returned to the UK. (Ten British residents remained in Guantánamo Bay.)

31 January 2005 DC federal judge Joyce Hens Green rules that the CSRTs held to confirm the status of the prisoners in Guantánamo as 'enemy combatants' are unconstitutional. The government appeals.

15 March 2005 Professor Tim Valentine reviews the videotape that purports to be the British Libyan refugee Omar Deghayes brandishing a Kalashnikov in Chechnya, and concludes that it is not him. Through the work of BBC *Newsnight* correspondent Peter Marshall, the person is shown to be a dead Chechen rebel, Abu Walid. The proof is delivered to the US military. Two years later the allegations against Omar remain substantially unchanged, he receives no trial, and he remains a prisoner.

June 2005 Members of the United States House Committee on the Armed Services visit Guantánamo Bay, describe it as a 'resort' and compliment the quality of the food.

6 July 2005 Widespread hunger strike begins at Guantánamo Bay, with prisoners demanding a fair trial or freedom.

12 July 2005 Members of a military panel propose disciplining prison commander Major General Geoffrey Miller (former base commander) over the Guantánamo interrogation of Mohamed al-Qahtani, who was forced to wear female underwear and threatened with dogs. The recommendation is overruled by General Bantz J. Craddock, commander of US Southern Command.

28 July 2005 Colonel Bumgarner and British resident Shaker Aamer negotiate a settlement of the hunger strike. Camp conditions temporarily improve.

5 August 2005   The short-lived agreement at Guantánamo begins to break down with the beating of Tunisian prisoner Hisham Sliti.

11 August 2005   The full hunger strike commences again.

29 September 2005   British resident Shaker Aamer, a member of the prisoners' council, is placed in total isolation in Camp Echo to prevent him organising the prisoners.

December 2005   First use of the 'torture chair' employed to force-feed those who remain on hunger strike in Guantánamo Bay. 'Pretty soon it wasn't convenient, and they decided it wasn't worth it,' US General Craddock subsequently says of the hunger strikers in the *New York Times*. 'A lot of the detainees said: "I don't want to put up with this. This is too much of a hassle."' The number of hunger strikers drops to a handful.

20 December 2005   President Bush pushes the Detainee Treatment Act (DTA) through Congress, seeking to forbid prisoners from bringing challenges to their detention in federal district court. It includes a prohibition against torture, but explicitly denies Guantánamo prisoners a forum in which to bring any challenge to their treatment.

13 January 2006   German Chancellor Angela Merkel criticises the detention of prisoners at Guantánamo Bay.

15 February 2006   UN report condemns Guantánamo, finding that conditions there amount to torture.

17 February 2006   Prime Minister Tony Blair issues his strongest condemnation of Guantánamo, suggesting that is 'an anomaly and sooner or later it's got to be dealt with'.

23 February 2006   US District Judge Jed S. Rakoff in New York orders the Defense Department to release uncensored transcripts of detainee hearings.

6 March 2006   Reprieve delivers evidence to the US military proving that Ahmed Errachidi, dubbed The General of al-Qaeda by the US military, was actually working as a cook at the Westbury Hotel in London at the time he was supposedly training as a terrorist in Afghanistan. A year later the charges against Mr Errachidi remain unchanged, and he is still a prisoner in Guantánamo.

April 2006   Reports surface that five Uighur prisoners in Camp Iguana have managed to plant a garden using seeds taken from their food.

15 April 2006   Under compulsion by the courts, for the first time since the opening of the Guantánamo detention centre the Pentagon releases a list of the prisoners being held there.

7 June 2006   Al Zarqawi, al-Qaeda leader in Iraq, killed by US bomb.

10 June 2006   Three prisoners in Guantánamo Bay allegedly commit suicide.

The Pentagon brands this a 'PR stunt'. The media are banned briefly from the base.

29 June 2006 US Supreme Court declares the Military Commission system unconstitutional in *Hamdan v. Rumsfeld* on the basis that the President could not create such a system without congressional approval.

25 August 2006 US Congressional Record states that there are currently 14,000 prisoners in US custody in secret detention centres around the world: 450 in Guantánamo, 500 in Bagram Air Force Base (Afghanistan); 100–200 in Kandahar (Afghanistan); 12,900 in Iraq; 30 in other secret prisons.

6 September 2006 In the run-up to the 2006 congressional election, President Bush announces that fourteen 'big name' al-Qaeda prisoners (including Khalid Sheikh Mohammed, allegedly the mastermind of September 11; Abu Zubaydah, allegedly al-Qaeda's field commander; and Ramzi bin al-Shibh, allegedly a planner of the September 11 plot) have been transferred from their secret CIA detention centres to Guantánamo Bay. The Bush Administration claims that there are no more prisoners held in secret CIA detention centres, and presses for urgent passage of a law undoing the *Hamdan* decision and allowing military trials.

September 2006 In another videotape released in the run-up to a major US election, bin Laden discloses evidence of Ramzi bin al-Shibh's involvement in the September 11 attacks (evidence that could clearly sustain a conviction of al-Shibh without the need to rely on any evidence obtained under torture).

17 October 2006 President Bush pushes the Military Commissions Act (MCA) through Congress creating a new system that is very similar to the previous one.

November 2006 Camp VI opened as a maximum security facility at Guantánamo Bay, housing up to 178 prisoners.

7 November 2006 US elections result in a majority for the Democrats in both the Senate and the House.

8 November 2006 President Bush accepts the resignation of Secretary of Defense Donald Rumsfeld.

11 December 2006 Three prisoners at Guantánamo Bay complete 16 months on hunger strike, being force-fed for well over a year.

15 December 2006 Al-Jazeera journalist Sami al-Haj reaches his fifth anniversary in custody without charges or a trial.

1 January 2007 British resident Shaker Aamer remains in isolation in Camp Echo after sixteen months.

APPENDIX B

A BRIEF HISTORY OF GUANTÁNAMO BAY

Guantánamo Bay sits at the eastern end of Cuba, its huge natural harbour well sheltered from the often hostile storms of the Caribbean. The name was originally given to the bay by the Taino, the indigenous people who lived in the area before the Spanish arrived. The two sides of the bay currently held by the United States are named after the prevailing direction of these storms – the Leeward side and the Windward side. From a Western perspective, its history began on 30 April 1494, when Christopher Columbus, then on his second voyage of exploration to the New World, anchored briefly in the bay. He called it Puerto Grande, or Big Port. The land around the bay was semi-arid, and when Columbus found neither water nor the gold of El Dorado, he sailed on the next day. A plaque commemorates where he came ashore, just fifty yards from the present-day ferry landing on the Windward side.

Europeans showed no interest in the place until 1741, when General Wentworth landed 3,400 British troops at the bay during the War of Jenkins' Ear. He renamed the bay Cumberland Harbour, and planned to attack Spanish forces nearby. He advanced sixteen miles inland, by which time more than 2,000 of his soldiers had been struck by tropical fever, and he abandoned the bay after a four-month occupation.

A century later, in 1854, there was a brief visit by HMS *Buzzard*, a British man-of-war, to land a number of yellow fever patients for isolation and treatment on the tiny island now known as Hospital Cay. But the modern history of the base began in 1898, when the declining Spanish empire found itself at war with an emergent United States. On 10 June of that year, the American marines landed to prepare for the decisive battle of Cuzco Well, two miles to the southeast. The Spanish were defeated, and Cuba gained its independence – albeit an independence that would be closely monitored by the United States for a long time.

In 1903, President Theodore Roosevelt signed a treaty with the new government of Cuba. This included a lease for a coaling station for the US Navy. The lease had no fixed expiration, and could be voided only by mutual consent of both countries. For a minimal sum – originally $2,000 in gold and now, a century later, still only $4,085 per year – the US was granted about 45 square miles, divided into three roughly equal areas, the windward side to the east, the harbour itself, and the leeward side to the west. The lease was protected by a clause written into the Cuban constitution, and at that time the US also asserted its right, under the so-called Platt Amendment, to intervene to protect the fledgling Cuban democracy if it came under threat. The US did not hesitate to exercise this power over the next thirty years – during the 'Negro Rebellion' of 1912, the 'Sugar Intervention' of 1917, and on various other occasions.

In 1934 the Platt Amendment was repealed from Cuban law, and the original lease was superseded by a new agreement. The terms remained essentially unchanged. Then and now, the lease barred the US from using the area for anything other than a 'coaling or naval station'.

Gradually the base expanded, finding use first as a major training ground for the US Navy, particularly in winter. Pictures from the base from the second decade of the twentieth century show more than fifty battleships anchored in parallel lines across the bay. Later came an expanding air force. The leeward runway was progressively extended so that it could handle very large aircraft.

Shortly after the Second World War, the roads on the base were named for the first time. On the leeward side, there was not much to name – First and Second Streets run roughly parallel from the western extremity beyond the CBQ to the ferry landing. (The CBQ is the Combined Bachelors Quarters, the motel where the lawyers and the media stay.) On the windward side, the main road is named Sherman Avenue, after Admiral Forrest P. Sherman, the senior officer in the Navy at the time of the Korean War, and author of a tract on the British occupation of the bay two centuries earlier. The smaller roads commemorate historical Cuban heroes, soldiers who died in the 1898 war, and former commandants of the naval station. One exception is Recreation Road, which runs along the side of the Guantánamo golf course.

In the Fifties, a period of relative calm at the base came to an end. Just forty miles to the west, a group of revolutionaries led by Fidel Castro began a march on the capital, Havana. They took power in January 1959. At the time, as reported in the naval history of the base by Rear Admiral M.E. Murphy, Castro had the 'complete support of the people of Cuba and the majority of nations in the world'.

The honeymoon was brief. As Castro declared his left-wing colours, President Eisenhower severed diplomatic relations with Cuba on 4 January 1961 – but was careful to assert that the status of Guantánamo Bay would not change.

Castro took the position that the lease was illegal. 'The Naval base is a dagger plunged into Cuban soil,' he complained, not long after the Revolution. 'A base we are not going to take away by force, but a piece of land we will never give up.'

Tensions rose on 17 April 1961, with the abortive Bay of Pigs invasion sponsored by the CIA several hundred miles to the northwest. Later that year, Castro sought to stem the flow of refugees seeking asylum by building the 'Cactus Curtain' along eight miles of the northeastern border of the base.

If Cuban-American relations were then sour, they became acid with the Cuban Missile Crisis. In October 1962, the US learned that Russian missiles had been placed on Cuban soil, just 90 miles from the US mainland, capable of hitting American targets within minutes of their launch. This provoked a massive operation on the base, with the evacuation of civilians, a large influx of soldiers, and the creation of concrete bunkers along the defensive line. A field of 75,000 landmines was laid down along the boundary as well, creating what was then the second largest minefield in the world after Korea. In Admiral Murphy's book there is a dedication to fifteen US soldiers who died in the process of laying and maintaining the mines. Murphy also gives the names of four Cuban nationals who died trying to cross the field, and mentions one set of skeletal remains identified only as a 'Fence Jumper'. President Bill Clinton ordered the removal of all American mines in 1996, and the area was officially cleared by 2000. The corresponding Cuban minefield remains in place.

Meanwhile, on 6 February 1964, the Cuban government cut off the base water supply, in retaliation for the arrest of 36 Cubans accused of fishing illegally in Florida waters. A rather petty interchange followed, where the Cubans accused the US of stealing Cuban water, and the Americans responded by erecting a sign where the water pipe crossed the boundary: 'US Answer to Castro: Gitmo water Liberated from Cuba at this point.' Paradoxically, this incident began a drive to make the base environmentally sustainable in a way rarely seen in the mainland US. Later in 1964 a water desalination plant opened with a capacity to convert 2.25 million gallons of fresh water from the sea each day. Almost everything is recycled on the base (and has been for years), and in 2005, at a cost of $12 million, four massive wind turbines on the windward hills began delivering a quarter of the base's electricity, cutting dependence on diesel fuel that must be shipped in. Strict environmental laws protect the wildlife – a soldier who runs over an iguana is liable to ten years in prison and a fine of $10,000,

As the water was cut off, Castro moved to terminate the employment of Cubans on the base. Until that point, several thousand Cuban nationals would cross into the base each day for work, providing a huge bonus to the local Cuban economy. A grandfather clause operated to allow those who had jobs to continue passing through the border gate each day, but retirement had eliminated all but two Cuban workers by 2006.

In the early l970s, the attitudes of both sides oscillated. By 1974, Castro declared that continued US occupation of the base should not be an obstacle to normalising relations. Although the early Seventies saw various calls from influential Americans for a change in approach, intense hostility from the Cuban expatriate community in Florida vetoed tentative moves towards a resumption of omatic relations.

The opportunity for a rapprochement dissolved towards the end of the Seventies, with various Cuban interventions around the world that were unacceptable to the US. The Cubans sent military assistance to the communists in Angola, and supported the Nicaraguan and El Salvadoran rebels. Then came the *marielito* boatlift, when Castro dispatched 125,000 'unwanted' Cubans in boats to Florida.

In the early 1990s, the administration of George Bush Sr began using Guantánamo to house Haitian refugees who were fleeing privation in their home country. Haiti is the closest Caribbean island to Cuba, lying only sixty miles to the east. The US hoped that the unique status of the base would justify a radical curtailment of the Haitians' legal rights. Although Admiral Murphy had candidly observed that 'Guantánamo Bay is in effect a bit of American territory,' in theory the base was sovereign Cuban territory. If refugees are interdicted on the high seas, they enjoy substantially fewer rights than those who make it to American soil. The idea was that detaining Haitians on the base would make it easier for the US government to deny them asylum status, since many of them wanted to come to America to seek a better life rather than escape political persecution.

The base achieved some notoriety when the US immigration service invoked a 1987 statute to test everyone for HIV/AIDs and, when some unfortunates proved positive, 276 were taken to an 'HIV camp' on the base. Their case was taken to the federal courts in litigation led by Michael Ratner of the Center for Constitutional Rights, and a federal judge declared the policy illegal in a scathing opinion in 1993.

Unfortunately, later that year the Supreme Court repudiated much of the district court judge's ruling, and suggested that a person held in Guantánamo Bay did not enjoy as many rights as a person on the mainland US. The policy had been widely criticised, though, and political pressure led to the closure of the detention camp – the last Haitian left Guantánamo in November 1995. Yet, ten years later, it was this earlier experiment that would give the administration of the younger George Bush the idea that a law-free zone could be created on Guantánamo.

In the late 1990s, many thought the base had outlived its usefulness, and that its return to Cuba would be a part of the long-awaited reconciliation between the two countries. This was not to be.

On 11 September 2001, a little-known terrorist group called al-Qaeda attacked the United States. Within a month, the US and an international coalition began the invasion of Afghanistan, and across that region Muslim men were taken into custody.

The authorities at the Guantánamo naval base were only given three days' notice that prisoners were about to arrive, and the first planeload touched down in January 2002. The early, iconic pictures of the base showed open cages in Camp X-Ray, where prisoners were held without any solid walls, or toilet facilities. On 27 February 2002, work began to create a more solid facility, still hastily built, called Camp Delta, which opened in April 2002. This consisted of six camps – Camp I, II, III, IV, Echo and Iguana. Camps I-IV are divided into their own blocks.

Camp Echo was the original isolation block, where prisoners would be held in solitary cells divided down the middle – sleeping on one side, and coming out for interrogation on the other. Since August 2004, most legal visits have been conducted there, although it has still been used to isolate some prisoners.

Camp Iguana was used in 2002–3 to house three prisoners who were under the age of 16, and was closed when they were flown home to Afghanistan in January 2004. The compound was reopened in mid-2005 to house some of the 38 prisoners who had been found innocent at their Combatant Status Review Tribunals (CSRTs) held earlier that year.

The first permanent, concrete facility was Camp V, a maximum security prison opened in 2004 and housing up to 100 prisoners. Camp VI, originally intended to be a medium security unit, was modified to maximum security and opened in November 2006, housing up to 178 prisoners. Kellogg, Brown & Root (KBR), a subsidiary of Halliburton (well known as the company run by Vice President Dick Cheney prior to the 2000 election), was hired to do the main construction work on these two prisons.

The formal military trials under rules cobbled together by the Pentagon in April 2003 are called military commissions. By the start of 2006, only ten prisoners (1.5 per cent of the prisoners who had been held on the base) had ever been charged in such a proceeding. None had been brought to trial, and the process was declared unconstitutional by the Supreme Court in June of that year. The Bush Administration successfully pressed Congress to estab-lish a new (and very similar) military commission process in the run up to the November 2006 elections. In November 2006, the military announced plans to build a new $125 million courthouse, but congressional opposition prevented the Pentagon from merely recommitting this money from other sources and, as of March 2007, congressional approval has not been obtained for this.

Much print has been expended on how the detention centre violates the law. Guantánamo Bay seems to be an onion with many layers of illegality. Civilian employees play a major role in the daily life of the base. Large numbers of people – primarily from Jamaica and the Philippines – perform every task from operating the lodging quarters and the restaurants to keeping the ferry running. For the most part these employees are paid sub-minimum wages, some as little as $1.25 (70p) per hour. This is not a novel problem. Admiral Murphy wrote in 1953 that, 'Naval activities at Guantánamo Bay had lagged far behind those in [the] continental United States in the field of industrial relations. It was noted ... that no wage survey had ever been held at Guantánamo Bay and that the wage schedule was unorthodox and undoubtedly inequitable in many ways.'

There are still refugees held on the base. As of December 2006 there were 46 Cubans who had fled Castro seeking asylum. They are held under stringent conditions – forbidden from using the telephone to contact their families or lawyers. One man was given 30 days' detention in 2006 for trying to call his mother in Cuba on Mother's Day. A second was given 60 days for wearing a T-shirt with the words, 'I'm a Cuban Immigrant, I Need Work'. A third was given 90 days for speaking with the press about his situation.

The US also violates the original lease in any number of ways. The base was intended as a naval station, to supply fuel for US ships patrolling the Caribbean. Under the express terms of the agreement, no private enterprise is permitted on the base. When Admiral Murphy wrote his history in 1953, he noted that the only exception allowed had been the laying of a private cable that ran through the site, and this was only permitted because 'the Cable Station is really a relay station between New York, Panama and other points, and does not of itself operate for profit on the Reservation.'

While the use of the base as a prison probably does not fit within the term 'naval station' either, the Cuban government would struggle to find a court where it could enforce its rights. It seems unlikely that the prison will close before the US government chooses to close it.

APPENDIX C

WHAT YOU CAN DO

I very much hope that when you read this book you will want to take action against Guantánamo and the secret prisons. There is always something that you can do to protect powerless people from those who would do them harm.

Reprieve is a UK charity that I helped establish in 1999. Reprieve's goal is to save lives and deliver justice on behalf of people facing the death penalty or detention without trial in Guantánamo Bay. Getting between the stone-throwers and their victims has been my uncomfortable vocation for many years, one shared by everyone who works with Reprieve.

Our original focus was on prisoners facing the death penalty, especially in the United States, a country that should be championing human rights, not violating them. I have spent more than twenty years representing people on Death Row, and we still spend much of our time on death penalty cases at Reprieve. But in January 2002 it became clear that the men in Guantánamo Bay were even more despised than those condemned to death on the US mainland. President Bush announced with a certainty born of ignorance that they were all terrorists. And the Guantánamo prisoners were the lucky ones: they comprise less than five per cent of the prisoners held in secret American prisons. Reprieve now devotes a substantial proportion of its time to bringing justice to the prisoners in Guantánamo and beyond.

Today there are 3,700 people on Death Row in the US alone, more than a thousand in Pakistan, and many more in China; there are thousands being abused in secret prisons around the world. It is the ambition of Reprieve to reach as many of them as possible. To do this, we need your help.

There are dozens of ways in which you can make a difference. For a start, you can write to our clients in Guantánamo. When Mohammed el Gharani (seized in Pakistan when he was just fourteen) got a stack of post cards from Amnesty International activists, I saw his broad smile. Previously, he had not received a single letter in three years of imprisonment. If you want to help by joining in a letter-writing campaign, then contact Amnesty International at www.amnesty.org.uk. Amnesty, like Reprieve, opposes the death penalty and is calling for the closure of Guantánamo Bay and all secret detention centres. Amnesty is running an ongoing campaign to bring an end to human rights abuses perpetrated in the name of security. The campaign enables you to take action on behalf of prisoners detained without trial, who undergo torture and ill-treatment under the auspices of the 'war on terror'. Amnesty can give you all the information you need to write letters, send greetings cards and lobby your MP. Mass public pressure is sometimes the only way that human rights can be improved – and even a single card sent to a prisoner can bring hope.

You can do more than just write letters. Lawyers and law firms can volunteer their time and resources for the direct representation of prisoners. Journalists can help tell the stories of individual prisoners facing the death penalty or secret imprisonment. Campaigners like Cageprisoners can educate the public and politicians. Photographers and painters can prove that a picture speaks a thousand words by creating images of the condemned. Actors can team up with the Tricycle Theatre to put on plays like *Guantánamo*. Musicians can write songs and take them to the road, like the band Seize the Day, who performed 'The Guantánamo Shuffle' outside the headquarters of Hiatts, a Birmingham corporation that makes a profit out of the handcuffs used to manacle the prisoners at the base. Doctors can emulate David Nicholls, who has made himself a thorn in the side of the US military physicians who are force-feeding prisoners in violation of their medical ethics. Horticulturalists can plant Guantánamo gardens, highlighting the plight of prisoners who are denied even their Geneva Convention right to grow flowers in captivity. Everyone can join an organization doing this work and volunteer some time.

And if you have disposable income that you wish to give to this cause, please become a regular donor to Reprieve and help us find the evidence, trace the witnesses, publish the facts and stand up for justice around the globe. Visit www.reprieve.org.uk, send an e-mail to info@reprieve.org.uk, write to PO Box 52742, London EC4P 4WS, or call 020 7353 4640 to get in touch.

Thank you for what you have already done, and what you will do in the future.

Clive Stafford Smith

INDEX

Aamer, Shaker, 11–12, 50, 128–9, 130,
139–40, 147, 190–2, 193–6, 197,
198, 202, 203, 205–8, 209–12,
213–14, 215, 216–17, 226–8, 245
Abbasi, Feroz, 135
Abdullah, Crown Prince, 261
Abdullah, Maher, 180
Abdurrahman, 202
Abu Ghraib, 34, 41, 46, 75, 185, 248, 271,
279
Abu Kabir, Usama, 12
Abu Munder, Sami, 259
Abu Salim, 261
Abu Walid, 256
Abu Zubaydah, 63, 69, 78, 87, 88, 236,
239–40
Addington, David, 243
Afghanistan
Abu Zubaydah in, 240
Ahmed Errachidi in, 167–8, 169
Ahmed Errachidi suspected of
attending training camp in, 164, 166,
168
American attacks on, 1, 22, 52, 167–8,
280
Binyam Ahmed Mohamed's visit to, 52,
69, 73, 122
'embedding' journalists in, 172
Hisham Sliti in, 199
Khalid Sheikh Mohammed in, 231, 232
Moazzam Begg in, 133, 190
Mohammed Atef killed in, 239
Omar Deghayes in, 258, 262
Omar Khadr in, 145
prisoners held in, 230, 242
problems involved in interrogation of
prisoners arrested in, 46–7
Sami al-Haj in, 174, 175–6, 181
Sami al-Haj attempts to return to, 177
Sami al-Laithi in, 154–5
Shaker Aamer in, 190, 191
refugees from, 253

brief references, 60, 98, 162, 179, 263,
275
African-Americans, 24
Ahmed, Ali Abdullah, 218
Ahmed, Rhuhel, 274
Ahmed bin Salman bin Abdul Aziz,
Prince, 240
Air & Space Power Chronicles, 97
Ala, Sheikh, 203
al-Bahlul, Ali Hamza, 92
Albania, 265
Algeria, 31, 178
Algiers, battle of, 30
al-Haj, Asim, 174–5
al-Haj, Sami, 150–1, 174–8, 181, 182–3,
213
al-Hayla, Abdulsalaam, 202
al-Jazeera, 6, 150, 174, 175–80, 181, 182,
233, 236, 237
al-Laithi, Sami, 153–7, 158, 162, 185, 226,
263, 264
al-Libi, Ibn Sheikh, 69, 78, 79, 249–51,
252, 275
al-Masari, Abu Qatada, 150
al-Muhajir, Abdullah *see* Padilla, Jose
al-Odah, Khalid, 219
al-Otaibi, Mana, 218
al-Qaeda
and Ahmed Errachidi, 164–5, 226,
274–5
and al-Jazeera, 181
big-name members transferred to
Guantánamo, 263
and Binyam Ahmed Mohamed, 52, 54,
63, 69–70, 72, 73, 78, 79
bounty payments for supposed
members of, 169–70
growing numbers attracted to, 273, 276,
279–80
and hunger strikes, 189
and Jose Padilla (Abdullah al-Muhajir),
49, 78

298